William Bloom PhD is considered by many to be Britain's leading holistic teacher. He co-founded Alternatives and is the founder of the Spiritual Freedom Network and the educational consultancy Holistic Partnerships which is promoting *Endorphin Effect* techniques amongst organisations and individuals. He is the author and editor of many bestselling books including *Psychic Protection* and *Working with Angels* (both Piatkus) and *The Holistic Revolution*.

The Endorphin Effect

WILLIAM BLOOM

PIATKUS

In loving memory of my parents,
Philip Bloom and Freddy Wenzel Bloom,
and
For my sister, Virginia

He that has once the Flower of the Sun,
The perfect ruby which we call Elixir . . .
Can confer honour, love, respect, long life,
Give safety, valour, yea, and victory,
Ben Jonson, *The Alchemist*

First published in 2001 by
Judy Piatkus (Publishers) Limited
5 Windmill Street
London W1T 2JA
e-mail: info@piatkus.co.uk

Reprinted 2002

The moral right of the author has been asserted

A catalogue record for this book is available
from the British Library

ISBN 0 7499 2158 7

Text design by Design 23
Edited by Esther Jagger
Illustrated by Lesley Wakerley

This book has been printed on paper manufactured
with respect for the environment, using wood
from managed sustainable resources

Typeset by Phoenix Photosetting, Chatham, Kent
Printed and bound in Great Britain by
Butler & Tanner Ltd, Frome, Somerset

Contents

Preface and Acknowledgements

The New Buffet of Knowledge

This book is the result of thirty years' research and practice. I have reached a stage where, finally, I think I know what I am doing. For that gift – however temporary – I give thanks to the times in which we live. In the whole of human history, there has never been an age like this. Information is exploding on our planet like a cosmic fireworks party.

Compare the twenty-first century with the seventeenth. Four hundred years ago it was difficult to get hold of information. For a start, most people could not read – and even if they could read, there were no local resources. People were restricted to the local priest and belief systems. If someone wanted more information, he or she had to travel. Even if they did travel, there were no centres of learning that contained all the knowledge and wisdom of other continents and distant cultures. Worse than that, people lived in societies that told them what to think and how to think it. Break those rules and you could end up in prison, on the rack or burnt at the stake. To research was hard. To investigate freely the nature of human consciousness and the meaning of life was almost impossible.

But in our time, the third millennium, all the information in the world is down the road in the local bookstore or one click away on the web. With almost complete freedom we can research our interests, different approaches, different options. In particular, we are able to investigate the meaning and process of life – the big questions of who, how and why we are. We are no longer trapped by narrow answers that come from a single source. 'This is the one and only way' sounds ignorant in today's world.

The information offered in *The Endorphin Effect* comes out of this modern culture. There is an incredible amount of new knowledge from which we can build more up-to-date models of how the world works and how we work. Every day there are breakthroughs in science, in our understanding of the world of electromagnetic phenomena and quantum dynamics. The most profound secrets of human biology are being revealed. There are also revelations from modern psychology, with its dramatic insights into the unconscious mind and emotional dynamics. All of this knowledge is freely available.

We also have access to what were once closely guarded secrets in the fields of spiritual development and energy medicine. In the past, the wisdom and techniques of, for example, yoga, chi gung and tantra were restricted to an initiated few. Today, they are widely accessible in books, videos and classes.

For anyone working in the field of human development, therefore, this is a blessed time. All across the world, people interested in a holistic approach to life are looking at this rich array of information which provides a new and far wider perspective. Revolutions in our understanding of health and the nature of existence are inevitable.

Two Holistic Premises

The understanding of endorphins presented in this book comes originally from rigorous scientific research, but to appreciate their full significance requires a more holistic perspective. There are, in my opinion, two crucial concepts that must be integrated – two ideas that sit at the very core of Eastern medical traditions and the holistic approach to healthcare.

- *The Mind-Body Connection* – There is an intimate connection between the body and the mind. In fact, it is possible to effect biological changes simply by using your mind.
- *The Electromagnetic Field* – The physical body is not just solid, but is also electromagnetic. As such, it can connect with the other magnetic wavefields in nature and the universe.

These ideas are, however, sometimes alarming to the Western medical approach. We live at a time of two very different worldviews which often clash when they meet.

The Western scientific paradigm is very powerful and has been extremely successful. It explains how the physical world is constructed and has provided the backbone to the industry and technology of modern society. Holistically minded people, however, often forget its brilliance and its startling success, especially in the fields of life expectancy and the quality of life in general.

On the other side, scientifically minded people often dismiss all holistic ideas as metaphysical nonsense. Whilst it is true that many holistic ideas are difficult to subject to rigorous scientific scrutiny they nevertheless work in practice, which is why millions of people espouse them. They can also be fully explained from an energetic perspective.

The two sides need to be more sympathetic to each other and recognize that ultimately their marriage is inevitable, as they both carry crucial aspects of the truth.

Neuroscience, Emotional Intelligence and Energy Medicine

The Endorphin Effect may seem an ambitious project. It has required familiarity with four fields – physical healthcare, psychology, spiritual development and energy medicine traditions such as yoga and chi gung. As a proponent of the holistic worldview, I am accustomed to putting these fields together for an effective approach to total health and growth. Usually, however, these different perspectives are kept separate. It was my publisher, Judy

Piatkus, who first pointed out to me that *The Endorphin Effect* combined all these areas for the first time in a way that was accessible to a widespread contemporary audience. I was so immersed in the work and took it all so much for granted that I had not noticed this inter-relationship.

In particular, this work is the first generally accessible approach that combines neuroscience, emotional intelligence and energy medicine. This is a powerful synergy. It stands, however, on the shoulders of many other important teachings and traditions. It is also, I believe, part of an enormous movement all around the globe to combine these fields into one integrated whole.

Because we are at the early stages of creating an all-embracing and rigorous holistic approach, I must confess to a certain reductionism in the book. Initially I have drawn heavily on the new fields of psychoneuroimmunology and the allied neurosciences, focussing in particular upon one biochemical, the endorphins. There are other biochemicals, such as serotonin or adrenalin, which also have immense influence on an individual's emotional and physical state.

I have chosen, however, to work from the particular opportunity provided by the discovery of endorphins and from that gateway to open up to the psychological, energetic and spiritual implications, knowing full well that I have chosen a very specific and exclusive starting point. I am a holist and not a professional biologist, and I hope that those with a more rigorous grounding in the biological sciences will understand and be sympathetic towards my endeavour to build an approach that is immediately relevant, accessible and helpful.

Equally, I hope that students of psychology, holistic healthcare and mysticism will approve of the way in which I have also taken key insights from their fields and attempted a new synthesis.

The Book's Structure

The book is structured like a sandwich.

- The first three chapters present the theory and underlying concepts. Chapter 2 is particularly concerned with the actual science of endorphins and the mind-body connection. Chapter 3 is concerned more generally with the whole area of metaphysics, energy and magnetic fields. In these chapters (and, indeed, throughout the book) I try to use language that is acceptable to both mainstream scientists and holists.

- The central part of the book, Chapters 4–11, presents the actual strategy and exercises.
- Chapters 12–14 are concerned with how this approach integrates in daily life and what it says about the future.

Thanks and Acknowledgements

My gratitude is owed to many people, books, schools and organizations.

I need first to thank those people who have in one way or another helped or inspired me, as friends, coaches, speakers and teachers: Austin Arnold, James Bloom, Sabrina Dearborn, Allen Gold, Roy Arbuckle, David Spangler, Oyvind Solum, Gry Solum, William Johnstone, Thich Nhat Hahn, Marko Pogacnik, Marika Pogacnik, Frances Howard-Gordon, Jamie George, Cary Meehan, Micheal Meehan, Leo Rutherford, Eileen Caddy, Peter Caddy, Osho, Baba Gi, R. J. Stewart, Jan Cisek, Caroline Myss, Gary Zukov, Peter Dawkins, Donald Reeves, Caitlin Matthews, John Matthews, Richard Glynn, Chris James, Roxy Grimshaw, Jonathon Horwitz, Jean Houston, Ram Dass, Ian Gordon Brown, Edward Glover, Alex Lobba, Zhixing Wang, T.W. (Bill) Shepherd, Nick Williams, Serge Beddington-Behrens, James Baldwin, Nicholas Janni, Kathy Jones, Martin Gerrish, Meir Schneider, Mary Aver, Gabrielle Roth, Appollon Leontas, Robin Monro, Taj Deeora, Morvin Fyffe, Page Bryant, Scott Guynup, Jaine Smith, Roger Harrison, Margaret Harris.

There are also particular traditions, organizations and schools that I must thank: International Co-Freemasonry, Lucis Trust, Knights Templars, Rosicrucianism, hatha yoga, raja yoga, agni yoga, pranayama yoga, Tibetan Bon, Christian Gnosis, the Ignatian Exercises, tai chi, chi gung, Kabbalah, Alexander Technique, holotropic breathwork, rebirthing, kahuna, psychosynthesis and the Mevlevi Dervishes.

I am grateful to all the individuals and organizations who have supported my teaching and, therefore, my research: Findhorn Foundation, Alternativt Nettverk, Triom, Open Center of New York, California Institute of Integral Studies, Alternatives of St. James's Church, Gaunts House, LifeTimes, the Glastonbury Abbey Retreat House, Paul Hover, Paul Martin, Darinka Gomiscek, Nevena Barakov, Plamen Barakov and Ole Nielsen.

In researching and grounding the methods and ideas presented in this book, I am mainly indebted to my colleagues and students who are part of Holistic Partnerships and the Open Mystery School. Without them, this work would really never have appeared. Jacqueline Moore has been supportive and wise from the very beginning, administering Holistic Partnerships. A number of wonderful people have worked directly alongside me, supporting and enriching the teaching, starting with Sabrina Dearborn and David Spangler, then Ashley Akin-Smith, Helen Martin, Judi Buttner, Christal Storm, Judith Bone, Colette Barnard and Rachelle Wolfe. I want to give particular thanks to Ashley Akin-Smith for some conversations that helped to clarify the potential of this work. There is the original core group of coaches who saw the value of our approach and were prepared to invest at all levels to support it: Chris-Michael Bartel, John Ward, Mary Priest-Cobern, Nicky Marchant, Lizzie Smosarski, Leigh Jackson, Marella Buckley, Freda Matassa. Several coaches immediately ran with the ball: Dai Owen, Jenny Kirk, Jay Bosisto, Terry Larter, Steve Griffiths and Angela McCaul.

There are also the friends, students and colleagues who worked with me in the early experimental years. Without them, none of this would have been possible. In naming them, I risk missing a few names and apologise for their omission: Vicky Oliver, Frank Walsh, Steve Burson, Elisabeth Braun, Rob Purday, Suzanne White, Julia Zalazar, Julia Sparkes, Naomi Adler, Jo McAndrews, Joyce Crawford, Marina Broussole, Elke Counsell, Carole Lakomski, John Cahill, Ruth Godwin, Don McLaren, Tony Zucker, Maria Pascual, Margit Azar, Nina Adamovicz, Dean Jonathon Gregory, Fiona Watson, Sally Barker, Sue Ramsden, Gordon Green, Callum Elliot, Elaine Walker, Sasha Paravina, Mishcon de Reya, Ken Knight, Marjory Morrison, John Coyne, Simon Kelly, Esmeralda Sanz,

Grierson Ramsay, Mark Jones, Clive Lees, Fiona Phillips, Jan Maloney, Tom Cook, Adrian Lunney, Gideon Ries, Marolyn Burgess, Sharon Thomas, Barbara Mahel, Allan Tyrer, Cherie Seed, Rhiana Levy, Elizabeth Hamer, Linzi Arundale, Mandy Webb-Johnson, Mary McLaughlin, Helen Hannah, Kim McLean, Mika Akagi, Francis Meynell, Joanne Sharpe, Cynthia Harris, Ralph Harris, Simon Lord, Maria Barsema, Jane Turney, Richard Dunkerley, Liz Baxter, Christina Waldock, Paul Kitchener, Frank Bartholomeus, Liz Lloyd-Jones, Phyllis Higgins, Mark Anderson, Christopher Twigg, Sue Aldridge, Chris Base, Helen Battistini, Toni Edwards, Michael Gabriel, Elizabeth Giambrone, Chris Higgins, Debbie Hogg, Surya Monro, Carmel Morris, Angela Packer, Paula Quant, Juliet Stokoe, Helen Yates, Glenda Young, Nick Allison, Anna Appelmelk, Jane Bartlett, Karen Bresloff, Joanna Burgess, Cavell Douglas, Sarah Frankel, Maria Kotke, Heidi Oravasaari, Mandy Smith, Hilary Thomas and Jo Worsley.

As other authors will appreciate, having good neighbours is an especial boon, so I want to thank Tony and Anna Richards on one side and François Joly on the other.

Editorially, I must thank my literary agent, Liz Puttick, who set the ball rolling with useful ideas. Paul Leigh, Stacey Camfield and Marella Buckley were helpful at various stages of the manuscript. My Piatkus editors, Sandra Rigby and Gill Bailey, were assiduous and inspiring in pushing me to write the best book possible; they and Philip Cotterell suggested the title; Esther Jagger also did some very good editing on the final typescript; and alongside them all was Judy Piatkus who had faith in me and the project all along. I am grateful for these professional relationships, which are friendships too.

PART 1:

The Concepts

CHAPTER 1:

The Elixir of Life

The ideas and the strategies in this book have changed my life and those of many colleagues, friends and students. When I think of the people who have trained in the Endorphin Effect techniques, several faces immediately come to mind. They include John, the head of a property management company; Marie, the manager of a trauma centre in Northern Ireland; Michael, a medical doctor; Scott, a factory worker; and Hazel, a painter.

What did these people really want when they came on my courses to learn holistic strategies for self-development which they could use in their own personal and working lives and for helping others? They wanted physical and psychological health. They wanted success, a sense of integrity and fulfilment. And they also wanted connection with the beauty and wonder of life – call that spirit, or God, or whatever you will.

The people who train with my colleagues and me do not come in order to achieve a temporary buzz or feelgood. They need a practical strategy that is of positive use in their daily lives. To manage an effective clinic, to develop a successful business, to maintain a harmonious family – all of these require substantial energy, emotional resources and life skills. The Endorphin Effect can deliver these because at a very practical level it teaches a new, simple and accessible method that people can use without effort whenever they want.

The foundation of this work is the fact that when the hormones known as endorphins are produced in the body, they reduce tension and allow the body to absorb the vitality of nature and the universe. Endorphins, however, are only consistently produced by particular emotional and mental triggers. When they are being produced, there is a further range of strategies that are needed to maximize their effect. This book explains how the system works and how you can immediately put it into practical effect.

It clearly asserts that enduring physical health is entwined with emotional and mental wellbeing; and this psychological wellbeing is itself entwined with a positive spiritual experience of life. By positive spiritual experience, I mean a deepening sense of connection with the wisdom, power and beauty of all life – including yourself.

- Physical health.
- Psychological wellbeing.
- Positive spiritual experience.

All these three are inter-related. By integrating them, the Endorphin Effect gives people a fundamentally new and effective strategy.

The Benefits

I believe that the Endorphin Effect is a genuine breakthrough. It provides a simple strategy whereby absolutely anyone – regardless of time, mood or previous experience – can create wellbeing and build a lasting foundation for all other forms of personal development.

First and foremost, it provides

- A clear and accessible way to integrate the physical, psychological and spiritual

From this foundation, it delivers a quantum leap forward in the following specific fields:

- Health maintenance
- Stress control, relaxation, transforming burnout
- Confidence-building, self-esteem and clear boundaries

- Developing the clear and positive vision needed for clarifying next steps, goals and purpose
- Crisis management in families and organizations
- Building the supportive and visionary attitude necessary for effective leadership, cooperation and caring
- Developing emotional intelligence and effective life skills
- Staying centred and clear in disturbing circumstances
- Self-healing and healing others
- Managing and welcoming change
- Transforming fatigue and crisis into times of creativity and nurture
- Creating and sustaining the motivation and energy needed for achieving goals and positive change
- Bringing people back to and deepening their sense of connection with a meaningful and benevolent universe

Endorphins – Legend and Reality

How is this integration of the physical, the psychological and the spiritual to be achieved?

The legends of many ancient traditions tell of a miraculous substance which bestowed upon mortals the gift of celestial immortality. In classical Greece it was known as Ambrosia, the food of the gods. In Hindu mythology it was called Amrita and was made by churning the milk of the great cosmic ocean. In alchemy, it was named the Elixir of Life and Flower of the Sun. In Ben Jonson's play, *The Alchemist,* written in 1610, the leading character asserts that the Elixir can give anyone honour, love, respect, long life, safety and valour, and turn an eighty-year-old man into a child. How could anyone not be interested in such a warm and golden fluid that gives physical and psychological pleasure, health and confidence, and that connects us to the beauty and creative power of nature and the universe?

This mystical substance is also supposed to exist in many dimensions at the same time. In one dimension it is a physical fluid, a nectar that can be drunk from a chalice or from the horn of plenty. In another dimension it is an invisible cosmic energy that flows through the universe. In yet another dimension it is an emotion – a feeling of love, wisdom and wellbeing that expresses itself through the power and beauty of nature, as well as through the generosity and tenderness of a human heart. It is always there, this ambrosia, but we cannot see it. It is like the moisture in the air that becomes dew in the morning – invisible until it distils. This, I believe, is a wonderful way to look at and understand endorphins.

Physically, endorphins are biochemicals which are naturally produced in the human body. They are chemically similar to opium and its derivatives such as morphine, but as part of the body's normal hormone system they are not addictive or damaging. The basic properties of endorphins are that they:

- Create physical pleasure and kill pain. In extreme situations the body is capable of producing endorphins a thousand times stronger than chemical morphine.
- Work towards the healing of wounded and diseased tissues.
- Boost the immune system, providing a foundation for maintaining strong and vital health.
- Create physical feelings of wellbeing, which in turn translate into emotional and mental wellbeing, psychological health and happiness.
- Create euphoria and bliss states in which people experience a deep spiritual connection with all nature and the universe.

Endorphins are responsible for the euphoric rush experienced by athletes during continuous exercise. During lovemaking and sexual climax, a cascade of endorphins saturates the body. Endorphins, in fact, are created every time that someone experiences a moment of pleasure. It may be a sunset or a song or a friend or an achievement; it may be a soccer goal or a flower or a touch or another's smile. But the result, the physical sensation of pleasure, is always brought about by these same internal chemicals.

This is not, of course, the same as saying that happiness or pleasure are just a chemical in the body. It does mean, however, that the actual *physical* experience of pleasure – whatever its original source – is produced by endorphins.

Imagine, then, that endorphins are indeed the elixir of life, the ambrosia and nectar of the gods. Imagine that they are not only of the solid three-dimensional world, but that they also exist as a psychological and a spiritual essence. Imagine that endorphins are indeed the dew, distilled from experiences of pleasure. All this, of course, is poetic metaphor – but close, so close, to the truth.

The Miracle – Endorphins at Will

Whenever you want – in the midst of family pressure, anxious colleagues, an urgent crisis or seemingly unbearable stress – you can trigger the production of your endorphins, feel better and once again sense the good things of life. This book explains precisely how to do this.

To create your own inner feelgood through deliberately producing endorphins is a basic life skill that I believe everyone should possess. It brings immediate and long-term benefits. In the short term, it stimulates physical health and feelings of happiness. In the long term, it is a strategy for building a deep sense of being at ease with the world, without any dependence upon other people or external circumstances.

From a psychological perspective, what really matters is how you feel privately inside your own skin. There have always been people who instinctively remain positive even in the direst of situations. They can do this because their internal experience of life remains positive and hopeful, despite their circumstances. They feel good inside regardless of what is going on outside them. This skill and attitude can be learnt.

To work with endorphins places in your hands the power to control your basic experience. This golden nectar is freely available. Moreover, you can increase its production and guide it through your whole body so that every part of you fully experiences its benefits. Whoever you are and whatever you do, the strategies of *The Endorphin Effect* can only enhance and enrich your life.

There is an ancient Chinese saying from the *I Ching*: 'You can change the town, but you cannot change the well.' The lesson here is that people can do everything to change their circumstances – new job, new relationship, new home – but it will not change their essential experience. Real happiness and fulfilment come from within.

Inevitable Challenges

Although I am inspired by and devoted to the holistic approach, there is also a need for realism. I know that every few weeks I am going to be told about some wonderful new method for achieving everlasting health and success. Having studied or worked in the holistic field for most of my life, I am used to this quick-fix syndrome. And it is not a new phenomenon: there were always saints' bones, false miracles and cure-all snake oils for the gullible.

Sadly, I have become accustomed to seeing the euphoria and certainty of self-help enthusiasts melt away after their panacea does not deliver the results they actually want and need. People may emerge inspired and confident after reading a book or attending a training, but the positive attitude disappears as they deal with the strains of daily life and realize that deep down they have not really changed at all. They lose energy and hope. Their euphoria evaporates and they slip back into their habitual experience of life.

It is of course absolutely normal and good that we should want health, success, happiness and personal development in our family, careers, sports, hobbies, relationships and spiritual lives. And there are thousands of books, courses, techniques, gurus, strategies and life skills to help us. But the reality is that these approaches cannot bring enduring results unless they also provide a core strength and positive attitude to sustain us through the difficult changes and inevitable challenges.

There are also many people who appear to have achieved high levels of personal and financial success but feel that their lives are hollow. They gain no real sense of satisfaction from their achievements, which may only camouflage a human being who really needs some far deeper form of comfort and contentment. People need to *feel* happiness and success, not own it. It needs to be inside their skin, not outside. A lasting sense of success and wellbeing requires a foundation that sits in your cells.

Any self-help approach which ignores these issues is less than complete. I was touched by Alice Miller's powerful book *The Drama of Being a Child*. In it, she attacks those schools of therapy and personal growth which aim for quick fixes and temporary feelgoods but fail to deal with relevant and tragic childhood histories. Her most poignant criticism is that the trainers, gurus and therapists themselves are trying to re-create with their clients the sense of family that they themselves wanted as children, but never had.

To face one's past is not always easy. It is usually more comfortable to stay in denial. Facing the truth about your emotional past, recognizing your patterns of self-sabotage and then managing them through to health is tough work. It requires motivation, support, appropriate strategies and many other dynamic factors.

At the very least, then, a sustained endorphin experience provides a benevolent and strong foundation for that kind of effort. It is obviously easier to embark on and sustain challenging self-improvement if the basic physical experience is coloured by ambrosia and not by the acid of tension and adrenalin. The later chapters of this book contain specific exercises for working with deep emotional pain whilst using the endorphin effect as a supportive foundation.

Cats, Soccer, Sex and Chocolate

My own understanding and appreciation of this endorphin-based approach did not come easily. In fact, one of the things that blocked me in the first place was that it all seemed too easy.

In my early twenties I gave up a career in publishing and novel writing, which had brought me material rewards and a good press but no satisfaction. I then took a two-year spiritual retreat living amongst the Saharan Berbers in the High Atlas Mountains, started a daily meditation practice, sometimes of five hours a day, and began teaching energy medicine back in Britain. When I decided that I also needed mainstream education I became a mature student, did two undergraduate degrees and a doctorate, and began to teach at the London School of Economics, later leaving to work with special needs students in an inner city college. Throughout this time I was still teaching meditation and energy work, and I was also initiating and working with various holistic projects. Do you catch a pattern in me here? I was Earnest Ernie, the workaholic meditator!

My bubble of earnestness, however, was finally popped by listening to students in my Open Mystery School, a project that I started in the early 1990s specifically to investigate new ways of teaching and practising meditation and energy medicine. One day, working with a very experienced group, I used a classic meditation to take them into an atmosphere of calm, bliss and a sense of unity with all life. I had done this exercise many times before, but I had an intuition about what might be interesting and instructive. Keeping the group in the calm atmosphere, I put a question to them.

'In your normal daily life,' I asked, 'what circumstances take you most easily into this same atmosphere, into this sense of connection? In response to this question see what thoughts and ideas surface in your mind.'

A while later I took the group out of the silence and then went round the circle listening to people share their thoughts. I was in for a shock that changed my whole style of teaching and my personal practice. There was a woman in the group who simply stated:

'Sitting at home, stroking my cat on my lap.'

Several other people in the circle nodded appreciatively, but I tensed up. A cat on the lap was no way to enter into the experience of deep cosmic connection! I kept my facial expression friendly and attentive, but inside I had gone into judgemental hyperdrive.

I repeated the same exercise with other groups. Over and over again, I found myself listening to answers that had nothing at all to do with meditation or any other classical spiritual practice. It was not just cats on laps. People mentioned walking, sports, eating, cycling, making love, gardening, reading, painting, managing, singing, succeeding, hobbies, eating chocolates . . .

This was all a spectacular revelation for me. All the structures and disciplines of the classical spiritual practices, which I knew so well, fell away. The puritan in me died a shocked death. The whole spiritual culture of the last two millennia is constructed on the idea that connecting with the benevolent wavefields – with 'God' or 'Cosmic Consciousness' or the 'Universal Mystery'– is very difficult. Only saints, the enlightened or the 'chosen' can achieve it. But here I could see that people were frequently making their own connection, in their own private way – though it was not being recognized or valued.

What I eventually learned and will explain in detail later in the book is that the fundamental religious experience – that sensation of pleasure and connection with the grandeur and wonder of life – is biologically experienced through the effect of endorphins. This is why, as my students taught me, there are so many different gateways to that experience. Any experience of pleasure can produce endorphins. And any one of them, in the right circumstances or with the right guidance, can create a cascade of endorphins.

Exercising Your Spiritual Muscles

Different people have different moments when they are moved by the beauty and excitement of life. For some people it may be the sunrise. For others a sunset. The mountains. The ocean. A good book. A sudden understanding. Music. Food. Sport. Children. Art. Suddenly an emotion and a feeling that life is perfect or wonderful can overwhelm you. There is a deep satisfaction, a sense of belonging, of being in flow. Your heart may open. A strange inspiration can touch you.

To have this moving experience requires no work or preparation – it is a natural part of being human. You only need to be alive and awake. But these events do not last long. Most people notice the sunset and the euphoria, perhaps pause for a few seconds, and then turn their attention elsewhere.

Imagine, though, what would happen if, when the beauty of an event temporarily moved you, you paused for a little longer. Imagine that you allowed yourself to stay in the experience, to feel and absorb it fully. (Perhaps you already do this.) Suddenly, questions that might previously have seemed naive take on real meaning.

- Do you sense the creative power of nature and the universe?
- Do you have a sense of peace, of deep contentment and of knowing that you are one with life?
- Can you sense an inner strength and a calm certainty that your life has meaning?

In normal daily life, you might not be able to answer 'Yes' to any of these questions. In fact, the questions might even seem embarrassing. But caught in the power of a euphoric moment they can feel very different and it becomes possible to respond with a clear, authentic 'Yes.'

At moments of powerful beauty, emotions can penetrate even the thickest and most cynical of skins. Endorphins flow. There is a release of tension. Energies, internal and external, flow and connect. The experience is not only soft and calm, but also contains the power and creativity of nature and the universe.

To create and to work consciously with these moments of connection is to exercise what we might call our spiritual muscles and our spiritual intelligence. What do I mean here by 'spiritual'? I simply mean that whole reality and dimension which is bigger, more creative, more loving, more powerful, more visionary, more wise, more mysterious than materialistic daily human existence. There is no theology or belief system that relates to this meaning of spiritual.

> **Exercising your spiritual muscles is to connect regularly with the powerful beauty of life and to allow it to enter you as an endorphin-filled full-body sensation.**

Religious Does Not Mean Religion

Obviously, from the perspective of this work, formal spiritual disciplines and rituals are not the only way to approach spiritual connection and wellbeing. They may be absolutely appropriate for some people, but for others spiritual experience is indeed the touch of their cat or a brilliant goal.

A man once described to me his own most awesome spiritual moment. As a teenager, he was taken to his first football match at which his superhero, George Best, was playing for Manchester United against Newcastle. Manchester won eight goals to two, six of which were scored by Best. The teenage spectator, standing only yards away from the goal posts with his fellow supporters, went into ecstasy.

When the endorphin effect is flowing with full power, it creates an emotion of bliss with its sense of the beauty and unity of all life. This is the classic mystical and religious experience. For a student of religion, this is revolutionary information, because it empirically demonstrates that the religious experience – euphoria, joy, bliss, connection – is not restricted to particular faiths or particular types of people. It is an integral part of the human condition, of being a healthy and harmonious human being.

Recognizing how endorphins work, it is possible today to understand and map the spiritual experiences that were previously thought to be restricted to great saints and mystics. Whilst this does not for one moment detract from the great mystery and beauty of creation, it does detract from human spiritual pomposity.

How deeply threatening this can be to religious fundamentalists was brought home to me in 1998 when I attended the United Nations Oslo Conference on Freedom of Belief as an official delegate representing the holistic approach to religion. Several controversial views were listened to respectfully. Those who spoke them included, for instance, a Buddhist monk sent from Beijing to denounce the Dalai Lama and a rabbi who ranted against the Palestinian Arabs. I, however, was booed for suggesting that there was a natural human instinct and ability to connect with the wonder and beauty of the universe, and that this was the true foundation of religion. I received the disapproval of a group of fundamentalist rabbis, Christian priests and Islamic mullahs who were, interestingly, sitting together. My statement challenged their view that human beings are imperfect creatures and that God alone selects the chosen ones who will experience divine beauty and bliss.

I was shocked by their hostility, but also happy to be in open conflict with them. Their way of interpreting religion is passing away as surely as we now understand that the Earth is not flat but round. Fundamentalist approaches may once have predominated, but a recent poll in the United Kingdom showed that 65 per cent of those asked believed either that 'all religions offer a path to God' or that 'there is a way to God outside organized religion'. Only 9 per cent of those polled said, 'What I believe is the only way to God.'[1]

The freedom and the ability to enjoy spiritual connection and inspiration belong to everyone, regardless of their faith or background. We are all, just because we are alive, able to feel and be at one with the universe.

From Mystery to Management

Recognizing the link between endorphins, pleasure and spiritual connection allowed me to develop and modernize many techniques from energy medicine – such as yoga, chi gung and spiritual healing – and meditation. The effectiveness of these new strategies gradually resulted in many of my students wanting to coach and teach them as well. So my experimental Open Mystery School courses transformed into formal training, many of whose students were already professional carers, educators and consultants. The techniques I developed, therefore, are now being taught on a one-to-one and group basis in therapy and life coaching, as well as in commercial and non-profit organizations.

At a gathering of these coaches in 1998, we decided that the work which had evolved out of the Open Mystery School should be called Core Energy Management (CEM). 'Core' because it is at the heart and centre of things. 'Energy' because, as one of our slogans states, 'The Universe is made of energy. So are you. It makes sense – knowing how to manage it.' And 'Management' because that was an accurate description as well as an appropriate word for taking the work out into mainstream situations. We also started a training and consultancy organization, Holistic Partnerships.

The applications of CEM are very wide. From my perspective, its most meaningful feature is that it gives people the most powerful tool available for looking after themselves. Through this approach, people get a genuine experience of their own private source of support. It plugs them into a limitless source of benevolent energy. Burnout is healed. A confident strong centre is built and maintained, which also delivers a supportive attitude and atmosphere for others. At the same time, purpose and next steps are easily clarified. This is powerful stuff when applied to any individual, family, relationship or organization.

These strategies are very practical and can sometimes work very fast. For example, one of our coaches, Jenny Kirk, a counsellor and ex-junior schoolteacher, was asked to work with an eleven-year-old by his parents. Their son was behaving abusively at home and being bullied at school.

> ❝ Having achieved a rapport with the boy, I took him through the basic CEM strategy encouraging him to use his own Star Wars language and imagery to make sense of it. His positive response was immediate. Almost overnight it gave him a sense of wellbeing and personal power which both stopped the bullying at school and his abusiveness at home. ❞

Ashley Akin-Smith, an experienced facilitator and energy worker, has also applied the strategy to teams.

> ❝ At an annual international convention for fund-raisers I was in charge of the fifteen-strong hospitality team who worked to welcome and host the thousand delegates to this week-long event. In the middle of the first day, tension was rising as delegates arrived late, could not get on the programmes they wanted and generally began to move the whole event into a sour mood. I pulled my team off the floor and over thirty minutes ran them through the basic Core Energy strategy. Within half an hour of them being back on the floor, the whole atmosphere of potential crisis was transformed. ❞

Ashley has also used the CEM techniques in large organizations to envision and plan their new computer and communications systems, an approach that I describe later in the book.

Over much longer periods of time, I have seen people using these techniques to heal the wounds caused by the worst and most tragic kinds of childhood abuse. I have also watched it support people coming off addictions and compulsive behaviour. And at the other end of the spectrum, I have seen successful and hearty people using these same strategies to deepen their sense of fulfilment, to expand the support they give others and to clarify their purpose and next steps.

I am very grateful to the woman who told me about the cat on her lap. She did not know what she was starting.

CHAPTER 2:

The Feelings Factory – Understanding Endorphins

Struggling with Ease

It is Oslo, July 1997. Sitting directly opposite me in the seminar room is a powerful man in his sixties with a high-domed forehead and a mane of white hair swept back from his face. He is leaning forward, his shoulders hunched and his face frowning. Every few seconds, he shuffles and sighs. He is struggling with the information that I am sharing. The other students are more relaxed.

It is impossible for me to ignore him, and I wait uncomfortably for him to say something. Finally, in one of my pauses, he simply interjects:

'It cannot be that easy.'

The rest of the students, a group of all ages, watch him but are not too bothered by his scepticism. It is a difficult moment for me. I could open up a discussion with him. Or ask the group what they think. Or call a tea break. Instead, I follow my intuition. All I do is nod to acknowledge what he has said and continue teaching.

Twenty minutes later he lets out a loud, exasperated sigh and slumps back in his chair shaking his head. I stop talking. This time, with a bemused smile, he says something very different.

'I do not want to believe it, but its true. I do it all the time.'

I ask him to say more. He sighs and again smiles his bemused smile. He no longer looks so intense or intimidating.

'I am an academic,' he explains. 'A theologian and an art critic. I came to your training as part of my research. I am writing a critique of the new approaches to human meaning and philosophy. They are too shallow. I know how difficult life is. You offer a quick fix based, you say, on what is natural for us. Of course, I have to reject it.'

He pauses and looks round the group.

'This is embarrassing for me. What Dr Bloom describes is indeed natural. I do it myself! In my dining room I have a wonderful copy of the *Mona Lisa*. Every day, sometimes several times a day, especially if I am depressed, I go and look at her. Looking at her changes my mood. I begin to feel lighter, more optimistic. Sometimes, looking at her, I breathe in a way that I was taught by Buddhists and my calm deepens. This is very good for me – and for the people around me. Without her, I would be hell to live with.'

Feeling the Smile

The Norwegian scholar's experience of his painting is precisely the same experience that other people have in hundreds of thousands of other situations. The *Mona Lisa* may not be what touches *your* mind or heart, but there will be other things that do touch you – places, people, activities, arts, sports, smells, tastes, memories.

And when you are touched by them, you know that something has happened because your emotions shift. How you feel – your mood – shifts from one type of sensation to another. You know this because you feel it within you.

Some people, not understanding what I mean by 'feeling it within you', tell me that they never feel anything, that they are unemotional or insensitive. When this happens, I ask them to close their eyes and think of some person, place or activity that they adore. I do not know what they bring to mind: perhaps a lover, a symphony, a beach, a motorbike, a meal, a book, a sport, a mountain. Almost immediately their facial expression changes. There is a universal body language at work here. A slight smile appears. The face lightens.

'Are you feeling anything?' I ask.

'No,' they invariably reply.

'Are you happy to be thinking about your friend or activity or place?'

'Yes,' they respond.

'What do you mean by "happy"? Is it a feeling inside you?' I query.

'Yes,' they say, smiling.

'That's it! That's all it is, that slight feeling inside you, the change of mood that makes you smile,' I say. 'You know it's happening because you feel it. It's physical and it's within you.'

The Feelings Factory

This ability to feel your mood, physically to sense and experience it, is the result of biochemical changes that take place inside your body. Organic drugs, naturally produced by your body, alter the biochemistry of your cells, which you then experience in the way you feel.

The feelings with which this book is particularly concerned are pleasure, happiness. Right from the beginning I want to be clear about what I mean by 'happiness' and 'pleasure'. This book is not about a superficial or narcissistic add-on to real life. We are talking about a fundamental aspect of what it means to be a complete and fulfilled human being. It is not by whimsical chance that the United States Constitution explicitly asserts and protects the pursuit of happiness as one of the most basic of human rights.

Happiness is not a simple thing. It might be spoken about glibly, but it is a complex entity and no shallow emotion. It touches the very roots of what it is to have a meaningful life. It contains profound sentiments such as confidence, fulfilment, success, connectedness, integrity and courage.

Pleasure and happiness are described by psychologists as one of the six primary or universal emotions, the others being sadness, fear, anger, surprise and disgust. You might possibly want more surprise in your life, but I doubt if you want more fear, sadness, anger or disgust – even though they are all necessary for effective survival and a whole life. But it is a natural and healthy instinct to want happiness.

From the perspective of biological science, pleasure and happiness are not abstract psychological or philosophical ideas. They are a biochemical state, a precise experience happening in the physical body.

That chemicals can create moods is not new information. This is exactly why doctors prescribe drugs for psychological illness and distress. Many of these drugs are organic and to be found in nature; others are manufactured. What has been discovered, however, is that the human body itself is capable of producing many of these drugs purely within itself. In fact, your body is a biochemicals factory.

The particular biochemicals that create the physical feeling of happiness are, as already explained, endorphins. The basic claim made by this book – that it is possible to trigger the production of endorphins and create feelings of happiness at will – is possible because of some remarkable recent breakthroughs in biological science, particularly in the scientific field known as psycho-neuro-immunology. These breakthroughs have mapped precisely how moods and feelings are chemically transmitted through the body. ('Psycho-neuro-immunology' is not usually hyphenated, but if you are meeting the term for the first time it is more easily grasped than the usual 'psychoneuroimmunology'.)

Discovering Endorphins

It is worth spending a little time looking at the actual science of endorphins. (Yes, we are about to get boffiny, but not for long.) Their discovery and an appreciation of their significance are in fact very recent.

The best known public figure in this field is Candace Pert who began her doctoral research under Solomon Snyder in the pharmacology department at John Hopkins University in Baltimore by looking at how opium and morphine 'landed' in human cells and created their powerful effects. The idea was that a deeper understanding would be very helpful, for example, in developing more effective and less addictive painkillers. In October 1972, using a technique developed by Avram Goldstein of Stanford University in California, she identified what was known as the 'opiate receptor', that part of the cell which accepted and then reacted with the drug.

It was then logically suggested that, if the body contained a mechanism for receiving these drugs, perhaps they were naturally produced within the body. In other words, within the body itself there would be a chemical equivalent to opium or pharmacologically produced morphine. And so the hunt for them was on in laboratories all around the world.

The search ended in 1975 when John Hughes and Hans Kosterlitz of Aberdeen University in Scotland published a paper identifying certain substances that they called 'enkephalins'. The American scientists working in the same field, however, named them 'endorphins', which means endogenous morphine – morphine produced within the body itself. And it is this term which has come into common usage.

Twenty types of endorphin have been discovered in the nervous system. They are part of a family of chemicals, known as neuropeptides, which carry information around the body. There are approximately a hundred different types of neuropeptide and they are all amino acids. DNA, the beautiful double spiral molecule which carries our genetic coding, is the most well-known of these amino acids.

Research was then developed to discover exactly where endorphins were produced in the body and what stimulated their production. Originally, it was thought that their production was restricted to the brain, but in the 1980s it was discovered that they were secreted not only in the brain but also throughout the whole body.

This was a revolutionary discovery as it led to a new and profoundly important understanding – that the body's nervous system, immune system and endocrine (hormone) system are all intimately interlinked. Endorphins can be produced at any location in the body and they can also flow through the whole system like waves in an ocean. In *Molecules of Emotion* Candace Pert described this process as follows.

> ❝ The point I am making is that your brain is extremely well integrated with the rest of your body at a molecular level, so much so that the term *mobile brain* is an apt description of the psychosomatic network through which intelligent information travels from one system to another. Every one of the zones, or systems, of the network – the neural, the hormonal, the gastrointestinal, and the immune – is set up to communicate with one another, via peptides and messenger specific peptide receptors. Every second, a massive information exchange is happening in your body. Imagine each of these messenger systems possessing a specific tone, humming a signature tune, rising and falling, waxing and waning, binding and unbinding, and if we could hear this body music with our ears, then the sum of these sounds would be the music that we call the emotions. ❞ [1]

Old models of the human body have therefore been forced to expand to include a new one. The body is not just bones, levers and muscles; not just a transport system of blood, nerves and juices. The psychoneuroimmunological perspective argues that we should also see the body as a flowing information system, with all its parts engaged in the business of conveying, receiving and processing information. This is crucial for understanding the relationship and feedback system between the body, feelings and mind. The endorphins and other neuropeptides flow through the body conveying this information in a way that resembles a cauldron of soup being stirred and filled with different nutrients and flavours. These nutrients and flavours are, from one perspective, chemicals. From another perspective they are our moods, emotions and feelings.

Endorphins, Health and the Immune System

Endorphins are directly implicated in the following physiological functions:
- Central nervous system and peripheral analgesia and pain modulation
- Chronic pain
- Gastro-intestinal physiology
- Cardiovascular regulation
- Temperature regulation
- Control of food consumption and taste preference
- Respiration
- Vomiting
- Immunological processes
- Regulation of anterior pituitary hormones
- Neuroendocrine control of reproduction
- Childbirth

They are also indirectly implicated in the following psychological functions:
- Stress
- Spontaneous behaviour
- Learning and memory
- Motivation
- Psychiatric disorders

Endorphins remove stress and pain. Their general effect is to relax tissue so that all the necessary antibodies travel into the affected body region in order to repair and heal. Under stress, your immune competence is reduced to a high degree. An ongoing flow of endorphins throughout the body avoids constriction and maintains a state of biochemical fluidity. In this way the immune system is maintained in its optimum state.

Specifically, endorphins enhance the immune system by activating the natural killer cells (NK cells), which destroy defective cells and cancer cells. They also maintain the flexibility and openness of blood vessels, thereby supporting an ongoing and normal flow of blood into all tissue; this prevents many of the adult diseases, such as strokes and cardiovascular problems. (Most adult diseases start from clogged blood vessels.)

Happy Blobs

Another significant discovery was that endorphins are found not just in humans but in all living creatures. Even tiny single-celled organisms, the most basic of life forms, have opiate receptors and endorphins. This basic amino acid, then, which creates pleasurable feelings in people is a fundamental part of biological life.

Imagine looking down a microscope and seeing a tiny single-celled creature floating around in its liquid. For me, it is stunning that this little being carries the feelgood chemical in its body. This leads to a major question: does this creature experience happiness? I do not know, but maybe it is a very comfortable little blob.

That tiny single-celled creatures possess endorphins is a profoundly optimistic piece of information. It means that every cell of our multi-celled body is capable of experiencing endorphins and that the propensity to experience happiness and euphoria is biologically built into each one of us. This allows us to put forward an unexpected but exact scientific statement: *Happiness and pleasure are built into the biological foundation of the human body.*

Inside

How, then, are we to create pleasure and happiness? It is certainly within all of us, latent as endorphins, but where exactly does the emotion of feeling good begin – in the mind or the body? Which comes first, the chicken or the egg – the biological mechanism or the psychological trigger? This question is of crucial importance when it comes to understanding why some people are happy and others are not. Does someone produce endorphins because they have a naturally upbeat disposition? Or are they happy because their biology is predisposed to produce natural opiates? Is it psychological or genetic?

The relationship between body chemistry and psychological state is a core issue for psychiatry and healthcare. The purpose, for instance, of prescribing drugs such as Prozac is precisely to create the chemical physical experience of an upbeat calm which in turn supports psychological stability. In the long term, it is hoped that the anti-depressant will jump-start the patient's own natural anti-depressants, both biochemical and attitudinal. The patient will get accustomed to feeling good and will, therefore, stay in the groove even when the medication ends.

In *The Feeling of What Happens,* Antonio Damasio, professor of neurology at Iowa College of Medicine, describes emotions as 'complicated collections of chemical and neural responses, forming a pattern; all emotions have some kind of regulatory role to play....their role is to assist the organism in maintaining life.'

It is challenging, however, for many people to accept that the experience of our emotions is based *purely* in chemical changes, because the actual experience of these 'chemical and neural responses' is so very psychological, so very emotional. They make us feel good. They make us feel bad. They are the stuff of life's daily drama and passion. How can it all just be molecules?

Well, it is quite evidently not just molecules. The molecules are part of a complete system that includes our mind, psychology and how we respond to our environment. Damasio recognizes this and suggests a helpful distinction between feelings and emotions. '*Feeling* should be reserved for the private mental experience of an emotion, while the term *emotion* should be used to designate the collection of responses, many of which are publicly observable.'[2] So, yes, a change in the molecules, an injection of morphine, can change how we feel, can alter our emotions and our thinking and, therefore, how we behave to the world around us.

The sequence has a clear logic:
1. The body produces neuropeptides.
2. The neuropeptides change how the body feels.
3. The new feeling affects our emotions, our mood and how we think.
4. The new mood affects our behaviour.

To put it graphically:

> **Neuropeptides –> Change how body feels –>**
> **Change psychological mood –> New behaviour**

In the specific case of endorphins, this could be described as:

> **Endorphin –> Feeling of pleasure –>**
> **Mood of happiness –> Friendly behaviour**

Outside and Perception

But outside events affect us too. Our moods do not always just emerge out of cellular chemistry beyond our psychological control. We are continuously stimulated and triggered by the circumstances around us.

When my students described what took them into bliss, joy and a sense of connection, we ended up with a list of stimuli longer than this book. Of course, there were general categories like places in nature, particular people and animals, special activities and hobbies, certain smells and sensations – but such a list could be almost endless. In fact, it is perfectly clear that outside events trigger our endorphins.

So we can easily state that:

- Chemical endorphins create a happy mood.

And

- Pleasurable events create endorphins too.

Obviously these two dynamics can benevolently reinforce each other:

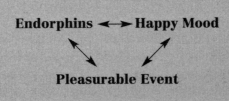

But how people respond to external events is very much a matter of perception. There is a mental and emotional filter at work here, which judges and selects what is liked or not liked. If something external is perceived as pleasurable, it triggers endorphins; but if something out there is perceived as threatening, it triggers adrenalin.

Let me give some simple examples. On the following list, which do you find pleasurable (or nice) and which do you find threatening (or nasty)?

- Chocolate cake
- Motorbike racing
- Female bodybuilder
- Male bodybuilder
- Bottle of whisky
- Carton of goat's milk

The perception of an external stimulus as being pleasurable or threatening, nice or nasty, depends on the psychology and taste of the individual. One man's *Mona Lisa* is another man's yawn. What is erotic for one person is a turn-off for another. One of the great riches of life is to appreciate and uncover the different things that give people pleasure, and not to expect everyone to like the same things.

We must, therefore, add perception to our formula:

External stimulus –> Perceived as pleasurable –> Triggers endorphins

Pleasurable Internal Events

But it is not only pleasurable external events that trigger endorphins. Pleasurable events that happen *purely within the mind* trigger endorphins too.

In fact, the biological mechanism that produces endorphins does not care about the source of the pleasurable sensation. It can be real or imagined. When I ask people to close their eyes and think of something they adore, the internal biological reaction can be as immediate as if they are encountering the real thing. The Norwegian scholar discovered that he could evoke as much pleasure just thinking about the *Mona Lisa* as when he was actually looking at it. (And his painting was a reproduction anyway.)

A pleasurable caress that stimulates endorphins can be physical or imaginary. Everyone knows that fantasy, for many people, is as stimulating as reality.

> **The unconscious mind and the psychoneuroimmunological system cannot tell the difference between what is real and what is imagined.**

The crucial practical point here is that people can actively choose to use this mental and imaginative ability in order to change the biochemistry of their own body. This can be seen clearly in the extreme examples of yogis and fakirs who masterfully trigger their endorphins in order to manage self-inflicted injuries.

Holistic Healthcare and Harmonious Flow

Understanding how endorphins work and the body-mind connection are crucial issues for healthcare. Endorphins are not only essential for maintaining good health, they are also an indication of whether you experience psychological wellbeing. There is here, then, an extremely obvious benevolent feedback loop:

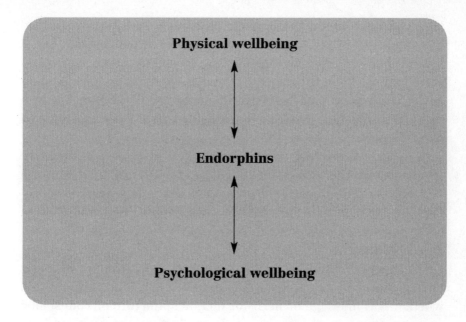

Mainstream Western medicine is cautiously moving towards accepting the implications of this. This caution is understandable because there is something intangible about the body-mind connection when compared with the apparent efficiency and logic of chemical and surgical intervention.

The holistic health movement, however, has enthusiastically embraced the insights about neuropeptides and the body as an 'information soup'. They substantiate the holistic approach's core tenet that the human body is not a conglomeration of bits and pieces, but a complex whole. For ongoing health, therefore, the holistic approach strongly asserts that all the different aspects of a human being must be in harmony.

Harmony is also a concept much used in Eastern systems of medicine. The mind, emotions, breath, muscles, blood, nervous system and so on need to be in harmony. Another way of putting this in Eastern language is that the body and mind must be in a healthy and contented 'flow'.

From a Western medical perspective, the words 'harmony' and 'flow' can seem to lack a certain scientific rigour. But endorphins need to flow in order to boost the immune system and to open up tissue that is tense, crystalline or coagulated. Disease is combated by a healthy flow of the necessary antibodies into affected areas. A healthy body necessarily means that blood, nutrients, hormones and so on are flowing smoothly around the system. In fact, one definition of illness is that the body's elements are not flowing easily. A damaged limb demonstrates its regained health by moving and being flexible.

If there is a blockage of this normal flow anywhere in the body, mind or spirit, the whole system will be affected and the result will be some form of illness or distress. Put in the language of neuropeptides, the normal and healthy background hum and flow of endorphins is replaced with an unhealthy coagulation of tension and constriction.

The purpose, then, of holistic healthcare is to remove blockages and tension and bring the whole system back into harmony. So, whether it is massage or herbs or diet, acupuncture or counselling or aromatherapy, yoga or sport or meditation, the purpose is to remove physical and mental obstacles so that the system can come back to a natural state of flowing harmony.

It is worth noting a fundamental idea here: *Harmony is the normal state in which we are supposed to live*. Real healthcare is maintaining this harmony.

Lessons for Western and Eastern Medicine

What the study of neuropeptides specifically gives to holistic healthcare is a much more acute awareness of the primary influence of emotions and attitudes – and the kinds of mood that are good for ongoing health.

The bottom line is, I believe, very clear: a sense of internal pleasure, or enjoyment, is fundamental to good health. I have noticed that many health practitioners describe harmony and flow as if they are almost technical concepts, like plumbing a house efficiently. But they are not technical, and they need a much more sensitive understanding of people's emotions. This is crucial because, psychologically, it is only a pleasurable mood that produces endorphins. Flow that is not pleasurable does not create the desired effect.

A famous example of the complementary approach to health, *Anatomy of an Illness*, shows how this works. In this book Norman Cousins describes how in 1964 he was struck down with ankylosing spondylitis, a severe connective tissue disease.[3] He decided to explore the nature of the disease himself and designed his own treatment, which was basically a regimen of very high doses of vitamin C and laughter. He found his laughter in a steady diet of *Candid Camera* and the Marx Brothers, and discovered that 'ten minutes of genuine belly laughter had an anaesthetic effect and would give me at least two hours of painfree sleep'. Cousins then went on to work in affiliation with the University of California's School of Medicine in Los Angeles, working to inspire a holistic and compassionate perspective in healthcare professionals.

His book, which attracted huge attention, was published in the 1970s, almost three decades before the startling revelations of psychoneuroimmunology. What we can understand now is precisely how the laughter created the pain-free comfort. The laughter was genuinely pleasurable to him and created a mood of optimism and harmony, healing the feelings of depression or pessimism that might contribute to destroying his health. He created for himself a lasting pleasurable mood which triggered the endorphins.

I think also of an acquaintance who suffered two severe strokes with complications and whose health was deteriorating. He is absolutely certain that he attained full recovery almost purely because of the regular visits of his granddaughter. In her grandfather's eyes, she was so delightful that she sustained him in a mood of pleasure despite his physical distress.

When neuroscientists at Chicago University conducted research into endorphin flows, they confirmed that laughter produced high endorphin surges. However, they also discovered that the people who produced the highest sustained flow were not those who laughed the most uproariously, but those who had a consistent smile and a twinkle in their eye. This 'twinkle in the eye' is a symptom of someone who is living a consistently pleasurable, happy and harmonious life, something that we shall return to in Chapter 5.

Understanding the relationship between endorphins and the mood of pleasure also gives useful insights into Eastern healthcare methods. The health-giving properties of yoga or chi gung, for example, are well known, but they both actually possess two distinct styles. One style is very efficient and disciplined; the other kinder and more focussed on a happy and pleasurable attitude.

The 'hard' style of yoga and chi gung produces a toned, vital and vigorous body, but does not necessarily produce the endorphin-based internal flows, which make for flexible and open arteries and tissues, true essentials for enduring health and longevity. The 'soft' approach, however, creates an emotional mood of happiness and pleasure, guaranteeing a much deeper wellbeing. The 'hard' style is also restricted to the able-bodied, whereas the 'soft' style can be practised by anyone.

Including the Environment

But our endorphins and our pleasure are not just triggered by things we psychologically perceive as pleasurable. Most of us instinctively respond to kind touch, to physical warmth, to a safe, beautiful and supportive environment.

Sometimes people even swoon with physical pleasure, leaving the mind in confusion. This makes me believe that there is a primal ability in all of us to experience beauty and pleasure. Just as a single-celled organism can soak in endorphins, so can we. It is part of our biological structure.

In this context, the idea that we need to experience harmony with nature and our environment becomes a key piece of the health-care package. To be blunt, how can you possibly experience safety and pleasure in a hostile or alienated environment? Whether you like it or not, you are an interdependent and creative part of your environment. You are not an isolated unit inside your private shell and closed universe – or at least you should not be. You are literally a creature of nature and of the universe and you need to know and feel this. A healthy body, a positive emotional state, an enduring and happy psychology are not separate from your ecology.

For sustained health, you need a harmonious relationship with your surroundings – people, plants, animals, landscape. And relationship is not a one-way flow. Just as you find harmony and plea-sure in your environment, so the community of life around you must also be able to find harmony and pleasure in you.

To live in a community that sustains your pleasure and towards which you are positively beneficial is a recipe for heaven on earth. Once again, we can see here the crucial link between physical health, psychological attitude and spiritual experience.

We therefore have to expand our original equation (see p.26) to include the whole community of life, so that the equation becomes a fully holistic and benevolent feedback loop:

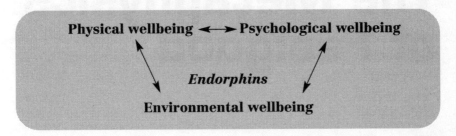

Physical wellbeing ◄—► **Psychological wellbeing**

Endorphins

Environmental wellbeing

This ideal of harmony with all life is not a mental attitude, but a full emotional mood experienced throughout the body. Good health, then, is to access this state and to be in it as much as possible. Let me affirm that I believe such a state of harmony to be possible – not only possible, but biologically built into our very essence. To be healthy, to experience harmony, is how we are meant to be.

CHAPTER 3:

The Metaphysics of Feelgood

Not Mad

In February 1972 one of the most distinguished psychiatrists in Britain declared that I was sane. Edward Glover was eighty-three years old, wore a pinstripe suit and bow tie and had a few feathers of white hair. I was twenty-four years old, had bell-bottom jeans, an earring and a large motorcycle parked outside. He declared me sane towards the end of three years' psychoanalysis which I had entered whilst suffering what can best be described as an identity crisis. His actual pronouncement in his precise Scottish accent went something like:

'So, do you still think you're mad?' He paused. 'I don't think you are. In fact, I think you're rather sane.'

I was Edward's last client and he seemed to enjoy my company. We often swopped cigarettes and occasionally he told me stories about the early days of psychoanalysis and his own analysis that sometimes took place under an olive tree in Italy. He once talked nostalgically about the time when there were only a dozen psychoanalysts in the world and they were all filled with a sense of wonder and discovery at what they were doing.

This kind of conversation, which is against the usual rules of psychoanalysis, was in itself very healing for me. Perhaps he did it with all his patients, or perhaps he did it deliberately to encourage me.

It was very important to me that he asserted so clearly that I was sane, because at the time I seriously thought that I might be crazy. The way that I experienced life did not fit any of the maps I had been given by my parents or my education. Since I was a young child, I had been very sensitive to the atmospheres of people and places. I was easily spooked, but I was also easily touched by beauty. Sometimes the experience of beauty – for instance, of the blue sky – was so powerful that I was transfixed in wonder. But I was not able to express any of this to my family or teachers. When I tried to talk about it, I was greeted with misunderstanding or sarcasm. So I kept quiet and wondered if I was sane.

Then in my teens, in the 1960s, there was an explosion of information about altered states of consciousness, vibrations, energy, meditation and different mystical and magical paths. Following the attitude of my parents and peers, I was mainly contemptuous or cynical, but then I began to realize that this information spoke about my own experience of life.

So I became strung out between two positions. On one side, I was having experiences of altered states of consciousness and the energy underlying all life. On the other side, I was still caught up in the idea that anything mystical was for the psychologically deluded and emotionally insecure. My patronizing attitude was also directed at holistic forms of medicine. I was typical of my cultural and intellectual group, many of whom are still around today – normally open-minded, but at the slightest sign of any concept beyond the norms, anything metaphysical, they react defensively and aggressively.

No wonder that I took myself into psychoanalysis. I was two people at the same time – an aggressive intellectual and a flower-power psychic. No wonder that Edward Glover's pronouncement of my sanity was so meaningful for me. No wonder also that today I so appreciate the insights of contemporary science – quantum physics, cosmology, complexity, psychoneuroimmunology. They provide a bridge between the rigour of a mechanistic scientific

approach and the less logical world of body, mind and consciousness.

Retreat into Feelgood

It was in the midst of psychoanalysis that I discovered I was a natural meditator. It began when I went through a period of finding my
working life very stressful and was prescribed tranquillizers. I took
them for a couple of weeks, but did not like their overall effect.
Without any planned strategy, on the way to work I began to stop in
quiet places such as churches and parks in order to calm myself
down. I would sit for ten to twenty minutes, eyes closed, allowing
myself to slow down and settle. Within the tornado of my busy mind
and speeding body, I began to find a space of inner quiet. This deliberate sitting and slowing down worked more effectively than the
tranquillizers. It also felt better.

The sitting and being quiet became part of my daily rhythm. I
was not consciously doing meditation or stress control, but just following my instincts. A few months into the practice, however, my
general calm began to deepen. I found myself able to observe and
witness my erratic and intense personality. I sat there, feeling calm
and happy, watching myself, looking at my life.

But who was this person within me who was watching myself? I then
began to realize that I was more than just my frenzied daily personality and that I possessed a deeper identity. This deeper identity was quiet
and observant, and was always in a very content and pleasurable mood.
From within this mood, it seemed as if the whole world was also filled
with a pleasant and benevolent atmosphere. The terrible intensity and
cruelty of human life were still there, but they were framed by this other
much wider context, by a universe of benevolence.

It was this pleasurable atmosphere which drew me deeper into
practising meditation. I wanted more of it. I knew nothing about
endorphins, but the longer I stayed in meditation, the more I began
to access this pleasurable state. I then began to read books about
meditation and altered states of consciousness in order to understand and explore what was happening within me. I also started to
visit many different meditation groups.

Although the different meditation traditions taught different tactics for achieving inner silence, they all supported the experience I was already having – discovering my inner self, becoming a witness to myself and connecting with the benevolent fields of consciousness that permeate the universe. I loved this inner world and I knew with overwhelming certainty that my life needed to be dedicated to moving more deeply into that reality. The 'illusory' outer world was filled with anxiety and suffering, whereas the 'real' inner world was filled with a calm and wise contentment that did not deny but could encompass the pain. This was why I chose to go on retreat and to go so deeply into meditation.

I talked to Edward Glover about all this and he reassured me that I was not an emotional cripple seeking solace in fantasy. As the psychoanalysis drew towards a close, I made up my mind that I needed to ditch my job and life in London and I prepared to take two years' retreat.

Three weeks before I left London for my retreat, Edward died. It felt, in a way, that he had prepared me for my journey and I had prepared him for his.

Entering the Bliss Fields

What drew me forward in this whole endeavour was the incredible pleasure that I was experiencing within meditation. My mind was beginning to access states that were not simply calm and benevolent, but were also filled with bliss. I could feel these bliss states hovering like clouds around me, and I was trying to open my mind and consciousness in order to let them in. It was tantalizing. Sometimes they felt so close, but I could not quite catch them. It was like a multi-dimensional chess game in my mind and consciousness.

Over the two years of retreat and for years afterwards I maintained a long and deep meditation rhythm, sometimes in silence for five to six hours a day. I practised the mindful observance of Zen and Vipassana, but I also practised the more active meditation approaches such as those of the Taoist, Kabbalistic and Tantric traditions. In these active traditions, you guide the focus of your mind and deliberately allow yourself to explore different modes of consciousness and different spheres of energy.

This may sound wacky to people who are not familiar with the techniques, but if you sit in silence for lengthy periods of time you begin to become aware of subtle energies and feelings running through your body and your environment. It becomes almost irresistible to follow them with your mind and to interact with them.

My goal, of course, was to go fully into the ecstatic states of consciousness and there was no other purpose in my life. I approached it all with intense fervour. My passionate intention was to expand my consciousness so that it opened to and merged with the bliss fields of universal and cosmic consciousness. I did not want just to taste the bliss. I wanted a full and ongoing experience.

I remember the first time that I went fully into the bliss fields. I had been struggling for months to keep my mental focus up in the area above my head, whilst at the same time keeping my body completely calm and my breath absolutely relaxed and rhythmic. Then suddenly one day I popped or rose into that completely new state of consciousness. It was extraordinary. All the books from the many different traditions teach about this state of consciousness and there I was in it. Using Eastern language I had taken my meditation into 'samadhi'. It was even more beautiful than had been described. I was calmly observing everything and yet at the same time I was enveloped in bliss. My consciousness was bliss. The whole universe was bliss.

Having dedicated myself so thoroughly to achieving this state, there were now two major pieces of work to undertake. The first was to keep going back into that bliss state so that I could become completely accustomed to it and explore it more fully. The second was to bring this new consciousness down into my daily life so that it coloured the whole way in which I lived. It was a process of normalization and integration. Thirty years on I am still happily working on both projects.

But in that time I have learnt that accessing the bliss fields does not require such a dedicated meditational approach. There are easier and more accessible ways of making that connection, which I am happy to share in this book.

Are the Bliss Fields Real?

You can see that my interest in endorphins began in a very different way from the neuroscientists. They start with studying a very specific chemical which kills pain and creates feelings of pleasure. I, on the other hand, in the company of thousands of meditators throughout the ages, begin with an experience of the bliss fields that permeate the universe.

With such different backgrounds and motivations, it is not surprising that the scientists and the meditators might look at each other with mutual suspicion. So what can be said about these bliss fields which might make sense to someone looking for empirical evidence?

Consistent testimony

To begin, there is consistent testimony about these fields from traditions and cultures all around the world. When meditators discuss their experiences with each other they find themselves describing the same sensations and perceptions. The various traditions use the symbols and language of their own culture, but the maps are essentially alike. Whether Jewish, Buddhist or Taoist, their general blueprint is the same and their results are the same – there is a multi-dimensional world of energy and consciousness that human beings can access using certain strategies for calming the body and guiding the mind.

Testability

These strategies can be tested repeatedly in different circumstances by different people, and will deliver similar types of consciousness and experience. I know them to be accurate from personal experience.

From the experienced meditator's perspective these fields are known to be true because, sitting in a state of calm observation, with no attachment to any outcome, they are experienced time after time. They are subtle fields of energy which cannot be denied by modern cynics simply because there are no scientific instruments sensitive enough to detect them. Either there is a massive cross-cultural and historical hallucination and fraud going on here, or there is some truth.

From a scientific perspective, the exercises of the different traditions meet the criterion of testability and repeatability. (I challenge any hard-nosed cynic to spend three months in a meditation or energy medicine school before passing judgement on whether it is all real or not.)

Drugged hallucination

Another damaging criticism that can be put forward by mainstream scientists is that the bliss fields of meditators are in fact only the hallucinations of endorphin-soaked brains. Control your mind and your mood well enough, they assert, and you become totally stoned! It is all just the result of the internal chemicals.

This is an interesting accusation, but the meditators can easily refute it. The endorphins are simply the way in which the body registers and anchors down the pleasurable experience of the bliss fields. *The endorphins are not the bliss fields themselves*, any more than a television picture is all there is of the studio, actors, and broadcasting technology that create it. What you see on the screen is just the medium which communicates the message. Likewise the endorphins are communicating a message, but are not its source.

Hard evidence

There is also hard evidence that these invisible fields of energy exist. The great medical traditions of India and China, both of which are much older than Western medical science, achieve cures based on a method that presupposes fields of energy. Indian Ayurvedic and Chinese Taoist medicine – both of which are highly effective – are founded on an understanding that the world is suffused with a benevolent subtle energy called 'prana' and 'chi'. This energy is also clearly described in all other spiritual and tribal healing traditions. The energy flows of the human body are minutely described in the meridian maps of acupuncture and their use in surgery, for example, creates anaesthesia which is quite as effective and less dangerous than that produced by chemical substances.

In general, I prefer to trust Buddha, Lao Tse, Pythagoras and my own experience, rather than the contemporary reductionist scientists who might be very clever within the rules of their own logic but miss the bigger picture. Anyway, not all scientists are so reductionist. Albert Einstein once wrote, 'The most important function of art and science is to awaken the cosmic religious feeling and keep it alive.'

The Quantum Fields

The challenge, then, is to clarify what is meant by bliss fields, fields of consciousness and fields of energy. In fact, to describe the world as permeated with energy is an accurate scientific statement. The most famous equation in the world is Einstein's $E = mc^2$, which states that energy and matter are interchangeable.

'Matter', in the words of the physicist David Bohm, 'is like a small ripple on this tremendous ocean of energy.'[1] In fact, at an international conference in 1998 the world's leading cosmologists recognized that the universe as a whole is filled with some unknown form of energy, 'an ethereal energy that threads empty space'.[2] In a very real sense dense matter, solid material, is the exception rather than the norm in our cosmos. There is more energy than matter.

The twentieth century has indeed seen a clear movement within science away from a simple mechanical model, in which the world is made up of solid bits and pieces, to something far more fluid and energetic. The old scientific model, as far as it goes, has been brilliant and transformational. But nature as a whole is more complex and unpredictable.

The new approaches of quantum physics, relativity and complexity have provided an understanding and methodology that are far more fluid. The old Newtonian view of the universe as a beautiful clock is melting. It is still partly a beautiful clock, but the apparently solid boundaries are, beneath their superficial appearance, plastic and permeable.

Matter, energy and consciousness are, it seems, part of the same spectrum. Atoms do not behave like billiard balls, bouncing logically off each other, but melt and distil, dance and flow. One moment they are particles, the next waves. Their location and their mass cannot be measured simultaneously.

Two classic books, Fritjof Capra's *The Tao of Physics*[3] and Gary Zukov's *The Dancing Wu Li Masters* describe how the models of modern physics so closely resembled the maps of Eastern mysticism.[4] In particular the notion of the quantum field, the basis of so much modern science, is very similar to Eastern ideas of the all-pervading wave fields of prana, chi and consciousness. According to quantum theory, the quantum field provides an underlying reality to the cosmos. Capra wrote:

> ❝ In these "quantum field theories", the classical contrast between solid particles and the space surrounding them is completely overcome. The quantum field is seen as the fundamental physical entity; a continuous medium which is present everywhere in space. Particles are merely local condensations of the field; concentrations of energy which come and go, thereby losing their individual character and dissolving into the underlying field. ❞

This quantum world exists within and behind the solid world that we can see and touch. This is the same as the radio and television waves, sounds and colours, cosmic rays and vibrations, electricity and electromagnetism, which are also there but beyond our normal spectrum of perception. The world is filled with things that exist beyond our normal ability to perceive them. We may not see the electromagnetic field of the Earth or the electricity running down a wire, but we do not deny their presence.

The Body as Energy

It is consistent and logical to talk about the universe and the things within it as being made of energy and wave fields. This description includes all material objects including the human body and, of course, the human brain. Just because we tend to experience ourselves as solid does not mean that, in reality, we are excluded from the realities of quantum mechanics. Our own cells, molecular structures and atoms are as wave-like and as eccentric as all the other material observed by subatomic physicists.

Year by year new evidence is also emerging of how plants and animals are biologically sensitive to electromagnetism. Most recently, for example, the scientific journal *Nature* published a report describing how birds, amphibians and reptiles navigate by detecting minute changes in the magnetic field, using a form of 'biochemical compass'.[5] In fact, in the 1940s it was discovered that pigeons with darkened contact lenses could still find their way home following the earth's magnetic field. Another parallel piece of rigorous research has recently reported how magnetic fields of a certain kind can have a healing effect on damaged nerves.[6] Research by Dr Michael Persinger of Lawrentian University, Canada, is also working in this direction. He has built apparatus which applies minute magnetic fields to the brain to induce biochemical changes and altered states of consciousness.

We are, in the words of medical doctor Richard Gerber, 'a complex energetic interference pattern interpenetrated by the organising bioenergetic field of the etheric body'.[7] (By 'etheric body' he means the invisible electricity and vitality which permeates and surrounds the solid physical body.) To put it another way, we are more like waves and currents of electricity than we are like solid bricks.

As electromagnetic and energetic beings, we are connected to and interpenetrated by the wave fields and energies of the universe. We take no notice of it because, like the blood that pumps through our bodies or the oxygen being absorbed in our lungs, it happens below our threshold of awareness. Our conscious experience of life may be that we are isolated units, solid objects, but the underlying reality is that we are like currents in an ocean of energy.

The Energy is Benevolent

Having accepted that everything in the universe, including ourselves, is electromagnetic and energetic, how do we know, as energy doctors and meditators love to assert, that the underlying dynamic is essentially benevolent and creative? Can we accept that the quantum field has an essential goodness? It is, in fact, the testimony of all people from all traditions at all times in history who connect with the universal energy field. It feels good. It inspires people to behave well and generously. When it is accessed and utilized in energy medicine, the results are positive and beneficial. But is this persuasive evidence? Does it prove that the universe 'hums' with benevolence?

Perhaps I should appeal to your personal experience. I know full well that many people experience life as tough and painful, but in nature and the universe as a whole, a different harmonic is being played out. When people connect beyond their day-to-day cares to the greater environment, there is always a feeling of wonder at its magnificence and beauty. Do you look at the night sky or walk in nature and experience the acid of anxiety or the honey of pleasure?

Restrict your vision to the purely human realm, and the pain is only too obvious. Expand your perspective to include the planet and the universe, look into the soul of living creatures, and feel deep into your own core. Again, is all of this acid or honey?

Built into the universe there is an obvious harmonic that draws everything into coherence and beauty. Yes, there are cycles of decay and rebirth, but a leaf falling from a tree has its own beauty, as does a seed struggling to emerge from the darkness. In nature and the universe, the struggle to grow and even the decay of death have their own sense and their own beauty.

I frequently observe even the most aggressive cynics disappearing off into the countryside for their holidays where, in their own private way by the river or in the mountains, they experience precisely what is being described here. Away from the pressure of work, relationship and city, they come back into connection with nature and the universe. They feel good. Subtly, the bliss fields are flowing through them.

The magnetic fields of energy that flow through nature and the universe are good for us – indeed they are absolutely necessary for our health. If they do not flow harmonically into and through the human body, the result is discomfort and illness. Throughout history and today, in all cultures, natural mystics and healers have understood and worked with this universal harmonic.

I cannot present materialistic sceptics with a rigorous equation that proves that the universe is filled with this benevolent harmonic, but focussing only on the struggle and difficulties is certainly a dry experience. What a tragedy to live your life with cynicism, when you could be exploring and experiencing the benevolent creativity of the universe flowing through your body, emotions and mind. The evidence for its truth is all around.

At its most materialistic, the fact that the body contains a fundamentally important group of hormones whose sole purpose is to ensure pleasure and health, that these endorphins are to be found even in simple, single-celled organisms, is a signpost you can choose to ignore or notice. As is the beauty of a petal or a hundred thousand other things around you.

It's the Whole Body, Not Just the Head or Heart

In Chapter 1 I wrote that my first revelation in this work occurred when I asked people in my meditation classes to report what situations, outside of meditation, took them most easily into the same state of centred pleasure as deep meditation. I was knocked off my elitist perch by their responses. Cats on laps, exercise bikes and a hundred other experiences created moments of deep joy and connected pleasure.

My second revelation came as I researched exactly how people experienced these times of pleasure, and, began to realize how important the whole body is in this work. In response to my questions, people often mentioned where they experienced the pleasurable sensation starting in their body.

- 'I feel a warmth in my lap which comes up through my body.'
- 'My heart opens.'
- 'I experience this pleasure in my solar plexus.'
- 'In my head behind my eyes. My forehead starts to relax.'
- 'Across my shoulders.'

Consistently, students were describing how the pleasurable experience started in one particular area and then either stayed there or unfolded into the rest of the body. Interestingly, in men the physical sensation often began in their head or shoulders, whereas in women it often started in their heart or stomach.

In all the energy medicine with which I had previously worked, great stress was laid on focussing on the head or heart. It was through the head or the heart that you began the process of connecting with the bliss fields. A Christian meditation, for example, might begin with placing the thought of Christ in your heart. A Buddhist meditation might begin with repeating a sacred mantra or prayer in your mind. These very specific techniques followed equally specific maps of how the human energy body is laid out. The best-known of these maps are those of the Ayurvedic chakra system, the meridians of Chinese medicine and the Tree of Life of the esoteric Jewish schools.

What these maps all tend to have in common is an assumption that only the top third of the human energy body can cleanly and without interference access the clear fields of energy and consciousness. In fact, in some mystical circles it is an insult to accuse someone of 'being focussed below the chest'; it implies that they are still subject to the passions of lust and hunger.

This might seem an arcane discussion to people who are not familiar with or interested in these maps. Historically, though, it is very important, because these maps supported the idea that we needed to lift our consciousness up above our physical bodies before we could access universal bliss states. Many teachers and students believed that it was essential to reject and transcend our physicality in order to connect with the greater universe. This is the source, for example, of many celibate religious orders, not to mention those strange mystics, the flagellants, who literally whipped their own bodies into submission.

Again and again, however, my students were reporting that their feelgood could be located anywhere in their body. This reflected my own experience. Ever since my first samadhi meditations, I had instinctively known that the experience needed to be brought down into my whole body and then expressed out into life. I have worked for years to manifest the samadhi awareness in every cell and to access the bliss fields through every part of my body. For example, at one point I experimented for several months with allowing the bliss fields to enter me through my feet and hips. I did not like the imbalance I felt if the bliss fields were purely in my head. I felt disembodied.

Many people who experience good massage or other forms of body work, know how a warm and healing touch can open you, can 'melt' you, both to a flow of endorphins and also to accessing the benevolent field of the universe. I worked hard at studying and understanding this process – it was enjoyable research – and over many years experienced most forms of body work: movement such as tai chi, yoga and dance; breath-work such as pranayama yoga, rebirthing and holotropic breath; and touch-work such as deep tissue massage, kahuna and shiatsu. All of this affirmed the testimony of my students.

It also echoed the psychoneuroimmunological research, which had clearly demonstrated that the endorphins could be triggered anywhere in the body and not just in the brain.

Endorphins and Bliss Fields

The general energy field, which human beings experience as bliss, runs through all nature and the universe. We are surrounded by it and we are also part of it. So why don't we feel it all the time? And what is actually happening in those pleasurable moments when we do feel it?

As I pondered these questions, my conceptual world began to turn upside down. All my previous models had seen the attainment of bliss as reserved for an elite of pure and disciplined practitioners. But if the bliss fields were always there, perhaps it was perfectly normal to have a continuous experience of them, a continuous sense of connection, of being part of a benevolent and creative universe. This seemed to be the case in healthy children. It also seemed to be the lifestyle that many tribal and aboriginal peoples claimed for themselves. So why didn't the rest of us feel this benevolent connection? Original sin? Lack of wisdom? Lack of enlightenment?

The answer, I now believe, is very simple:

> **We do not experience the bliss fields around us because we are too tense and armoured.**

I believe that this is an absolutely crucial insight. If we understand this, we can see that experiencing the bliss fields is easy. They are always there. We just are not able to notice them.

Where body tissue is tense or frozen, there are two negative effects:

- The production of endorphins is blocked
- The flow of benevolent energy is blocked

It is a tiny biochemical change that allows us to register that something pleasurable is there. When we are tense, we inhibit that chemical change.

A pleasurable experience – be it a physical caress, a memory, music or whatever – softens our usual body tension. This happens in localized body areas. In classical meditation, the mind relaxes and endorphins are released in the brain; so there are many pleasurable sensations, openings and insights that occur in the mind. In heart-centred meditation exercises, endorphins are released in the heart. The cat on the lap stimulates endorphins in the lap. And so on.

But it is not just a biological experience. Something else is happening. Not only does pleasure stimulate the production of endorphins and the relaxation of tissue, it also allows the body to let in the benevolent vitality. The body moves from being frozen to being in flow, both internally and externally, biologically and energetically.

Let me put in graphic form the basic premise which underlies this book. It is a very significant proposition for holistic healthcare and personal development, and is the key to understanding the Endorphin Effect.

The Key Endorphin Effect Concept

Physically triggers the
production of feelgood
endorphins and
→ relaxation

→

A pleasurable event or thought

→

→ Energetically 'melts'
body tension so that
benevolent wave fields
can be felt and
absorbed

Bioenergetic Tension

That tension in the body prevents a healthy flow and flexibility was clearly described by Wilhelm Reich, a medical doctor and psychoanalyst, in the 1930s. He developed a therapeutic approach known as bioenergetics, which recognizes that psychological and physical traumas anchor down into musculature and tissue, causing permanent freezing or 'bioenergetic armour'.[8]

Reich also understood that the vitality or energy flowing through a human body is the same vital energy that flows through nature and the universe in general – the *prana* of Indian medicine and the *chi* of Chinese. He even began to measure its electric charge. Most Western scientists and doctors of his time rejected his insights, but now they are becoming an accepted part of holistic healthcare.

Reich also put forward the idea that one way of assessing an adult's health was by virtue of whether she or he was capable of enjoying sex. This seemed an absurd and embarrassing idea to many people, but in the light of endorphins it makes a great deal of sense. The pleasure of lovemaking comes from the flood of endorphins. This flood is only possible if the whole body is sufficiently fluid and open to allow it.

The importance of our body armour and how it affects our ability to experience pleasure and connection cannot be underestimated. Most of us have learnt to live with our armour and take it for granted. The tragedy here is that we have become accustomed to an ongoing subliminal level of tension, little realizing how profoundly it can hurt our physical and psychological health.

Our bioenergetic armour has developed over years and carries the full history of our past distress. Memories are not just psychological imaginings, but sit as patches of tension in our bodies. Infants emerge from the womb soft, floppy, vulnerable, energetically open, receiving and feeling everything. Every child, simply by virtue of the fact that she or he is alive, is connected with and flows with the benevolence and creativity of life. Children throb with a natural connection. But the slings and arrows of outrageous fortune start hitting early on. Careless parents. Bullying elders. Competitive siblings. Tough schools. Harsh media. Dangerous streets. Social injustice. All the 'noise' of modern life. Hunger and pain. Each of these events, every childhood injury, physical and psychological, creates tension in the physical body.

The result is that by the time most of us are teenagers we have lost that bubbling continuous ability to feel life's natural beauty. Of course, we feel it every now and again when we do things we enjoy and our armour temporarily melts. But the loss of that ongoing pleasure and connection damages us. The *Tao Te Ching*, a Taoist text on health and development, puts it very simply:

> When people are born they are supple
> And when they die they are stiff.
> When trees are born they are tender
> And when they die they are brittle.
> Stiffness is then a cohort of death,
> Flexibility a cohort of life.

Sadly, many people are so stiffened emotionally that they are even sceptical about the possibility of benevolent energies. The Endorphin Effect, however, provides immediate and long-term strategies for bypassing, working with and healing bioenergetic armour.

The Kinaesthetic Sense

By now, I hope you are beginning to appreciate how important it is to be aware of what is happening in your body. Your whole body is an organ of perception which senses and feels what is happening. If endorphins or benevolent vitality are flowing, your body feels it. Just as the eyes are the organs for vision, and the ears are the organs for sound, so your whole body is the organ for sensing how you feel. Close your eyes, think of something that you adore and there will be a change of feeling in your body.

The ability to notice the sensations within your body is known as the kinaesthetic sense. One dictionary describes kinaesthesia as 'the sensation by which bodily position, weight, muscle tension and movement are perceived [from the Greek *kinein* to move].'

To give kinaesthetic attention to what is happening in your body is an important skill to develop. Normally, the kinaesthetic sense happens below one's threshold of consciousness, but it can be brought into full awareness simply by giving it focus. Normally you do not notice the pull of gravity or your weight upon a chair, but if you are asked to, it is easy to give it your attention and feel its effects upon your feet, thighs and buttocks. Equally if you are asked whether your stomach or your brow are tense, it is easy to turn your focus in their direction and monitor what you are feeling.

In exactly the same way, as chemicals and energies move and change in your body, they also create very tangible physical sensations which are easy to feel and notice. It is this basic ability to monitor and to notice what you are feeling that makes the strategies of this book accessible to anyone. There is no need for any special skills or sensitivities. All you need is the ability to monitor how your body and emotions are feeling. Pause and notice what is going on inside you. This is the first step in taking small experiences of pleasure and turning them into a full-blown and satisfying lifestyle, of benefit to yourself and all those around you.

I write that this work will benefit 'all those around you' not because that is a nice idea, but because it is absolutely necessary. Biologically and energetically, the full flow of endorphins only happens when your pleasure and happiness spill over into goodwill and generosity. Personal happiness that is totally self-centred contains the tension of self-protection and is marked by anxious or aggressive boundaries. This tension, inhibits the flow of endorphins and benevolent vitality.

Real pleasure and happiness possess a relaxed flow that is generous to life and the surrounding community.

PART 2:

The Exercises

CHAPTER 4:

Your True Environment – Your Body and the Universe

The Panic of Being Lost

Have you ever been lost – in a forest, for example, or on a complicated highway system – and found yourself going into panic and disorientation? It is an experience that most people know. Children have it when they get separated from their parents and suddenly find themselves alone in a strange place. They look around for reassuring faces or signs. They see none and become overwhelmed by fear and hysteria. Their survival, they feel, is threatened.

We are biological creatures, part of earth and nature. Our habitat might seem to be the modern world of houses, careers and human communications, but really it is nature and the universe. If you never pause to remember that this is your true context, you deny yourself its natural reassurance.

But somewhere deep within us is an innate biological intelligence which recognizes the goodness of this connection. The capacity of every cell to produce endorphins is an indication of this comfortable and happy solidarity with all natural life.

The True Context

The first commitment I ask of my students is to decide where they really live. Do you live in nature and the universe, I enquire, or are you inhabitants only of the purely human world? How, I challenge, can you expect to be happy and to experience an ongoing endorphin flow if you cut yourself off from your true home?

There is a childish sketch that I like to draw in my classes. It is a long curve representing the surface of the earth with a couple of trees and an animal on it. Above it is the sun, the moon and a star.

I remind my students that this is our true environment. There is something incomprehensibly good about it which is nothing to do with visual beauty, for blind people have the same experience. Nor is it purely to do with what we hear or smell or touch or taste. There is an atmosphere, a magnetic field, which we sense and which feels good – it has good vibrations. I represent this in the childish picture with the musical notes. It *feels* good to be part of all this. Even the toughest and most cynical people have this experience of nature.

I know many people who have increased their sense of inner stability and confidence simply by pausing to recognize where they are physically located. In the centre of the city or in the buzz of their office, they pause to notice the sky and the position of the sun. They orient themselves to the points of the compass and know the direction in which their home is located.

> 6 My home is in that direction. My best friends live
> west from here. My favourite landscape is there.
> Beneath the concrete of the city is the soil, the clay and
> the chalk. I am human and I am a creature, an animal, of
> this earth and universe. 9

Our physicality is no more separate from nature than any cat or tree. The Zen teacher Alan Watts expressed this very beautifully:

> 6 We do not "come into" this world: we come *out* of it,
> as leaves from a tree. As the ocean "waves", the
> Universe "peoples". Every individual is an expression of
> the whole realm of Nature, a unique action of the total
> Universe. This fact is rarely, if ever, experienced by most
> individuals. Even those who know it to be true in theory
> do not sense or feel it, but continue to be aware of
> themselves as isolated "egos" inside bags of skin. 9 [1]

Lost in the 'Noise'

For much of the time, then, we are alienated from the wonder of the universe. We do not remember or feel it. We tend to be aware only of a world that is very immediate, always in our face – an environment created by only our species.

With its dense population, relationships, complexity, industry, economics, media, telecommunications, income and so on it is incredibly stimulating, interesting, demanding and overwhelming. The modern world is constantly firing more and more information at us. We are trained from infancy to receive these communications of human civilization, but not those of nature and the universe. At the same time, we are bombarded by the incessant buzz of industrial and electronic technology. Pollution and 'noise' of various kinds are continuously swimming around our environment.

But this human world is not just the solid world we see, hear and touch. It is also full of the vibrations and energies of everything that human beings do. It is thick with the magnetism and wave fields of human existence, the good and the bad, the suffering and the pleasure, the sadistic and the brilliant. Can you imagine the wave fields created by the combined energies of six billion people with all their compulsions, desires, fears and anxieties?

The hassled single parent, juggling children and scarce resources in a small apartment is in precisely the same position as the harassed office executive, juggling time and surviving the rush hour. They are both separated from the comfort of their natural environment.

As we come out of childhood we forget that there is something else to life, something more beautiful, more meaningful, more lasting and more significant. This is hardly surprising. It is difficult to feel the hum of the stars and of nature when we are so fully engaged in the electric buzz of humanity.

The general intensity of this experience blocks the production of endorphins and encourages the hormones of stress. Instead of the Elixir of Life, we soak in anxiety. And we tend to think that this is normal.

The Universe is Bigger Than Blobsville

I then like to add something to my childish drawing. On the long curve of the earth's surface I draw a small blob. This tiny mark represents a human city like London or New York or Beijing.

We live inside these tiny blobs which I call Blobsville. We think that Blobsville is the true and most important environment. We completely forget the wider context and we imprison ourselves in this limited domain. It contains a lot that is wonderful and inspiring, but it also contains the tension, ignorance and suffering of everything human.

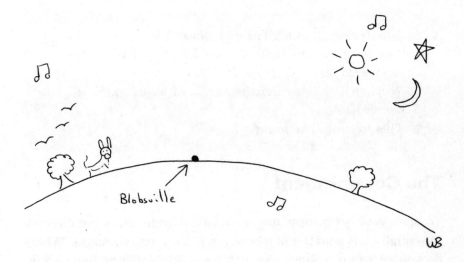

But Blobsville is not our true environment. It is tiny compared to the immensity of the earth, minuscule compared to the infinity of the cosmos.

So here are some crucial questions:

- Where do you really live?
- What is your true environment?
- Where do you choose to put your attention – in the daily confusion and stress of Blobsville, or in the beautiful and creative dignity of nature and the universe?
- Do you live *only* within the Blobsville of human culture and human vibrations?
- Or do you remember that you are part of nature and the cosmos?
- How can you possibly feel and experience the vital wave fields of nature and the universe if you do not even recognize that you live within them?

None of this is to negate or deny the good things about Blobsville. It is only to state the absolute reality, that the true context of our lives is far bigger and more wonderful. I have friends who have created for themselves an affirmative statement which they utter when they feel pressured. 'This is Blobsville.' They push it away attitudinally. 'I belong to nature and the universe.'

> You are not just a citizen of Blobsville.
> The mass energy field of humanity is not your only environment.
> You are a creature of the earth, of nature and of the universe.
> This is your true home.

The Commitment

To open your awareness to your true environment is not difficult. Essentially, it is a matter of where you place your awareness. Where do you *choose* to believe that you live – Blobsville or the cosmos. This is a stage at which I sometimes have to push my students. They have heard and understood all the information. They may even be amused by my passionate rant that they are beings of nature and the universe – and not of Blobsville. But they have not understood that they have to make an active choice.

We all have to make this decision. We have to commit to remembering where we are. We have to stop being lost in Blobsville. The hassled single parent has to pause and remember. The harassed executive has to pause and remember. We all do. Beyond the immediate pressures and stimulation, there is another dimension.

No matter how great the human success or crisis or joy, it is not bigger than the cosmic context. No human drama has a more powerful vibration than the earth. The greatest and most charismatic mortal on earth cannot compete with a mountain or an ocean, let alone a planet or a star.

> The pressures of daily human existence create tension and block the flow of endorphins and benevolent vitality.
> The expansiveness of your true environment relaxes and opens you up, so that endorphins and benevolent vitality can flow abundantly.

To reclaim some kind of sanity and truthful awareness, you have no choice but to make a clear and distinct commitment to remember the wider context in which you actually live.

Waking Up to Your Body

We may have created a culture and lifestyle that separate us from nature and universe, but we move around in physical bodies that are, by their very essence, part of the natural world. As Alan Watts reminded us in that wonderful phrase, 'As the ocean "waves", the Universe "peoples",' we emerge from nature and are as natural as any plant or animal.

Unfortunately, just as we forget our natural environment, so we also forget our bodies. We already know that there is an intimate body-mind connection and that the general state of your psychology can affect your physical condition. But there is an important issue here that is usually forgotten. Your body needs your mind's attention. If your mind ignores your body, your body will feel abandoned and will tense up, blocking benevolent chemicals and energies.

Your body is an animal, an intelligent and very sensitive ape, which has this amazing mind living in it. Sometimes these two aspects, body and mind, can be very separate. Even worse, some people disdain or dislike their body. This can have a terrible physical effect.

From the body's point of view, it is like living with a constantly disapproving adult. Children and animals wither in this kind of company and become defensive, resentful and victimized. A disapproving adult is a recipe for tension and anxiety.

This is precisely what happens in your own body if you do not appreciate and care for it. The monkey creature which is your biological body will feel disliked and alienated. Ignored and rejected by its own mind, the body automatically tenses. It lives in a state of subtle but ongoing fear and produces stress hormones but no endorphins. Frozen, it is unable to feel the positive vitality of life in and around you.

To maintain its health and wellbeing, its vitality and its feelgood, your body requires some of your attention. But all you happy couch potatoes can breathe a sigh of relief. I am not going to ask you to exercise. Nor am I going to demand that you change your diet. Nor are people with any physical disability excluded. What matters here is your attitude.

Let us start with an exercise that you can do any time – though I recommend that you do it morning and night in bed. Its purpose is to build some creative rapport between your mind and your body, and then develop awareness of your true environment.

REMEMBERING YOUR TRUE ENVIRONMENT: HOW TO WAKE UP AND FALL ASLEEP

THE FIRST STEP

Lying in bed, bring your attention down into your body.

Allow your awareness to scan and notice the whole of your body. Start anywhere you like, but do not forget the tips of your toes and your fingers.

Move and stretch your toes.

Move and stretch your fingers.

Remember that this is the physical vehicle in which you live and move.

Whatever it looks like and no matter what condition it is in, it is the only body you have and it deserves your attention.

If there is any part of your body in pain or feeling tense, then touch yourself in that area. Let the warmth of your hand comfort your own body.

Pause for a moment and give your body a moment or two of gratitude and affection.

THE SECOND STEP

Stay comfortably in bed.

Allow yourself now to remember your true physical environment.

You are on the earth and you are surrounded by nature.

Even if you are in a city, the wilderness of the clouds, winds and sky is still above you. Allow your mind to travel and expand beyond the city to where there is always nature – mountains, deserts and oceans.

Above you is the sun with its light and heat.

And all around is the universe with millions of stars.

Lie there, relaxed and patient, and softly allow yourself to be aware of earth, nature, sun and universe.

Remind yourself: 'This is my true environment.'

THE THIRD STEP

Turn your focus down into your own body again. It is a creature. Scan it again. If it feels appropriate, touch yourself again.

Do all this in a relaxed and even sleepy way.

Then stretch as much is comfortable for you.

If it is morning, begin to get up.

If it is night time, allow yourself to sleep.

Sometimes I am asked how often people should do this exercise. How often should a cat stretch? The answer is whenever you want. At the very least, do it when you wake up and before you go to sleep. It is like the television remote control. Pause and change channels. The hassled single parent and the harassed office worker are able quickly to shift their attention from the immediate pressured environment.

- *Pause.*
- *Turn your attention down into your body.*
- *This is your environment.*
- *Turn your attention out to nature, the earth, sun and universe.*
- *This is your environment.*

The chapters that follow give specific exercises for deepening and expanding this awareness.

Regaining a sense of your body and your true environment is like having been a lost child and finding your parents.

Remembering and Appreciating Your True Home

It can be hard for people engulfed in modern culture to remember the wonder and beauty of their environment. In the last part of this chapter, therefore, let me share some information that, I hope, will remind, encourage and inspire you to open up to the wider context. It can be read as straightforward information or used as seed thoughts for contemplation.

Aboriginal peoples say that nature and the land sing. The ancient Greek philosopher Pythagoras spoke of the harmonics of the planets and stars. In Japan, there is a saying that every blade of grass has its own spirit and its own song. In one sense, these are all descriptions of vibrations. Even the most urbane of people can sense the atmosphere of a powerful tree, mountain or river.

All of this is to affirm that we live in a cosmos filled with songs, atmospheres and vibrations beyond those of human culture. These vibrations, however, are not just out there. They are also within us. We are animals constructed of the same material that builds trees and plants and all of nature's other creatures. The water of the rivers and oceans is the same water that is in our bodies.

We are not separate. Everything, without exception, emerged from the same mysterious beginning. This is our home and, built of the same stuff, it feels like home. It is not a romantic construct but a physical fact that we are made of stardust.

Precisely the same dynamic that propelled the creation of the universe propels the growth of a human being. When a single sperm cell meets a single egg, these cells join and divide, and continue dividing to grow new life. This is the same dynamic in which the universe is still growing, expanding and changing.

The atoms and the molecules that make up our bodies are the same matter that makes up our own planet, the moon, the sun and the stars. The vitality that dynamizes us is the same energy at the centre of the sun and all stars. We share these same properties because we are made of the same fabric. This is a cosmic phenomenon, not limited to life on earth. We are participating in a great dance of life that flows through the infinity of the universe.

When we allow ourselves to connect with nature and the universe it feels good, because we possess the same substance and vitality that make up everything else in the world. When the essence of creation touches our minds and bodies, some primal essence in us responds to the harmonic: our tiniest cells respond with the production of endorphins and our bodies can laze in opiate pleasure.

Age by age, culture by culture, men, women and children have attested to this reality. This is a religious experience without any religion. It is natural spirituality with no pretensions or controls.

It is there as an instinctive wisdom built into every cell of your body. To ignore your true reality, to stay absorbed purely and solely in the stimulation of human society, is unhealthy, unrealistic and damaging. How much better simply to expand your attention.

There is no demand here to transform your life or commit to some uncomfortable discipline. The only request is to remember that you are already at home – the home of your body and of the universe. So many people are trapped in a cage, a limited sense of what life really is. Free yourself to the brilliance of your true home.

Remembering the Earth

There is a wonderful Homeric hymn, three thousand years old, that begins:

> ❝ I will sing of well-founded Gaia, Mother of All, eldest of all beings, she feeds all creatures that are in the world, all that go upon the goodly land and all that are in the paths of the sea, and all that fly; these are fed of her store. ❞

This song is just one of thousands that have been sung around the world, celebrating the beauty of our planet whom the ancient Greeks called Gaia. The earth is not just a spherical rock hurtling through space, but a living being with a presence and a life of her own. Again, if you can sense the presence and identity of a tree or mountain or lake, how much greater is the identity of the whole earth.

The material that makes up our physical bodies emerges from the earth. Our bodies recycle back into the earth. We are part of it. All life emerges out of the nutrients and warmth of earth. Place a seed in the dark earth and it will sprout, grain to wheat, acorn to oak tree. 'The Earth is our Mother' are the opening words of a tribal chant. These words are not sentimental: they describe a fact of life.

Have you ever laid your hand or your head upon a pregnant woman's stomach? There is a warmth and nurture there, filled with the power of new growth. It has an aura of strength and great comfort. The earth is continually like that pregnant stomach, all of nature emerging out of it. Volcanoes and earthquakes are but tiny hints of the power that is generated within it.

And just as earth is described in that chant as 'our Mother', so it is no poetic fancy to call ourselves 'her' children. What does this mean? It means that we feel safe, warm and nurtured within her aura. She is our natural parent. A mother's aura always comforts and strengthens her children. The earth's aura does the same for us.

To connect with the earth, to feel it, to open to its vibrations is always wonderful medicine. I wonder how many of you still lie on the earth, smelling the grass or earth or sand and feeling the comfort and strength. This is so normal. The earth is 8000 miles in diameter. It weighs 6600 million million million tons And it flies through the air orbiting the sun at a speed of 66,000 miles per hour. She is many millions of years old and will live many million more years. Most human beings are between five and six feet tall. We usually weigh somewhere between 100 and 200 pounds. We have trouble moving faster than ten miles an hour. And we live for around eighty years. Compared to the size of the earth, we are minuscule.

Lying in bed in the morning and evening, remember this great being who carries you.

Remembering Nature

Across the surface of the earth is that whole dimension of organic life which we call nature. As much as any other living thing, we are part of it. In a sense, nature is the earth's personality presented for everyone to see. There is always something playful, dramatic or serene about it. There are innumerable poems and ceremonies and dances which celebrate her. Here is an ancient Welsh song from *The Black Book of Carmarthen*:[2]

> ❝ *I am the wind that breathes upon the sea,*
> *I am the wave on the ocean,*
> *I am the murmur of the leaves rustling,*
> *I am the rays of the sun,*
> *I am the beam of the moon and stars,*
> *I am the power of trees growing,*
> *I am the bud breaking into blossom,*
> *I am the movement of the salmon swimming,*
> *I am the courage of the wild boar fighting,*
> *I am the speed of the stag running,*
> *I am the strength of the ox pulling the plough,*
> *I am the size of the mighty oak tree,*
> *And I am the thoughts of all the people*
> *Who praise my beauty and grace.* ❞

If humanity were to destroy itself, nature would reclaim even the greatest of our cities and return them to green wilderness. That small plant in your window box and the blade of grass in the brickwork are nature's scouts.

Places of worship all over the world are decorated with flowers and plants celebrating the creative glory of nature. We deliberately bring plants and animals into our homes. Offices everywhere are hung with pictures of landscapes to remind people of the beauty of nature. We do all this because we know it is healthy for us to remember nature.

Consider water too – the oceans, seas, lakes and rivers that roll through and across the planet. Many people need only to stand by a small dancing stream to feel bewitched and healed and nurtured. A single parent whom I know is almost overwhelmed by constantly caring for her young children stays sane by remembering nature. Washing dishes while the children watch a video, she pauses and looks at the water flowing from the tap. It reminds her of the rivers and oceans.

Many of us have pets – dogs, cats, mice, hamsters, budgerigars, lizards and so on. Some doctors and counsellors recommend pets as cures for various ailments of the body and mind, for to touch and smell and watch an animal is good medicine.

Lie in bed and acknowledge the smells and beauty of nature. Allow your awareness to travel out to your favourite landscape, to beaches and mountains and rivers. Sit in your office and notice the plants or the pictures; look out of the window. Remember the greater context.

Remembering the Sun

We are minute beings on this extraordinary planet, but the earth itself is also tiny in the context of the solar system. To get a handle on the size and power of our sun, imagine whether you could easily see a candle burning 200 yards away. You might possibly be able to see it, but could you feel its heat?

The sun, however, is not 200 yards away, but 93 million miles. Yet it is so big, powerful, hot and bright, that our skin and our eyes can be burnt by it. We take for granted its light and heat, and we ignore its size and power. But other peoples have fully understood the significance of the sun. It is no wonder that the oldest known prayer and poem, *The Gayatri* from Hinduism, was written to the sun, or that so many ancient religious systems centred upon the sun. And according to many energy medicine traditions, including Ayurveda, it is the vitality and energy of the sun, its *prana*, which vitalizes our own physical bodies.

It is a staggering reality that we live within the aura of this star. It travels through space at over one million miles per hour, carrying the planets with it. One scholar, writing in an early edition of the *Encyclopaedia Britannica*, evocatively describes its power.

> ❝ If the Sun were enveloped in a shell of ice 40 feet thick, it would thaw its way out in one minute of time. If an ice bridge two miles in diameter could be built, spanning the immense distance of 93 million miles from Sun to Earth, and if by some means, the whole of the Sun's radiation could be concentrated upon this ice bridge, in one second it would be water and in seven seconds more, it would be dissipated into vapour. ❞

The temperature at its centre is 27,000,000 degrees Fahrenheit, the result of nuclear processes in which hydrogen is converted to helium. Its magnetic field holds the planets in its orbit so that we do not go flying off into space.

People love to watch candles and burning fires. They are but a hint of the fire whose heat and light sustain the plant and animal life on earth. This is very personally relevant because it also sustains our own lives.

Lying in bed, having given some appreciative awareness to your body, turn your attention towards the sun. Relax, and contemplate how powerful and how close it is.

Remembering the Universe

And beyond our sun, of course, is the galaxy of which it is a tiny part. This galaxy is so thick with stars that when we watch it at night, we see a cloud of hazy light. This cloudiness has led it to being called the Milky Way – a very soft name for millions of stars, each one of which carries the same furious power as our own sun.

Sometimes I wonder if, in its naming, there was some unconscious recognition that our galaxy is also a parent to us.

'The Earth is our mother. She will take care of us,' runs that tribal chant. But the sun then is parent to the earth. The Milky Way, in turn, is parent to the sun. Certainly there were many ancient cultures which believed that the whole universe was the stomach of a Great Mother. Perhaps the stars of our galaxy were thought to be her nurturing milk.

Cosmologists and astronomers discuss the rays, waves, energies and particles that flow endlessly through the cosmos. Astrologers discuss the vibrational influences of the planets and the constellations. As you look up at the night sky, you may envision an empty space filled with sparkling little lights, but the reality is that you are looking into a rich and incomprehensibly wonderful environment. When people pause at night to look at the sky, they first feel awe and then a haunting companionship.

> **You live in a miraculous complex body, on a beautiful planet, in a radiant solar system, in a benevolent and wonderful universe. This is your true environment.**

CHAPTER 5:

Your Strawberries, Your Gateways – Working with the Events and Thoughts that Create Pleasure

The Wild Strawberry

❛ A terrified man was alone at dawn in the jungle. He was running in complete panic as animals howled around him and sinister eyes glowed in the dark. Damp creepers and roots caught his legs and stung his face. Insects, spiders and bats became tangled in his hair. Adrenalin pumped ever more intensely through him, driving his frantic pace through the thick undergrowth. He ran on and on, gasping, weeping and pathetic.

He could feel the dangerous animals getting closer, sensing their teeth and desire for blood. Suddenly he tripped and fell, but there was no ground beneath him. He was falling into a ravine. He could feel himself screaming, but there was no sound.

A small bush caught his fall. Hysterical, he hung on to the bush and looked down. Far below was a rushing torrent of water with sharp rocks and pools filled with alligators and piranha fish. Above him the wild animals were baying and howling.

The man was in living hell.

Then a mouse appeared on a small ledge and moved towards the bush from which he was hanging. The mouse looked at the man and twitched its nose. It then moved over towards the roots that were holding the bush to the rock face and began to nibble at them. Slowly but surely, the bush began to give way from the cliff.

Out of the corner of his eye the man spotted a flash of red. Next to the bush was a wild strawberry. He reached out and he picked the strawberry. 9

The story, which is to be found in several traditions, ends there. It is one of those fables at the end of which the listener is left hanging. It is like the Zen phrase: 'The sound of one hand clapping.' There is supposed to be something enlightening about leaving the mind with an unanswered question.

But there is an another interpretation to the story:

> **No matter how terrible your situation, there will always be a strawberry. There is always something to connect you with the wonder and beauty of life.**

The strawberry represents the thought, memory, sight, smell, taste, event or encounter which can focus your attention away from hellish circumstances and connect you with a different, more benevolent reality. Even in the worst situation, a strawberry can trigger endorphins and enable you to connect with the benevolence of life. And even if this connection is a tiny, thin thread, it can nevertheless be a lifeline to survival.

Heaven in Hell

The strawberry fable contains practical advice which many people already instinctively follow. Over and over, we hear stories about men and women who have found themselves in genuine hells, but have been able to hold on to their sanity and happiness by focussing on things which connect them with a reality beyond their present situation. Prisoners of war and kidnap victims find blessed relief in tiny glimpses of the sky, or in the miracle of some bug or spider, or in the memories of loved ones. Irina Ratushinskaya wrote a beautiful and moving poem about her time as a prisoner in a Soviet labour camp. It demonstrates profound moral courage and the power of encountering beauty. In the midst of that freezing hell, one day she saw a beautiful frost pattern on a window and its beauty transported her.

> *And I will tell of the first beauty I saw in captivity*
> *A frost covered window!*
> *No spy holes, nor walls,*
> *Nor cell bars, nor the long endured pain –*
> *Only a blue radiance on a tiny pane of glass –*
> *A cast pattern – none more beautiful could be dreamt!*

More recently, I was moved by the story of a German woman who was held captive for over a month by a serial rapist and killer. Heroically, she remained composed and hopeful by thinking of her family and loved ones. Finally she escaped.

In these situations the power of the human mind triumphs over real-life adversity. The strawberry is the gateway to a reality far more powerful than the actual physical terror. And this is a strategy which can also be used by those of us who endure lesser states of pain.

The Audit

The whole purpose of this book is to create a deep shift in your life, to change how you feel inside your skin and how you relate to your wider environment. If you follow this book's approach, you will substantially increase your endorphin production and your ability to connect with the positive field of life. But this can only happen if your experience of life is pleasurable. And nobody can invent what gives you pleasure. So you need to know the strawberries that work for you.

A strawberry is anything or any thought that brings you pleasure, makes you smile, opens your heart and makes you feel good about life. I have found it helpful for people to divide their strawberries into categories:

- Places
- People, pets and animals
- Activities
- Peak experiences
- Religious figures and symbols
- Textures, scents, tastes, sounds and colours

Places List

Get a sheet of paper and head it 'Places'. Then list the places that you adore.

These are places that you have visited or that you know about or that you want to visit. There is something about them which makes you feel good. They may bring you comfort or inspiration, healing or excitement, or a sense of the sacred.

Do not have a fixed idea about what these places should be for you. They really do vary from person to person. For some people it might be a meditation chapel, whereas for others it could be a football stadium. Some people love mountains, but others prefer the ocean. Here are some possibilities: your bedroom, garden, lounge, river, ocean, lake, where you had a great holiday, mountain, landscape, city, deserts, Great Pyramid, Taj Mahal, Battersea Power Station.

People, pets and animals list

Head another list 'People, Pets and Animals'. Under this heading, list all the people and animals you really like.

In one training I remember a man in his early forties saying that he could not think of a single person whom he loved or who made him smile. The group around him looked astonished and then dismayed. Then, suddenly, the man smiled. 'Charlie Chaplin,' he said emphatically. 'Yes, Charlie Chaplin.'

There may be many people who, when you see them or think of them, light up your life, make you smile and feel good. But do not include on this list any people who have recently died or left you. Until your grief has fully passed, memories of these people will probably trigger a mixture of emotions and not just pleasure.

On this list you can also place any animals or pets with whom you have a great relationship. Meinrad Craighead wrote of a dog:

> ❝ I held the dog's head, stroking her into sleep. But she held my gaze. As I looked into her eyes I realized that I would never travel further than into this animal's eyes. At this particular moment I was allowed to see infinity through my dog's eyes. ❞

Activities list

Head your third list 'Activities'. There are many activities which make people feel good, happy and connected. Some of them are very obvious, whilst others are ignored because they seem so mundane and ordinary. When you make this list, be certain that you do not censor yourself. It does not matter what you put on your list. It just needs to be authentic.

For some people, their favourite activity is to wander round an art gallery gazing at classical paintings. For others, sitting at home watching television and eating tomato ketchup white bread sandwiches is the very best. Some people are knitters and others are rugger players. See if any of these represent you: walking, sport, making love, the gym, fixing things, dancing, sitting under trees, reading, gardening, painting, cycling, understanding a problem and finding a solution, caring for others, looking after children, working, lazing, travelling, cooking, cleaning, being in bed, out at night, climbing, trekking, cinema, opera, meditating, massage, shopping, eating, sleeping, dressing well, spectator, the arts, religious events and ceremonies, crosswords . . . .

Peak experiences list

Head this list 'Peak Experiences'. From your past you will have some really wonderful memories – moments when you felt extraordinarily happy and at ease with the world. There were moments when your consciousness achieved a peak of bliss and enjoyment: perhaps childbirth, your team winning, succeeding at something, meditation, a holiday, lovemaking, when you fell in love, being in a religious setting. If you cannot remember any, move on to the next section.

Spiritual figures and symbols list

Head this list 'Spiritual Figures and Symbols'. For some people there are particular spiritual teachers and symbols that really touch their hearts and trigger a pleasurable response. Scan your own life and see if there are any religious icons that evoke a smile and a softening, or that inspire you. Intellectually you may want to dismiss them, but go along with what touches your heart.

Also, if you have a spiritual or religious background, take care not to choose a symbol or a teacher just because you think you ought to. It is important that you list only what genuinely evokes a warm and immediate response. I have worked with many people who are devoted to particular religions and they are often surprised by this exercise. Their deepest connection to the universal wave fields of benevolence – to what they would call God – does not necessarily come most easily to them through the personages and symbols of their specific religion. It may come through dancing or gardening or a grandchild.

Textures, scents, tastes, sounds and colours

Head this final list 'Textures, Scents, Tastes, Sounds and Colours'. For many people there are particular sensations in these categories which really switch on all their lights. It may be silk or marble or wood bark; the scent of a particular flower or food, or of mown grass or someone you know; birdsong; wind in the branches; waves lapping against the shore; the taste of chocolate or strawberries and cream.

Pause and Stretch the Moment

Every item on your lists presents you with an opportunity to pause, trigger endorphins and connect with the better things of life. Remember the key equation:

> **A pleasurable event or thought**
>
> → **Physically triggers the production of feel-good endorphins and relaxation**
>
> → **Energetically 'melts' body tension so that benevolent vitality can be felt and absorbed**

The power to manage how you experience life is in your hands. Every single time that you see, experience or remember anything on your lists, you can press the button on your psychological remote control and dramatically change channels. Life is not a dress rehearsal: if you want a good existence, then choose it now.

I wonder how many of you take for granted the people and things that you once found precious. I know a woman who bought a house specifically because of the beautiful tree that stood in the front garden. But after she had moved into the house, she forgot all about the tree. She never went to the window to admire it. She passed it every day on her way to and from work, but never paused to look at it or touch it. Yet the tree was always there, an opportunity for her to come back to reality. Your strawberries too are always there. It is you who forgets.

All you need to do is pause and notice – allow yourself a moment of appreciation. Your life is full of strawberries, but you have been taking them for granted. There are plenty of activities, people and places that you enjoy, but you simply walk past them every day. I know people who think they love their partners or their children, but never stop to appreciate their presence. There, in front of your nose all the time, are opportunities to take pleasure and enhance your health – but you just wander past them. It is the same when people notice rainbows and beautiful sunsets, then move swiftly on without pausing to soak in the value of the moment.

Do not be casual about those things around you that you love. From a selfish perspective, each one provides the pragmatic potential for endorphin production. From a spiritual perspective, each one is a potential opening to the wonder of life.

Pause and stretch the moment. Allow a much deeper experience to be triggered. This pause need only last a few seconds. Each stretched magic moment is a valuable deposit in the bank of your overall health. A few seconds of appreciation repeated several times a day can bring a completely new dimension and rhythm into your life.

THE ESSENTIAL STRAWBERRY EXERCISE:

PAUSE AND ABSORB

When people ask me whether the strategies presented in this book will work for everyone, I reply that they will work for anyone who is prepared to pause. Pausing is a mental and psychological act. It does not necessarily require that you stand still or stop what you are doing. All you need, for a little while, is to go into an attitude of *watching yourself* and noticing what you are feeling. Everyone can do this unless they are being swept along by a wave of emotion or compulsive behaviour.

This exercise is the gateway to triggering endorphins when you want and to turning up the volume on their production. The trick is to pause and notice what is happening within you when you are having a pleasurable moment.

This pleasurable moment can be spontaneous or it can be deliberately created.

This pleasurable moment can be a real event, person or place – or it can be a thought or memory.

Then, in the pause, you notice your pleasurable response. Somewhere in you there will be a warmth, a glow, a twinkle, a satisfaction, a happiness. Just by pausing and noticing it, the pleasure will become greater.

SPONTANEOUSLY

As regularly as you can, get into the habit of noticing and acknowledging the strawberries in your life. These are all the strawberries on your lists. Stop taking them for granted.

Notice that some activity, event, person, place or thing is giving you pleasure.

Pause and turn your attention to the strawberry. Stay relaxed. Notice that this strawberry is giving you pleasure. The pleasure is a tangible sensation somewhere in your body – a smile on your lips or in your eyes, a warming and opening of the heart, a relaxation in the shoulders.

Relax a little more. Imagine, sense or visualize that you are like a sponge. Allow the good feeling to come more deeply into you. Absorb the pleasurable sensation. Like a sponge, allow it to soak into you. Breathe in slowly and, on the in-breath, allow the pleasure into you. Let it sink into you.

You can do this exercise for only a few seconds or you can draw it out for as long as you like. Sometimes the experience will be very subtle and sometimes it will be strong.

The basic sequence is Notice –> Pause –> Absorb

You see a beautiful tree. Notice your pleasurable response and pause. Allow the pleasure to enter you more fully.

You see your children in the morning. Notice your pleasurable response and pause. Allow the pleasure to enter you more fully.

You see the blue sky. Notice your pleasurable response and pause. Allow the pleasure to enter you more fully.

You like the taste of your breakfast. Notice your pleasurable response and pause. Allow the pleasure to enter you more fully.

Your team scores. Notice your pleasurable response and pause. Allow the pleasure to enter you more fully.

You enjoy walking. Notice your pleasurable response and pause. Allow the pleasure to enter you more fully.

DELIBERATELY

A thought or memory

Whenever you feel like it or have the opportunity, close your eyes and bring into your mind one or more of your strawberries. (You do not have to do this with your eyes closed, but most people find it easier this way.)

The sequence is now the same as above: Notice, Pause, Absorb.

Notice that the thought of the strawberry is giving you pleasure.

Pause and be aware of the actual sensation of the pleasure.

Absorb the pleasurable sensation more deeply into you.

An activity, person or place

Again, whenever you feel like it or have the opportunity, *choose* to do or look at one of strawberries on your list. If, for example, you love the sky, choose to look at it and enjoy. If you love music, listen to some. If you love sailing, look at a picture of a yacht. The sequence is the same:

Notice that the thought of the strawberry is giving you pleasure.

Pause and be aware of the actual sensation of the pleasure.

Absorb the pleasurable sensation more deeply into you.

Marking the Lists

There is more work that can be done on your lists. It is very useful to divide your strawberries into the following categories:

- *Daily* – Those you can easily meet, see or do on a daily basis.
- Occasional – Those you can easily meet, see or do on an occasional basis.
- *Picture* – Those you would like to have a picture of in your home or workplace.
- *Big Smile* – Those that, when you think of them, always bring an irresistible smile.

So please go through your lists and mark them in the following way, or use symbols of your own choice:

- ★ Put a star beside everything that you can easily see or do every day in real life.
- ✚ Put a plus sign beside everything that you can only do or see occasionally in real life.
- ▲ Put a triangle beside everything that you would like to be reminded of by having a picture or some object connected with that person or place. For example, if you enjoy sailing would you like a picture of a yacht or a model boat in your home or workplace? Or your sailing cap hanging somewhere you can always see it? If you had a fabulous holiday somewhere, would you enjoy having a photo of it some-

where? Or would you like a rock from your favourite
beach?

● Put a circle beside anything on your lists that, if you close
your eyes and think of them, immediately make you smile
and open your heart.

★ Daily strawberries

You have marked the activities that you love and that you can easily
do on a daily basis – but do you actually do them? Even if you do, do
you really appreciate them and get the full benefit? There are millions of people, for example, who love dancing or listening to music,
or sport or gardening, but hardly do them at all. They simply forget
to. This is madness. Why deny yourself the positive benefit, the
health, the pleasure of what you love? It is better to dance or stretch
for sixty seconds than not at all. It is better to pause and smell a
flower for a few seconds than not at all.

Sometimes in my training sessions, I can feel a stodgy inertia in
the air as we talk about people's favourite activities. It is like taking
a thirsty but old and world-weary horse to a trough full of fresh
water. The horse just stands there, scarcely able to notice the water,
let alone actually make the effort to bend its neck and drink. 'You
are mad,' I shout, 'not to do the things you love! How can you expect
to have a healthy happy life if you yourself ignore what you love?
Commit now to doing what gives you pleasure! Throw away your
inertia and psychological chains. Do what you love to do.'

- **If you like singing, sing – and enjoy it.**
- **If you like eating, eat – and enjoy it.**
- **If you like jogging, jog – and enjoy it.**
- **If you like watching television, watch it – and enjoy it.**
- **If you like reading, read – and enjoy it.**
- **Whatever gives you pleasure, do it – and enjoy it.**

Let me clearly repeat the logic of the exercise. For health and connection, you need to trigger endorphin flow and melt your bioenergetic armour. This can be achieved by experiencing pleasure.
Therefore you must work with what gives you pleasure. It is only by
working with such things that you will achieve the Endorphin
Effect.

I have seen jaws dropping as people realize the implications. They are being given permission to enjoy themselves, to do what they like. And not because it is an egoistic activity, but because it is the foundation of healthcare. Moreover, nobody is telling them what they should enjoy. It is all coming from their own lists.

I work with many people from the caring professions who have a tendency to burn out. As they begin to understand the logic of the Endorphin Effect, they realize the emotional and spiritual intelligence of doing what brings them pleasure. Burnt out, they cannot serve any useful purpose. Supported by the ongoing elixir, they can deliver their work more creatively and productively.

Giving yourself permission to do what you enjoy is the basic thread that needs to run throughout your life.

You also need to go through your list of daily strawberries and notice how many of them you are ignoring. You are surrounded by things that would give you great pleasure if only you paused and quietly appreciated them.

✚ Occasional strawberries

You have placed a plus sign next to all those places, people and activities that you love but can only experience occasionally. You need, therefore, to arrange your life so that you can enjoy these occasional experiences. They feed your soul.

- The mere expectation of doing it will trigger pleasure.
- The actual event will be great.
- And the memory will also give you pleasure.

If you are making decisions about where to go, what to do and whom to visit, everything on your list guides you. Go and see the people and places that touch your heart. Make an effort to get there. If you have a person or a place that is a really powerful strawberry for you, doesn't it make sense to lay some long-term plans for visiting them? Again, why deny yourself the pleasure? And even if they seem financially out of reach, there may still be a way of reaching them if you save over a long period.

In one of my classes a man once complained that the most beautiful thing in his life was opera, but that he was unemployed, living off social security and did not have a penny to support such an expensive taste. He found this very depressing. Then, one by one, the group asked him questions and gave him suggestions.

'Why not save one pound a week for a few months and then go?'

'Do you listen to opera on the stereo? You can always borrow tapes and compact discs from the library.'

'You can listen to it on the radio.'

'Have you considered the local amateur opera society?'

'You could get a job selling ice cream or tickets in the theatre.'

This whole conversation was embarrassing for him. It was not the lack of money that was blocking him, but a lack of imagination and motivation. He agreed with the group and committed to giving himself the boosts he needed.

There is a general lesson here for some people. If for some reason you are blocked from enjoying your passion, do not push it out of your life completely. Do not cut off your nose to spite your face just because you cannot have all of it.

> **The occasional and tiny dose of your passion is better than none at all.**

I met another poignant example of a thwarted passion in the Bulgarian capital, Sofia. One of my students was a woman who had a university doctorate in forestry management. Being in the mountains and the forests was the passion of her life, but because of political and social circumstances she was forced to live on the tenth storey of a high-rise block in a tiny apartment with her husband and children. She also had to work as an underpaid languages teacher in an inner city school. This was hell for her. She wanted to be out of the city, away from people and in her beloved wilderness. She felt sad, depressed and victimized.

'I love working with plants,' she said. 'They are my life.'

'Then why don't you?' she was challenged by another student in the class.

'I am stuck in this city with no time and no money,' she answered sharply.

'But you have a small balcony. Why not grow something there, nurture it and enjoy its growth?'

'You can see the mountains from everywhere in this city. Don't you ever just look at them and give thanks?'

Someone was even more direct: 'Get off your high horse! Don't complain so! Accept reality and enjoy what you do have. You want mountains? Look out of the window, there they are! You want plants? Like she said, grow them! At least you're alive and not tortured.'

The forestry expert was embarrassed by how obvious this all was. In her mind, the only way she could enjoy her passion was by having it in a full and complete way. She was fixated on being in the mountain forests and felt oppressed by the poverty and pollution of her city life. But she could see the absolute sense of the advice that was being given her. There was no reason that she should completely deny herself the pleasure of her passion.

She bought some pots, earth and seeds and carried them to her balcony. She planted and tended them carefully. She took notes of growth and replanted some of the tree seedlings out in the landscape. She had recovered her strawberries in an apparently hopeless situation.

> **Whenever you want, pause. Be aware of a strawberry and absorb the pleasure.**

▲ Images and medicine bags

Surround yourself with images and objects that remind you of what you love. These can be very evocative and powerful. As described in Chapter 3, the memory or thought of what you enjoy can be as powerful as the actual physical reality and sometimes more powerful.

To have these images and objects around you is normal and many people instinctively do this. Most homes are filled with photographs, pictures and objects which give their occupants pleasure. It is also normal to find images and sculptures performing the same service in workplaces and offices. Desks carry family photographs and office walls images of landscapes, oceans or sporting events and heroes.

On your list you have marked those people, places and events whose images you would like to have around you. Having these images around you and pausing before them will evoke pleasure, enhance your surroundings and trigger positive emotions of pleasure.

You should feel free to surround yourself with objects or images that support you. Do this in any way that suits your taste and style. Some people are happy with postcards or pictures cut from magazines, whereas others need properly framed paintings. One woman I know has postcards of her favourite beaches and waterfalls all around her bathroom. First thing in the morning she walks into the room, sees the images and smiles. Someone else who adores the ocean saved some money and bought a minor masterpiece of the sea, which hangs grandly in his lounge. I have a picture of a Hawaiian waterfall beside my shaving mirror. On my desk are pictures of my family, a penguin chick looking earnest and a baby elephant sitting under a waterfall with its trunk up in the air. These are the images that work for me.

Use what works for you. Wouldn't it give you pleasure to go searching for some work of art or a piece that is meaningful to you?

Some people create collages of places, faces and friends. I know travelling carers and salespeople who have carefully decorated the dashboards of their cars. Before they go to see a particularly difficult client or after a hassled journey, they park, and spend a little quiet time looking at these images, getting some comfort, amusement and support. It makes them feel better and gives them a more effective attitude. If you are embarrassed about putting such images where everyone can see them, stick them on the inside of the sun visor and turn them down when you need.

In many ways the traditional medicine bag filled with 'good medicine' which many tribal peoples carry around their necks or waists, is a small sack full of strawberries. In the language of the Endorphin Effect, all the objects in the bag, in one way or another, help the owner connect with the benevolent vibrations of the universe. In modern societies many people still wear images of loved ones around their neck.

In this context, it also becomes obvious what a real altar is. Its purpose is to connect people with the wonder and benevolence of life. The objects on the altar need to fulfil that purpose. A magnificent religious image is useless if it does not actually evoke from people a feeling of deep pleasure and a melting towards the goodness of life. Again different things work for different people, often in a culturally defined way. Jesus on the cross can only work as an image that connects people with the great mystery of life if you already understand and are at one with its significance.

I do not want to trivialize the great religious symbols, but they are only symbols and their true purpose is to open people up and link them with a greater and more benevolent reality. To that extent, and respecting that people genuinely have very different tastes, any image or object before which one pauses and experiences the Endorphin Effect is an altar. That postcard of the waterfall beside my shaving mirror is as much a religious altar as any magnificently decorated object in a church, temple or synagogue. A picture of a beloved grandchild or pet or tree may open us more quickly to the divine in life than an explicitly spiritual icon. In many ways, this has always been the message of pagan and animist religions: every natural object is a manifestation of life's beauty and an opportunity to worship the splendour of life.

It is important to have images around you that you find genuinely meaningful and not just because they are fashionable or expensive. One man I know had a room in his house reserved for meditation and filled with beautiful religious paintings and sculptures from around the world. After listing his strawberries, he laughed. 'There isn't a single object in my meditation room that is on my lists! All my pieces are just there for show.' He removed most of those objects and replaced them with images and objects that truly touched him.

In your workplace, relevant images can be real lifesavers. I know many people with stressful, demanding working lives who maintain their sanity and health by having relevant images and objects in their workplaces. Regularly throughout the day they pause and look at the image, bringing themselves back to centre and a sense of being comfortable inside their skins. The picture of the golf course becomes an opportunity to re-experience the enjoyment of the game. The plant or flowers are a gateway to nature.

● Immediate strawberries

For many people, the simple act of remembering a smell or colour is enough to trigger a full Endorphin Effect. On the lists, you marked with a circle those strawberries that immediately trigger a smile and a warm heart simply by thinking of them. You bring them into your mind and you automatically smile, open your heart and experience pleasure.

It is these strawberries that demonstrate just how powerful your mind and your emotions are. The remembrance of them is sufficient to trigger a powerful brain and psychoneuroimmunological response. The neural pathway linking the thought of them with the internal chemical processes is so well defined that there is an immediate pleasurable reaction.

This puts in your hands a very simple mechanism, a very powerful tool, for changing the way you experience life. Simply by thinking of your favourite strawberries you are able to change your body chemistry and how you feel inside your skin, simultaneously providing an opportunity to relax into nature's feelgood.

This can be used just as much when you are exhausted and in a bad mood as when you are feeling good. Imagine that you are in a lousy mood, but you manage to create a pause for yourself. In that pause, wherever you are – collapsed in bed, travelling to work, in your office – you bring into your mind your very best strawberries. In that moment, the thought of your strawberries will automatically trigger a positive chemical and emotional response. Imagine doing that every time that you are stressed.

I will discuss this strategy in greater detail in later chapters.

Using textures, scents, tastes, sounds and colours

Monitoring the textures, scents, tastes, sounds and colours that you like can also give you powerful support. The purpose here is to fill your life with the qualities that turn you on, then to enjoy them fully.

It is obvious that you should decorate your home and workplace with the colours that you like, but many people do not bother. Right this moment look around the space you are in and find in it some colour that you like. In a relaxed way focus on the colour and appreciate it. Notice how your mood changes.

If you have not previously used perfume, essential oils, incense and other sources of scent in your life, you might want to start experimenting. There may be a particular flower whose scent really works for you. It is sensible, therefore, to have those flowers in your home or garden, or to buy an aroma from that flower. I have a friend, for instance, who loves lavender and often carries a sprig in his pocket. It is a delight at any time for him to take it from his pocket and inhale it.

Textures can also be easily carried in your pocket or used at home. Again, preferences vary hugely. Some people swoon to the feel of velvet whilst others love the touch of wood bark. Next time you are with a texture you love, close your eyes and allow yourself fully to enjoy it.

New Strawberries

For some people, surprise, discovery and new things are their strawberries. If this is the case for you, make sure that they are clearly on your list and that you keep going into new situations or visiting new places where you can meet the unexpected.

The lists of strawberries are anyway not fixed. Over time some strawberries become jaded and are replaced by new ones. I know one woman whose whole life has taken on a new dynamic because she is always on the search for new strawberries. I also regularly receive messages from my friends and students that start: 'Hey, I just found a new strawberry!'

Strawberries of Compassion

For some people, images of tragedy and sadness evoke a sense of compassion and caring which also trigger the Endorphin Effect. On my own desk, for example, alongside photographs of my family and places and animals that I love, I keep two photographs of human tragedy. One is of a five-year-old slave boy in Pakistan carrying bricks. The other is of a two-year-old orphan girl in China who has been tied to a chair with a hole in it and has her trousers around her knees; she is left there for hours because there is no one who will care for her. These two images are a constant call to me to stay in my heart, to be present and to be compassionate. They help to keep me connected and in the flow of life.

If images of tragedy evoke compassion for you, they may be very useful and relevant. But if they trigger sadness and disturbance, do not use them.

The Football Strawberry

I have a fantasy. It was triggered by a night that some soccer fans may remember – the night in July 1999 when the England team lost their game and went out of the World Cup. The tension and disappointment were so great that my neighbour, for example, could not sleep.

I too had become involved in the progress of the English team and my wife, Sabrina, was astonished by my exclamations and explosive body language when England scored a couple of remarkable goals. After the sustained tension of waiting for a score, the experience of release was ecstatic.

So I began to wonder whether the experience of watching your team score can be stretched into a longer joy at the beauty and creativity of nature and the universe.

I began to contemplate huge stadiums of football supporters reaching that peak experience of GOAL!!!

I also imagined and dreamed something more. In my dream the crowd reaches the peak experience of their team scoring. GOAL!!! And then time stops. The frame is frozen. The ecstatic crowd is held in suspended animation. The crowd stays in the ecstasy of the experience and the length of the experience is stretched.

As they experience their joy at the goal, a voice begins to suggest gently to them: 'Relax your breath. Stay in the experience. Absorb it. Let it flow in, through and around your body.'

The voice then asks: 'How does the world feel to you now?'

'Ecstasy and love,' the crowd replies.

'How do you feel about other people?'

'We're all in the wonderful cosmic soup together. It's beautiful. It's wonderful.'

Then, slowly, the suspended animation is lifted and everyone in the crowd comes back into full ordinary consciousness and the soccer game is resumed.

But the atmosphere has changed. There is a haunting beauty and companionship. It is a different kind of score.

As the Chinese sage Mr Tut-Tut wrote in his *One Hundred*

Proverbs: 'Who does not enjoy his happy moments cannot after all be called lucky; who feels happy in extremities is the real cultivated scholar.'

> **Do not be casual about the people, places, activities, things and thoughts, which give you pleasure. These are the gateways to your health and fulfilment. These are the triggers for your endorphins and your flow of connecting vitality.**

Your Attitude and a Cracked Pot

This ability to work freely with, appreciate and value your strawberries is partly a matter of attitude. Is your glass half full or half empty? Where do you place your attention – in the pleasures or in the discomforts? The founding fathers of the United States were not unrealistic men, yet enshrined in the Constitution is the right of every human being to pursue happiness. The English political philosopher John Locke was startlingly clear about this: 'The necessity of pursuing true happiness is the foundation of all liberty.'

I encourage you, in the privacy of your own inner life, to embrace the idea that happiness is something that you deserve and which is your right. An anonymous fable is relevant here.

A water-bearer in India had two large pots, one hung on each end of a pole which he carried across his neck. One of the pots had a crack in it and, while the other pot was perfect and always delivered a full portion of water at the end of the long walk from the stream to the master's house, the cracked pot arrived only half full.

For two years this went on daily, with the bearer delivering only one and a half pots full of water to his master's house. Of course, the perfect pot was proud of its accomplishments. But the poor cracked pot was ashamed of its own imperfection, and miserable that it was able to accomplish only half of what it had been made to do.

After two years of what it perceived to be a bitter failure, it spoke to the water-bearer one day by the stream.

'I am ashamed of myself, and I want to apologise to you.'

'Why?' asked the bearer. 'What are you ashamed of?'

'I have been able, for these past two years, to deliver only half my load because this crack in my side causes water to leak out all the way back to your master's house. Because of my flaws, you have to do all of this work, and you don't get full value from your efforts,' the pot said.

The water-bearer felt sorry for the old cracked pot, and in his compassion he said, 'As we return to the master's house, I want you to notice the beautiful flowers along the path.'

Indeed, as they went up the hill, the old cracked pot took notice of the sun warming the beautiful wild flowers on the side of the path, which cheered it somewhat. But at the end of the trail it still felt bad because it had leaked out half its load, and so again the pot apologised to the bearer for its failure.

The bearer said to the pot, 'Did you notice that there were flowers only on your side of the path, but not on the other pot's side? That's because I have always known about your flaw, and I took advantage of it. I planted flower seeds on your side of the path, and every day while we walk back from the stream, you've watered them. For two years I have been able to pick these beautiful flowers to decorate my master's table. Without you being just the way you are, he would not have this beauty to grace his house. Know that in our weakness we find our strength.'

> **When you are enjoying something, really enjoy it.
> If you are not enjoying anything, find something to
> enjoy and really enjoy it.**

CHAPTER 6:

The Inner Smile

The Perfect Yogi

There was an Indian yogi who took a twelve year retreat in a cave in the mountains. He ate roots, grasses and leaves. He drank from a spring. He became extremely pure. He sat in deep meditation in the perfect lotus posture. He kept his breath in perfect rhythm and maintained a composed smile of detachment. He looked enlightened.

After the twelve years he descended slowly from the mountains, walking carefully and meditatively, prepared to bring his bliss down into the human world. He approached the first village where men, women and children were excited by his arrival. They ran towards him asking for his blessing. The yogi maintained his composure and felt his spiritual radiance blessing the villagers who had now formed a crowd around him.

'Bless me, guru, bless me,' people shouted from the throng.

He raised his hand in a saintly gesture and at that moment two five-year-old boys, who were wrestling, crashed into his legs. The saint was shocked by the impact as he staggered to the side. Unable to control his reaction, he hissed, 'Little brats!' and kicked out at them.

His kick missed the boys, but his toe stubbed hard into a rock. He winced in pain and hopped about holding his foot. The villagers looked at him, amazed. They did not know what to think. Was he simply an unpleasant, irritable old man who had lost his temper and did not like children? Or was he a very special 'crazy' guru teaching them a more mysterious lesson?

Within a few seconds the yogi calmed down, came back to centre and felt embarrassment and shame. His pain was twofold. There was the physical pain of the stubbed toe and the psychological pain of acknowledging his awful behaviour.

'I have learnt nothing!' he said to himself.

He turned around and began a slow, sad walk back up to the mountains for another lengthy retreat.

One simple strategy would have saved the poor man from this shame. He knew little about the Inner Smile.

The Vehicle and the Driver

To understand the importance of the Inner Smile, we need to remember the intimate relationship between physical health and state of mind. It is clear that someone's mental attitude directly affects their physical health. An attitude of fear and anxiety, for example, creates physical tension and blockages which can manifest in various illnesses. Equally, an attitude of confidence and goodwill creates pleasure, which in turn trigger endorphins, relaxation, a strengthening of the immune system and so on.

The Inner Smile is a technique that works directly to link a positive mental attitude with the biological vehicle. It is a method for communicating safety, reassurance and pleasure down into the physical body. When practised, it can immediately take the body out of tension and into a more relaxed endorphin flow.

It is an exercise that is taught frequently in meditation classes, but often misunderstood. Understanding the chemistry of the body, however, helps to clarify how the exercise works and how it should be practised. It is a soft, compassionate and affectionate smile, which really glows into and warms the body. It is kinaesthetic – it can be felt. It is not a clever smile of cold detachment.

This kind Inner Smile works successfully because the physical body has a life of its own. It is an animal – a complex mammal with powerful biological drives, including the drive to survive. Your mind and personality may be elegant and cultured, but your body is an ape with its own agenda. Food, sex and breathing are its priorities. It is programmed to survive and it has instinctive reactions over which you usually have little control. But it likes the Inner Smile.

So let me pose a question to you. What is the nature of your relationship with the vehicle that is your body? Do you like it? Do you care for it? Do you give it affectionate attention? In fact, do you have any awareness at all that your moods and thoughts anchor down into your physical body and general health? These are very important issues that most people have never even begun to consider.

Your body is one of the most perceptive and sensitive animals on this planet. It is continually watching its environment, observing signals, seeing what is safe, noticing whether people are friendly or threatening. If people are unfriendly or threatening, the body freezes. This becomes clear if you watch children – someone grimaces and they turn away; someone smiles and they move forward.

The most important person in your body's life is you, your mind. If you are cold towards your body, it will freeze. If you do not like your body, it feels abandoned and fearful. For its wellbeing, your body needs your affectionate attention.

There is precise body chemistry and electricity going on here. The mind, as it sits in the brain, generates different fields of electricity and different hormones. These are then distributed through the body. Fear and alienation trigger adrenalin, cortesol and survival mechanisms, which make the body taut. Safety and love trigger feelgood relaxants. The mood of your mind directly affects the state of your body. If your mind has an affectionate, accepting and encouraging attitude towards your body, your body will feel it. If your mind is harsh, your body too will experience this.

> **The body tenses if people appear threatening. The body relaxes amongst supportive friends.**
> **Your body tenses if your mind is unfriendly towards it. Your body relaxes if your mind is friendly and affectionate to it.**

The old Latin saying, *mens sana in corpore sano,* is far truer than people realize. It really should be translated as 'happy mind *in* happy body' and not 'happy mind, happy body'.

The Smiling Parent

Your body is hugely significant because, as I stated earlier, it is the organ of perception for how you feel. Your eyes mediate vision. Your ears mediate sound. Your body mediates how you feel. If your body is permanently frozen because of your own cold inner attitude, you will not feel anything except frozen.

If your mental attitude to your body is detached, frigid, utilitarian, stoic, embarrassed, ashamed, resentful or harsh in any other way, this sends an ongoing signal of disapproval and alienation into the body. This in turn causes ongoing tension and perpetual anxiety.

Your mind should give your body warmth, affection, encouragement, love, enthusiasm, care and extended authentic positive attention. This gets the endorphins flowing in abundance and releases all systems into an open flow.

Calm detachment is no good for your body, which will feel abandoned and cold as if left alone. Living things need positive feelings and communications expressed to them. All children and adults require this if they are to be healthy and stable. A cold mental attitude sends a frigid harmonic through the whole psychoneuroimmunological system. The vehicle tenses up because it is saddled with this unfriendly, careless driver. Over the years this may take a terrible toll on your health: the frigidity may anchor into debilitating long-term illness.

Ecologically, your physical body is also the major environment in which your mind lives. Your mind therefore needs to care for it in an environmentally friendly way. Food and exercise are important, of course, but even more important is the attitude that you direct towards it. If you have any kind of environmental or ecological awareness, remember that the nearest living creature for you to look after is your own body, the naked ape.

You cannot expect good health or expect to feel the benevolence of nature and the universe if, in the first place, you do not have a good attitude towards your own body. If your mind is frigid towards your body, it blocks endorphins and connection by creating ongoing background tension.

Switching on the Inner Smile

The Inner Smile is a private and personal affair, not something that anyone else need know about or see. Most people can do it easily with minimal practice. Essentially, it is a matter of just switching on a kind attitude and allowing your eyes to twinkle with a philosophical watchfulness. You then turn this attitude down into your own body, smile down into your body and communicate a warm feeling towards it. You let your body feel appreciated by you.

The true Inner Smile is a warm, caring and watchful sensation that is most easily started in the heart and the eyes, and which is felt through the whole body.

When you first do it, you may feel as if you are posing or being stupid or inauthentic, but if you just hold the attitude for a little while the scepticism will pass away.

THE INNER SMILE

It is most easily done with eyes closed, but can also be done with eyes open. You can do this whole exercise in a few seconds or over several minutes.

THE FIRST STEP

Close your eyes and place both your hands gently on your lower stomach.

Bring into your mind one or more of your very best strawberries any person or thing that you love.

As you feel the pleasure – subtle or obvious – triggered by the strawberry, allow an authentic smile to begin within you. Switch it on.

Stay relaxed and allow the Inner Smile to settle in you.

With some people, it starts most easily in the heart. With others, it starts in the head, the face and the eyes.

Allow your face muscles to soften and relax, especially around your eyes.

Allow a kind, friendly twinkle to be expressed through your eyes. The expression that many people find helpful is 'soft eyes'. Switch on soft eyes.

There you are – kind and watchful.

This smile is not aloof and separate.

It is not a smile of cleverness.

It is a smile of wisdom, kindness and compassion.

This smile does not distance you from life. It engages you.

It is a smile of warmth and understanding.

It is a smile with a sense of good humour.

THE SECOND STEP

Staying with the sensation of the Inner Smile, turn your attention down into your body.

Allow your focus to scan around your body, noticing every part of it.

If it feels appropriate, you may want to wriggle your toes or your fingers so that you feel the extremities of your body.

Notice that your chest and abdomen are like a huge cave or cavern. You can focus your attention down into this great cavern. Smile down into your cavern.

Pause and notice how it feels.

In particular, let your attention go warmly down into your lower stomach.

Then send a message of appreciation down into your body. This is not just a thought, but a warm feeling. Do it softly, with no tension or seriousness.

Allow the friendliness of your Inner Smile to flow down into your body.

Allow your body to relax and enjoy the affectionate attention and vibration.

> 'Loving yourself' then is not some kind of touchy-feely irrelevance. It is a practical method of inducing relaxation and health.

It's the Feeling, Not the Pose

You can easily tell if you are doing the Inner Smile correctly by using a very simple yardstick. Is it cheerful? Is it pleasurable? Somewhere in you, do you light up? These are not great intellectual questions. They are simply directed at how you feel emotionally.

In my classes, people have protested that they could not do the Inner Smile properly and it is always because they cannot believe how easy it is. I have had the following conversation with many students.

'I can't do it, William. I just can't do the smile.'

'Okay.' I accept their statement. 'May I take you through it again?'

'Yes.'

'So close your eyes and, if it feels helpful, put your hands on your lower stomach.' I pause. 'Bring into your awareness one or more of your best strawberries. And now, as you feel the pleasure, just switch on your kind and watchful smile. Let your eyes twinkle.'

I pause again and then ask: 'Are you feeling anything?'

'No,' comes the reply. 'It's the same as before.'

'Are you thinking of one or more of your strawberries? Do you have them in your awareness?'

'Yes.'

'Do you enjoy thinking of the strawberry?' I ask

'Of course,' comes the inevitable reply.

'How do you know you're enjoying it?' I ask.

There is usually a silence now, and I ask the question again: 'How do you know you're enjoying it? There must be some feeling going on inside you. Some tiny little feeling of pleasure.'

'Yes,' the person agrees.

'That's it!' I encourage triumphantly. 'That feeling is it. Does it feel like a smile?'

'Yes.'

'Can you get that smile, that gentle twinkle, to be in your eyes?'

'Yes.'

'Okay. Now turn your attention down into your body. Smile down into yourself.'

Even working with the most cynical and resistant of people, I have never met anyone who cannot do this.

Compassion Not Detachment

You know if you are having the Inner Smile experience, not because your mind has gone through some mental decision-making process, but because you feel it. It is a kinaesthetic felt sensation.

Some readers may think I am labouring this point about it being a sensation and not a detached mental attitude. But I have met many people, especially those trained in Eastern schools of meditation and energy medicine, who have been taught the Inner Smile in a wrong way. They have been taught that the physical world and the biological body are illusions that get in the way of true spiritual reality. And, because of this, they have been taught to detach themselves mentally from their own physical body and to observe it from a distance.

But they were never taught the other essential foundation of that practice, which is to observe themselves with compassion, love and wisdom. Without those qualities, their smile can be frigid and even sanctimoniously smug. Worse still, some of these people think that because they can observe everything with detachment, they are in some way spiritually enlightened. They are like the yogi whose story opened this chapter. They never turn the true smile of compassion down into themselves and so they are frozen and out of the flow.

The key here, as you will have gathered, is the feeling of it. Over and over again, people in my classes – especially those who have previously trained in energy medicine or meditation – let out a sigh of pleased recognition as a huge piece of the jigsaw drops into place. The *thought* of the smile must be followed by the kinaesthetic *sensation*.

Using the Inner Smile, when the yogi comes down out of the mountains, he is in a good mood. He does not lose his temper when two fighting boys come crashing into him. He flows with their impact and laughs and embraces them.

Whenever you feel harsh, switch on your soft eyes.

'Keep on Twinkling', Science Tells You

The chemistry and energy of the Inner Smile and soft eyes work directly into the neuroimmunological system of the body. The body feels the kind attitude of the mind and responds immediately. It is especially powerful when the smile is placed in your eyes, when you let them twinkle with compassion and understanding. This is because the eyes are exposed parts of the nervous system. They are literally stalks from the brain. Therefore, when you place a compassionate twinkle in your eyes you are sending a message directly into your nervous system.

In fact, because every part of the body is energetically, electrically and chemically linked, you can place this twinkle anywhere in it and the effect will be the same. It does not need to start or stay in your eyes. In many classical traditions of meditation the smile is started in the heart. In some Taoist work, it begins in the lower stomach. Feel free to experiment with the way that works most comfortably and easily for you.

It is the feeling of the Inner Smile, and the general wellbeing that it can create in the body, which form the foundation of good health through humour and laughter. The beneficial effects of humour are now so well recognized that there are even laughter clinics funded by the British National Health Service.

Let me also remind you of some information presented earlier in this book. According to an experiment conducted by Chicago University Medical Center, the people who consistently produce the highest level of endorphins are those who, in the words of the medical researcher, 'had an ongoing twinkle in their eye'. No wonder, then, that people who experience inner peace and practise the Inner Smile have always been so healthy.

> **Smiling eyes produce a continuous flow of endorphins.**

Strength and Confidence

The Inner Smile is also a powerful first step in building strength, confidence and a sense of safety. (In Chapters 7 and 8, I describe further exercises for building inner strength.) The Inner Smile balances out the endless stream of stimulation and information we receive from our commercial, industrial and electronic society. It also balances out the never-ending change of the contemporary world.

Remember that the body is also an energetic and electromagnetic creature. It simply cannot cope with the incessant stimulation. Sooner or later, it feels the stress of it all. The immune system becomes depleted. You run out of energy and inspiration. All this is a high price.

To create stability, confidence and strength, you must have a firm awareness of your body. Without this attention, your body is always hyped up to go automatically into instinctive biological defence and survival mechanisms. Tension means to be in a continuous state of frightened preparation, ready to flood yourself with the energy of adrenalin. The result of all this is a constant readiness for the three Fs – Flight, Fright or Fight. Because of this, some people are in a perpetual state of depression, low level anger and frustrated aggression.

If you give your body affectionate attention it is reassured that, despite all the external noise, you are still aware of it and caring for it. Every time you send it the Inner Smile, you will experience a tangible change in the way that you feel. Your body is like a child holding your hand in dangerous traffic. Give it reassuring signals and it will feel safe.

There is a well known and effective relaxation strategy in which, starting with the feet, different areas of the body are tensed and then released. I often think that its effectiveness is due not so much to the release of tension as to each part of the body being given attention, and thus reassured. This is particularly relevant to people who are physically disabled and may not be able actually to tense and release different areas of the body. It is the attention, especially kind attention, given to the body which produces the relaxation and feelgood.

In Taoist medicine and the Western alchemical tradition, each body part is regarded as a special being with its own personality and characteristics. These traditions incorporate specific exercises in which students are taught to scan down into their bodies and greet each organ and area separately. They greet each body part with a smile and then pause and feel or imagine the body part smiling back. Again, this highlights the absolute necessity for the smile to be a genuine one of experienced affection and not some kind of passing greeting that you might give someone on the street. It is the *felt* sensation of friendly warmth which triggers the Endorphin Effect.

> **The greatest reassurance and safety that can be given to your body is the warm attention of your own mind.**

Ideally, part of your mind should always be aware of your body, monitoring its signals. This is easy for people who are naturally earthy, grounded and 'in' their body. It is not so easy for those who are more intuitive, mental and spacey.

Grounding and Earthing

The practice of the Inner Smile can be usefully supplemented with other techniques that literally bring your body into greater connection with the earth. As the body is elementally made up of the earth, it finds comfort and reassurance in its contact with the earth. Lying on the grass, hugging a tree, swimming, gardening, working with clay – all bring the body into direct touch with the earth.

But there are also energetic and imaginative strategies which connect the body's energy directly with the earth. These strategies can be very effective in calming people down and bringing them to a point of confident centre. For people who have real trouble grounding, I recommend doing a short course in one of the following: yoga, chi gung, tai chi, belly dancing and martial arts. The exercises in Chapter 8 are directly relevant too.

EARTHING

What follows are several grounding techniques. Experiment with them and see which ones work best for you. They gain in strength and efficiency the more often you do them.

THE FIRST TECHNIQUE

Walking down the street, imagine that you are walking along ten feet under the ground.

THE SECOND TECHNIQUE

Sitting quietly, sense and visualize a stream of energy flowing from above your head down through your body into the earth. It goes deep into the core of the earth. Another stream of energy comes back up from the earth connecting with the base of your spine.

THE THIRD TECHNIQUE

Using the chakra system of Ayurvedic medicine, imagine and sense a stream of energy flowing down into the earth from your crown, forehead, throat, heart, solar plexus, genitals and base of spine.

THE FOURTH TECHNIQUE

Sense and imagine above your head a very dark-coloured cloud – black can be used – with the texture of velvet. Sense it coming slowly down, calming and dampening the cells of your busy brain. It comes down through your brain and spinal cord and deep into the earth.

THE FIFTH TECHNIQUE

Sense and imagine that you are:
- **A tree with a strong trunk and deep roots.**
- **A mountain rising out of the earth.**
- **The big fat smiling Buddha firmly on the ground.**
- **The wide-hipped goddess of the earth.**

THE SIXTH TECHNIQUE

Imagine and sense the energy and warmth at the centre of the earth coming up into your body and settling in your stomach.

CHAPTER 7:

Absorbing and Guiding the Golden Streams

Energy Follows Thought

Pleasurable moments trigger endorphins and melt tension. This feels good. In order to achieve the strongest possible foundation for health, this positive sensation then needs to be guided so that it floods through the whole body. The enjoyable sensation experienced by the woman with the cat on her lap or the man looking at the Mona Lisa, needs to be absorbed into every cell of the body.

So there you are, for example, sitting in a crowded train. You notice something that pleases you, or you have a thought that makes you smile. You then withdraw your attention from the crowded train and focus on your internal physical sensation of pleasure. You mentally direct your body to absorb the pleasure and begin to guide it through the whole of your body, taking it deep into every part of you. The crowded train journey is, therefore, transformed into an enjoyable inner process. By the time you reach your station you are feeling happy and relaxed. You have done some vital and pleasurable health maintenance.

It is possible to do all this because, within your body, energy follows thought. Simply by thinking about a particular part of your body you create what is called a 'neural pathway', a connection between your mind-brain and that body part. Using your creative mental faculties, you can deliberately imagine and guide good feelings through your body. This is not a mental or imaginative game played between brain cells, but an actual occurrence as neuropeptides, the chemicals that carry information around the body, respond to neural directions.

This process already happens unconsciously. For example, every time you injure yourself the body creates a sensation of pain in order to attract your attention. Simultaneously various healing agents are mobilized and stream towards the damaged area to heal it.

This automatic process can be instigated deliberately and consciously – and it is really worth understanding it more fully.

> **Notice your strawberries. Pause and allow the pleasure to move deep through you. Let this become second nature to you – automatic and normal behaviour. Receive life's enjoyment.**

Flows of Electricity

Your mind, working within the brain, is an electromagnetic entity seamlessly networked into the electrical streams of the whole body. Your physical body, in fact, is a dynamic energy system in which liquids, chemicals, electricity and vitality are flowing all the time. There is not a single part of your body that is dense or inert. You are an electric being. This is not a metaphor, but a fact.

I remember a science fiction movie in which a family of tiny travellers became stranded inside a human brain. This was very dangerous for them because of the crackling electricity shooting between the brain cells, and they had to jump across them in order to avoid being killed. Again, this is not a metaphor. The brain genuinely is a crackling system of highly charged electricity.

In *The Energy of Life* Guy Brown writes:

> ❝ It seems hard at first to believe that humans run on electricity. If we touch the body we do not get a shock, there are no visible sparks and our hair does not stand on end. This is because of the minute scale on which these biological electric circuits run. They are miniaturized beyond the dreams of any microchip designer. The electric charges are separated by the thickness of a membrane – about five nanometres or less than a millionth of the width of a finger nail. And the voltages are equally tiny, about 0.1 volts, so there is not much chance of getting an electric shock. However, 0.1 volts across a five nanometre membrane gives *an electric field of twenty million volts per metre and this is much larger than the field in a thunderstorm causing lightning – about a million volts per metre.* ❞ [My italics.] [1]

This is powerful electricity, powerful energy, and it is inherent in the basic biological structure of every single one of us. It is perfectly accurate, therefore, to describe yourself as a flowing electrical energy system. This is one aspect of what is sometimes called in holistic medicine your 'subtle' anatomy.

It is also a fact that your mind is capable of easily *guiding* energy – in the form of neuropeptides and vitality – around your body. As the mind turns its attention to one or other part of the body, the whole body's intelligence is also drawn towards that focus. There is a flow of subtle electricity and biochemicals towards the target. Vital energy also flows towards it. All of this is common knowledge and practice in all forms of spiritual healing and energy medicine.

> **The mind can deliberately guide benevolent vitality and endorphins through and into any part of your body.**

Absorbing and Guiding

The basic sequence that you can use to absorb and guide is very straightforward:

- *Strawberry* – Pause and focus upon anything that gives you pleasure.
- *Notice* – Notice the pleasurable feeling in your body.
- *Absorb* – Allow your body to absorb the good feeling more deeply. Let the good feeling in.
- *Smile* – Switch on your Inner Smile and kind eyes.
- *Guide* – Guide the good feeling around and deep into your body.

It is essential that the sensation, the energy, the good feeling, that you move around your body has a particular quality to it. It must be experienced as warm, benevolent and fluid. It is not sufficient to have a cold visual sense of the energy, which will not trigger the endorphins or melt your tension. Your mental imagery, your kinaesthetic sensation, the feeling that you project into the experience needs to be like warm flowing honey or golden oil. This is ambrosia, nectar, the Elixir of Life.

An understanding of what triggers endorphins clearly points to the necessity of this warm and pleasurable sensation. In some energy traditions – for example, in many martial arts and 'hard' forms of energy work – the vitality is experienced as cool, fast and electric. This is useful for building strength and toning, but it does not open up the tissues to allow healing and enduring immune system resilience. It does not open people up to that most psychologically beneficial experience, which is to feel a connection with and the support of a benevolent nature and universe. And it is irrelevant for people who are in any way immobile.

I recall several men and women who were adepts of martial arts and chi gung, but felt they were missing something for their personal and spiritual development. As soon as they started to move their energy and their internal sensations in a way that was warm and pleasurable, they experienced a quantum leap in their personal growth. Suddenly they were experiencing not just vitality, but sensations best described as beautiful, wise and loving. Without exception, they also recognized that this gave them greater power – a power which sat wisely in their core – than the simple strength of athletic vitality.

The best-known yogi in the West, perhaps in the world, B. K. S. Iyengar, gained this insight in his eighties. In a wonderful interview on BBC radio with Mark Tulley in the autumn of 2000, he described how he now at last properly understood what he was teaching. He was giggling and laughing as he said this, amused by how seriously and earnestly he had taught yoga in the past. He was now celebrating his knowledge that it was all to do with pleasure, laughter and love. It was a joy to listen to him.

> **The experience with which you are working is warm, benevolent, fluid, flowing honey, golden oil, ambrosia, nectar, Elixir of Life.**

The Hollow Body

Your body is not solid. It is a network of communications: electrical, hormonal, blood, oxygen and vitality. There are many maps from different medical traditions which display various aspects of this fluid anatomy.

For the purposes of this book, a detailed knowledge of these different medical maps is not necessary. But it is important to expand your understanding of the human body and appreciate that it is more than just a solid object. It is a hollow, flowing energy system. If you have this idea clearly in your mind, it is much easier to guide the endorphins and *prana* using your imagination and kinaesthetic sense.

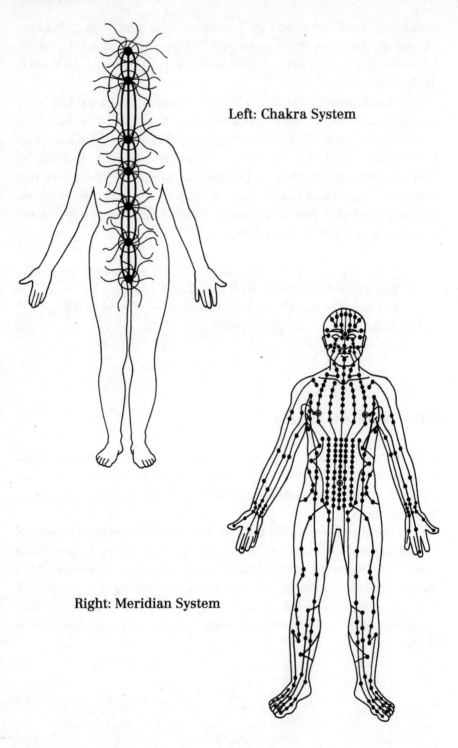

Left: Chakra System

Right: Meridian System

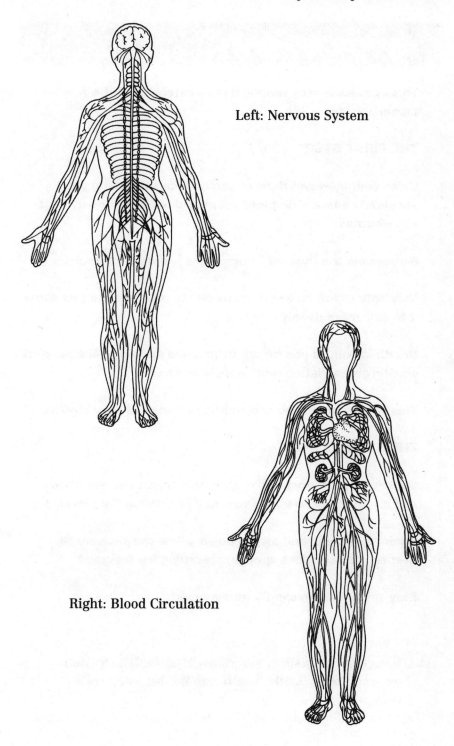

Left: Nervous System

Right: Blood Circulation

ABSORBING THE PLEASURE

This exercise is very simple. It is an extension of the very first technique. (see p.78)

THE FIRST STEP

Close your eyes and think of someone or something you absolutely adore. Bring into your mind one of your very best strawberries.

Notice how the thought brings you a feeling of pleasure.

Very softly, with no effort, focus on the pleasure and just allow it to sink more deeply into you.

Breath in and, as you breath in, imagine and sense the pleasure sinking and radiating more deeply into you.

This sensation may be very subtle or it may be very obvious.

THE SECOND STEP

Switch on your Inner Smile, and smile down into your body and into the area in which you may be sensing the pleasure.

Again, breathe in and as you do so, allow the pleasure to deepen. You are like a sponge, absorbing the feelgood.

Stay smiling benevolently into yourself.

Notice the pleasure. Let yourself absorb it. Switch on your Inner Smile. Guide the feeling deep into your body.

GUIDING THE ENERGY

The process of guiding the endorphins and benevolent vitality, the golden elixir, around your body is also easy. Most people take to it like a duck to water, although one or two encounter some initial difficulties which I shall discuss later in the chapter. However, in almost three decades of leading exercises like this, I have never encountered anyone who cannot do it.

Bring a strawberry into your awareness and notice the pleasurable sensation.

Breathe it in. Absorb it.

Switch on your Inner Smile and direct it down into your body.

Notice where you may be feeling some pleasure.

INSTINCTIVELY

Softly allow your mind to guide the sense of pleasure around your body. Allow it to move instinctively and intuitively.

Experiment with moving it a few inches in one particular direction. It really does not matter where it goes. Even for people experienced in the field, it is always a new experience.

In a relaxed and patient fashion, maintaining your good humour and a sense of kindness, allow the golden oil to enter more deeply into your body and allow it to move around.

Allow it to flow where it instinctively seems to go.

At the same time, experiment with guiding it where you intuitively sense it wants to go or where you feel it ought to go.

If a particular part of your body is tense, in pain or carrying illness, then experiment with allowing the elixir to go to those areas.

You will come to your own instinctive and intuitive knowing about where the energy should flow. Your body has an instinctive wisdom of its own. You will easily feel where you want to guide the flow. The energy wants to move. Its natural state is movement.

You will come to recognize that when you are in certain moods, the energy will be drawn to specific parts of your body or not flow so easily. When you are ill, the energy will be drawn to where it is most needed. This is all a very private process as you get to know yourself and learn what works best for you.

INTO AND THROUGH SPECIFIC AREAS

There are, I believe, four particularly important areas into and through which the endorphins and benevolent vitality need to be guided. All these areas, which are described more fully a few pages further on are crucial for health maintenance, strength and vitality. They are:
- Spinal cord and brain
- Bones and the bone marrow
- Acupuncture meridians
- Energy field and aura beyond the physical body

Spinal cord and brain

Guide and allow the feelgood, the warm honey, to sink deep into your spine and spinal cord. Allow it to travel all the way up and down your spine. Do this in a completely relaxed way, never losing your Inner Smile or soft eyes.

Take the elixir to where the spinal cord meets the lower part of the brain. Allow the feelgood to sink deep into that area.

Then allow the feelgood to move into and be absorbed by the whole brain.

Let your brain and spinal cord soak in the ambrosia.

Bone marrow

Become aware of your skeleton and bones. You want them to be both strong and supple.

Allow the feelgood to go deep into your bones.

Allow it to be absorbed by your bone marrow.

Experiment with sensing and imagining the bone marrow to be glowing with vitality, soaked in the elixir.

Acupuncture meridians

It is in the area directly beneath the skin, in the fascia, that the benevolent *prana* circulates.

Imagine the golden honey circulating under the skin and moving around your whole body. Allow the sensation to have a pleasurable tingle to it.

If you are familiar with them, follow the circuits described in acupuncture.

As you circulate the energy, make sure that it circulates around your body. Allow the tingle to penetrate far down into the tips of your toes. Sense it circulating around your legs and thighs. Bring it up your back and over your head. Let your ears tingle with the energy.

You are aiming for a general sensation of pleasurable tingling all over your body.

Energy field

Allow the feelgood to begin to move in your body.

Following your intuition and instinct, allow this warm energy to begin to move around your body anywhere that it wants to go.

Then allow and guide it to move in the energy field beyond your dense physical body. Again, follow your instinct and intuition about where it needs to go.

Allow it to flow and make wide sweeps through your energy field.

Allow it go all around you, over you, behind you and under you.

Allow it to come into your physical body and then out again.

Experiment with moving it in spirals and in different directions.

Let it go right to the edge of your aura. And let it flow deep into and through your body.

EXPERIMENT WITH THE VELOCITY

If it feels that you are blocked or you just feel like experimenting, you can accelerate the speed at which you guide the energy around you.

First, move it slowly and softly, as normal.

Then begin gently to accelerate the movement until you are visualizing or sensing it moving fairly fast. Do this for as long as is comfortable.

Then accelerate it so that it is moving as fast as you can possibly imagine. Let it zip in and around and through you.

Do this for as long as is comfortable and then bring it down to half speed and decelerate down into the soft movement. And finally to a halt.

Timing

People often ask how long should these exercises last. You can pause and do them for a split second. Or you can stretch them for minutes, hours, even a life time. How long you take is completely up to you. It is like surfing waves. Sometimes the waves are small and quick. At other times they are long and deep.

Why These Particular Parts of the Body?

This book is not a textbook of holistic anatomy. Nevertheless, it is useful to have some understanding of why you are moving the feelgood into these particular regions of the body.

Spinal cord and brain

'You are as old as your spine,' goes a well-known saying and, as many people know, the spine needs to stay flexible and strong for good health. The spinal cord, which runs down the centre of the spine, is also extremely important. It is the core of the nervous system, fanning its tendrils out into every part of the body, and is directly linked to the lower part of your brain. Physiologically it is in this lower area of your brain and in the spinal cord – together known as the reptilian brain – that all your survival instincts are lodged: it is here that you hold your instinctive patterns of defence and attack, addiction and compulsion. Guiding the golden flow of energy deep into them massages them into relaxation and release.

Taking the endorphins and benevolent vitality deep into the entire brain is an excellent counterbalance to the non-stop activity that some people experience in their brains. To place the elixir into the actual cells where thought processing happens changes their electrochemistry and facilitates a feeling of intelligent calm.

The bone marrow

The health of bone marrow is crucial as it produces almost all the cells that make up blood. It is blood that transports the necessities of life to all parts of the body and creates a stable environment. Vital bone marrow therefore equals healthy, vital blood, which in turn equals a healthy body. Vital bone marrow also supports supple and strong bones.

The meridian circuit

Chinese medicine of which acupuncture is a crucial part, is very specific about how vital energy or chi flows in and around the human body. Practitioners spend years studying these flows and how to enhance and balance them for strength and health. For our purposes here, however, you can take a very simple approach and recognize that in general the meridians – the flows of energy – are located directly under the skin in the fascia. The fascia is the area of tissue between the skin and the layer of fat or gristle or muscle or bone. If, for example, you take your finger and gently rub the back of your hand, you will immediately feel the fascia beneath the skin. It is through the fascia that vital energy circulates around the body. This is the layer into which acupuncture needles are placed.

Your energy field

As discussed in earlier chapters, the whole body is permeated and surrounded by an energy field or aura. From an electromagnetic or subatomic perspective, it is accurate to describe the entire body as being electric and energetic. This is also, of course, the perspective of all holistic medical traditions.

In a healthy human body, vital and benevolent energy is always circulating in and through the whole energy field. How it circulates depends upon the individual. A blockage in the circulation always manifests sooner or later as physical illness or lack of vitality. Blockages are caused by psychological and physical factors.

It is, therefore, always beneficial to guide and encourage the movement of benevolent energy through and around the whole of your aura. The field extends quite a distance from your body, and it is worth experimenting with swooping the energy at distances of up to twenty feet away from you.

Tension and Discomfort from the Exercises

During the exercises described in this chapter or immediately afterwards you may feel tension and discomfort. This is not unusual. As you turn your attention towards your body and circulate the feelgood, you will meet tensions you may have previously ignored. As the endorphins move into areas of stress, memories of past distress and anxiety may be released and you may suddenly experience uncomfortable feelings of sadness, tension, frustration, fear or loss. These may be experienced as physical and emotional discomfort. This work is simply revealing what is already there.

Later in the book, you will find more detailed instructions for working with this kind of discomfort. For the moment though, if you do experience distress during the exercises:

- Stay with your Inner Smile and soft eyes.
- Keep your attention affectionately down in your body.
- Think of your very best strawberry.
- Place your hands either on the tense area or on your lower stomach. This will help reassure your body.
- Greet the distress as an old friend. Do this in a style that is soft and accepting.
- Send a message into the tension, asking it to relax and melt.
- Take two or three long, slow, gentle breaths down into your lower stomach.

If you feel tense after the exercise, a good stretch, shake or shout can release constricted energy. Knowing when to stretch, shake or scream is not a life skill taught in most schools, but I would place it high on the curriculum of emotional intelligence. So much emotional time-wasting and psychological torture could be avoided if people monitored how their bodies felt and went along with the necessary releasing strategy. I am not suggesting that you start to embarrass yourself in public, but that you experiment with some 'active release' in the privacy of your own space. These are skills that everyone should have the freedom to exercise.

If you feel tense, allow yourself to stretch. Be like a cat waking up in the warm sun. Stretch and release tension. Do any stretches you have learned in yoga or gym work. If you feel frustrated, give yourself a good shake. If it will not disturb your neighbours, allow yourself the release of a healthy scream. Loud singing can also help.

DON'T GET TOO SERIOUS

Different traditions of energy medicine have different maps for how the energies should flow and be guided. In chi gung, yoga and Kabbalah, for example, very specific routes and gateways in the human body are described for accessing these greater wave fields. But, as all teachers of energy medicine know, in the final analysis everyone has to find their own way of working with the benevolent flow.

This work is not mechanical. It is to do with flows and floods and tides, and each individual will find his or her own best way of doing it. The teacher gives guidelines, but these are not rigid.

So, whilst I put forward my particular suggestions and strategies, I actively encourage everyone to experiment with what feels best for them. In fact, I enjoy and look forward to hearing different approaches from fellow practitioners and students. Everyone develops their own best way of doing this work. Experimentation is good.

It is also important to have a sense of humour and a sense of proportion. When I get too serious about the specifics of how this work should be done, I think of the different religious attitudes to hair which always make me smile.

There are, for example, many religious groups, such as Christian and Buddhist monks, who think short hair or a shaved scalp are essential for letting in God's blessing. Others, such as Sikhs and some yogis, are certain that long hair is crucial because the hair strands act as aerials picking up spiritual vibrations. Other monks, however, are certain that the hair should be retained but that you should shave the very top of your head and have a tonsure so that your soul can get in and out. And there are other monks who prefer exactly the opposite – a shaved head with a topknot of hair. Finally, of course, we must not forget those religions that want men to wear hats all the time and those other religions that contrarily need women to cover their hair.

There are obviously different courses for different horses.

Possible Difficulties

There are a few problems that some people may experience when absorbing and guiding the flow. It is useful to be aware of them.

It is just my imagination

Some people do not believe, when they start to move the feelgood around their body, that something real is happening. They say things like, 'I don't trust myself. This is all just my imagination. I'm making it up.'

When beginning this kind of work, it is natural that a part of your mind should be sceptical and questioning until it is proven, but do not let it stop you doing the practice. The sensation becomes more obvious the more you do it. It is perfectly normal that, if you are doing this kind of work for the first time, it may take a while for you to get accustomed to how it feels and to trust it.

It is subtle

The sensation of moving the golden elixir through your body may be very subtle for you. People have varying levels of kinaesthetic sensitivity in this work. Some people are highly sensitive and notice everything, whilst others are more stolid. Most of us are somewhere in between. In general, though, the sensations are subtle compared to being slapped across the face with a wet kipper.

Notice and stay with the subtlety. Do not be put off because you may have heard of other people having spectacular experiences. Subtle pleasure too is very enjoyable and it does the job.

The inner critic

A third problem is that some people have an inner voice which, for all kinds of psychological reasons, has to sabotage all pleasant experiences. It is usually the voice of a parental figure or stoic disciplinarian who thinks you do not deserve to enjoy yourself without paying for it. It is suspicious of pleasure and anything that is gained easily. It can also surface as an impatient scientist who finds this work illogical and too touchy-feely.

The best strategy for dealing with this internal saboteur is to adopt a sympathetic attitude towards it. It is possible to do the exercises even while you have a sceptical critic in your head. Let it burble on, but do not let it stop you. In Chapter 9 I shall give specific techniques for dealing with these internal saboteurs.

Breathing

Finally, it is useful to know how to work with your breathing. In different cultures all across the globe 'conscious' breathing – monitoring and guiding it – is taught as the fundamental skill for staying centred and dealing with distress and tension. Watching and guiding your breath is a powerful signal to your body that you are in control, in the driver's seat.

When you are relaxed and in a pleasurable mood, your breathing is regular and comfortable, and you do not have to give it any attention. But when you are in any kind of stress, your breathing will be tight and constricted.

CONSCIOUS BREATHING

The easiest way to work with your breathing is to use the Inner Smile and soft eyes.

Think of a strawberry and notice the pleasure. Turn on your Inner Smile and turn your friendly attention down into your body.

Notice your breathing – how your chest and stomach move.

Notice how the air feels in your nostrils as you breathe in and out. Just stay noticing it.

Stay calm and watchful, never losing your Inner Smile.

If you want to, start counting your breaths. Count as long as you like.

If you want to, guide your breath so that the exhalation is the same length as the inhalation. Count to seven on your inhalation. Pause. Count to seven on your exhalation. Pause. And so on.

Keep watching and feeling your breath.

Maintain your soft eyes and kind attitude.

Sooner or later, your tension will subside and you will come comfortably back to centre.

CHAPTER 8:

Curled Deer, Strong Centre – Conscious Retreat, Clear Boundaries

Relaxed and Strong

It is obviously impossible to maintain endorphin production if circumstances exhaust, irritate or overwhelm you. It is crucial therefore that you know how to replenish your vitality, stay strong and confident. This chapter specifically deals with those concerns and draws particularly on some insights from Eastern energy medicine. For endorphins to flow throughout your life, you must be able to deal gracefully with life's oppressions.

In the hierarchy of human needs, it is clearly recognized that you cannot get on with the business of self-development if you are threatened. Put in more biological language, you cannot fulfil your potential if you are stewing in the adrenal acid of anxiety and fear.

Being realistic, a genuine state of relaxed strength and confidence comes from an inner feeling which then spills over into dealing effectively with the people and events around you. It is no use feeling good and relaxed if you are also a walkover. I get concerned about stress control and relaxation techniques, which leave people limp and passive in the face of daily reality: 'I'm feeling great, but please walk all over me. I'm relaxed, so take no notice of me.'

Over and over, I meet people from all walks of life – teachers, parents, business people, managers and carers – who find themselves stressed because they do not know how to manage pressure. They feel as if there are only two alternatives – submit or lash out. I think immediately of a media executive, who desperately wanted to do the best for both his family and his colleagues, yet could not handle the pressures in a dignified way. He would try to stay calm and be kind, but beneath his smiling exterior he was writhing with nervous energy and resentment. If he was tired or ill, his fuse would become unbearably short and then he would behave either submissively or aggressively. At work he would be short-tempered, impatient and sarcastic, occasionally erupting with anger. At home, he was also impatient and sarcastic, but instead of lashing out he would collapse in theatrical self-pity at his wife's demands. Working with the techniques in this chapter, he managed to achieve a sense of balance and the skills to manage pressure.

I want to help people feel good and to de-stress. At the same time, I want them to be able to put up a firm boundary and communicate a clear 'No!' which other people respect. I want people to get relaxation with strength.

The first part of this longish chapter, then, is concerned with developing effective relaxation and harmonious inner energy. It then describes techniques for maintaining this inner strength in the face of crisis and for asserting clear boundaries.

> **In order to produce a consistent flow of endorphins you must feel relaxed, safe and confident. A consistent flow of endorphins makes you feel relaxed, safe and confident.**

A Good Rest and the Curled Deer

There is a very distinct texture and feeling to a good rest. It is warm and comfortable. The body is happy. The mind is also happy and relaxed – snug as a bug in a rug.

This is a universal experience for all human beings. It is caused partly by the hormones that are released during rest and partly by the absorption of benevolent energies. This may be a new piece of knowledge for many readers: when your body feels comfortable and safe, it acts like a magnet and absorbs vitality. This is a major reason why you emerge from a rest feeling better and vitalized. You have been absorbing *prana*, which happens automatically when you are asleep.

You can also deliberately create the same effect when you are awake, by guiding your body into the *feeling* of a good rest.

The easiest way to do this is through working with a loop of energy or meridian in the body which Chinese medicine calls the Microcosmic Circuit and recognizes as the foundation of health. This loop is described as running up the spine, over the top of the head, down the front of the face, neck, chest and abdomen, under the base of the spine and then back up. In Chinese energy medicine, to stimulate good health and a flow of *chi* practitioners are taught to visualize and guide energy around this circuit and then through the other meridians.

There are two crucial points here

- When this loop is in harmony it magnetically absorbs the benevolent wave fields from the natural and cosmic environment.
- This loop is in natural harmony when you are resting.

This may all sound strange to Western minds hearing it for the first time, but it is a basic premise of Chinese energy medicine.

This loop is at its most efficient and magnetic when it feels pleasurably soft and harmonious. Once again, we are encountering the essential fact that the only way to produce the desired effect is through a soft and pleasurable style. This softness is quite explicit in the original Taoist texts. Alongside the basic instruction to circulate energy around the loop is a beautiful pen and ink drawing of a deer curled up with its nose on its tail. The message of the curled deer is obvious. It tells students how the exercise should feel.

What would it feel like to be a young deer curled up and with your nose on your fluffy tail? Pleasurably soft and harmonious.

We are born with the Curled Deer sensation as an intrinsic part of our biological and energetic make-up. Think of a foetus in the womb, curled up and floating in an ocean of warm biological fluids. The foetus is absorbing both food from its mother and the benevolent and creative vitality of nature and the universe. Again, the loop can be clearly seen in the circular shape – head curled to tailbone – of the foetus. And, again, it is clear what this feels like.

So, you will know whether your loop is in harmony and effective because you will feel comfortable in your body. Or, to put it the opposite way, whenever you feel comfortable in your body, then the circuit is in harmony. You are in the classic energy poise of the Curled Deer. (It may be that you do not like to curl up when you rest, but prefer to stretch out. Nevertheless, the actual sensation of comfortable relaxation in your body is exactly the same.)

Microcosmic Circuit

> ## THE VITAL MESSAGE
>
> - **There is a circuit of energy in the human body which magnetically attracts and absorbs the benevolent vitality of nature and the universe.**
> - **This loop functions naturally when you feel relaxed, comfortable and at ease.**
> - **Your body energy instinctively 'falls' into this loop when it needs rest and revitalization.**
> - **You automatically go into this harmonious loop every time that you rest or sleep well.**

Peter Hanley, one of our CEM coaches and an ex-submarine engineer, describes it as being similar to an electric motor. Loops of copper thread spinning around a magnet create electricity. The fast oscillation of a magnetic field generates energy. The Curled Deer does the same.

You can see, then, how useful the strawberries and Inner Smile are. They support you in creating a pleasurable and harmonious sensation which can then be deliberately used to take you into a pleasurable rest, even if the circumstances are oppressive.

If, for example, you slump into bed or an armchair in a bad mood, you need to use your strawberries and Inner Smile in order to switch channels and feel better. It is a matter of where you place your focus. Instead of stewing in your lousy mood and letting yourself get obsessed with whatever has disturbed you, you can focus on something that gives you pleasure. In this way, you have a gateway out of Blobsville and back into where you really belong. Then, when you feel centred and strong, you can come back to Blobsville and manage its challenges.

THE CURLED DEER

THE FIRST STEP

You can do this exercise in any position. It is easiest when you are comfortable, so choose a position that suits you.

Once you are comfortable, just be quiet for a minute or so.

When you are ready, go through the basic sequence of contemplating strawberries, switching on your Inner Smile and lowering your focus down into your body.
- Strawberries – Think of some things that give you pleasure.
- Inner Smile – Switch on your Inner Smile and soft eyes.
- Focus down into your body – Turn your awareness affectionately down into the great cavern of your stomach and abdomen.
- Take a few soft breaths down into your lower stomach.

Now allow yourself to experience a slight heaviness running through your body, as if you are falling or caving into yourself.

Take a few soft breaths down into your lower stomach.

If it feels appropriate, place your hands on your lower stomach.

Become aware of the base of your spine.

Imagine and sense that your forehead is connected down to the base of your spine.

You feel like a deer or a cat curled up on itself, nose happily on its tail. (For some people, this imagery does not work. It may be more helpful to use the image of an animal stretched out and completely comfortable. Or it may be easier to go straight into the sensation of being relaxed and comfortable.)

Stay with your Inner Smile. Keep your focus down within yourself.

You are creating a feeling of comfort. If it feels appropriate, give yourself permission to feel childlike and comforted, like a foetus in the womb or like an infant sucking your thumb.

You are deliberately guiding yourself into the feeling and texture of a good rest.

Allow yourself to sink into the sensation of the Curled Deer. Enjoy the kinaesthetic experience.

THE SECOND STEP

Become aware of the actual location of the Microcosmic Circuit, just under your skin in a loop that runs over the top of your head, down your face, neck and chest, down your abdomen, under your groin, up your back and over the top of your head.

Allow the muscles of your neck, chest and abdomen to sink down.

Sense your spine relaxing and opening upwards.

Sense a soft warm energy looping this circuit.

Maintain your sense of comfortable containment.

THE THIRD STEP

As you rest in the comfortable feelings, become aware that you are now like a magnet. Good vitality is coming to you and being absorbed by your body.

When the human body is allowed to rest, it naturally regenerates itself and absorbs nurture, vitality and strength. This is built into its biological and energetic structure.

Retreat and Collapse Used Consciously

The Curled Deer strategy is so effective and so natural that it can transform times of crisis and fatigue into times of renewal and creativity. In fact, your body and psyche already use this technique every time that you have a good rest. Regardless of whether you are extrovert, powerful and successful, or introvert, meek and moderate, you still get tired and have to sleep. There is no one on earth who can keep going twenty-four hours a day, week after week. Sooner or later, you collapse. And in the collapse, something miraculous happens. The body and psyche put themselves back together and come out of it refreshed and ready for new activity.

To retreat into rest, therefore, is a natural pre-requisite for health. I despair at the gung-ho attitude that sometimes prevails in business and personal training programmes. Our workaholic society tends not to understand or value rest periods – it is all competition and war. But, believe me, Genghis Khan also slept and knew when to retreat. A good rest is a form of strategic retreat. It is a powerful and necessary tool.

You need, therefore, to develop the habit of deliberately using rest and collapse for relaxation and regeneration. All the exercises presented so far – Connecting with Strawberries, the Inner Smile, Guiding the Energy – can be easily done when you are resting. In fact, one of the greatest assets of the strategy presented in *The Endorphin Effect* is that it does not require a positive attitude to set it going. So many self-help techniques force you into a positive attitude, but the fundamental strategies in this book can be put into practice when you are wallowing in self-obsession, curled up with junk food and watching mindless television.

You also do not need to be sitting straight-backed in the lotus meditation posture or any other special position to do any of these exercises. Any comfortable position works.

Sometimes, of course, you have to pass through a bad mood before you are able to feel the comfort of rest. The key here is to allow yourself to collapse until you eventually find yourself feeling at ease. Most people are very familiar with this process. You come home in a bad mood or you have a row. You feel depressed and overwhelmed. You crash on to the sofa or into bed. You may watch a video or television, have some junk food and a glass of wine, or just disappear under the duvet. Then, sooner or later, the pressures of the world seem to lift off and you are left in the comfort of your own scent and your own warmth. In this state of withdrawal you no longer feel all the pressures of the outside world. You are in safe space. Blobsville is irrelevant.

It is, then, when you have withdrawn from the world and are feeling comfortable in the privacy of your own space that these exercises can easily be done. It is both pleasant and powerful to be in a sleepy mood and to ponder your strawberries. As you withdraw from the cares of the day or push them away, it is also pleasant to turn your focus down into your body with a friendly Inner Smile and then to guide the warm flows of energy around within yourself.

So the real trick here is to work consciously with these times of natural retreat.

ENJOY COLLAPSING

The next time you are feeling low or tired, deliberately allow yourself to collapse into bed or on to the sofa, and wait until you begin to feel some comfort. You can also do this slumped in a chair at your work or when travelling.

If it feels helpful and is not embarrassing for you, allow your body language to become quite childlike, as if you were happily sucking your thumb. It may feel appropriate to curl up physically.

Enjoy a feeling of self-satisfaction inside the isolation of your safe space. Allow yourself to feel infantile and comforted. Feel free to tell the rest of the world to back off and leave you alone.

Allow yourself to feel heavy and leaden. See if you can catch a sense of the Earth's gravity pulling you down and of your body collapsing downwards and inwards.

From within this very private space, allow one or more of your best strawberries to float around in your mind. Notice how thinking of them brings you a sense of pleasure. Enjoy and absorb the feelgood. Breathe it in.

Now switch on your Inner Smile and focus down into your body.

Then guide the pleasure around your body. Allow the energy to circulate and run through you. Bring it deep into your spine, your bone marrow and your brain. Following your instincts, allow it to move softly through your meridians and your aura.

Do this for as long as feels comfortable. Enjoy the sensation.

> Strategic retreat transforms difficult times into perfect opportunities for regenerating your energy and preparing for your next dealings with the external world.

The Power Nap

I know several people who have no knowledge of the strategies of this book, but are instinctively masters of it. John, for example, is CEO of an international media company and commutes into central London by train every day from his home in the country. His daily travelling time is three hours. On the journey, he never reads the newspaper or chats to fellow passengers, but always allows his head to fall forward and drops into sleep or a semi-conscious slumber. Instinctively he curls up his energy and looks after himself. He finds it energizing and is adamant that he would not survive the pressures of his job if he did not do so. It is a very economic use of his time.

When I run one-day training sessions, after lunch I insist that everyone takes a ten-minute nap. Many participants are shocked at this apparent waste of time, but I am being completely practical. There is always a lull in energy after lunch. The body needs to digest and people's attention span is very low. Trainers call the time after lunch the graveyard session. So I give people a ten-minute rest and also introduce the Power Nap.

THE POWER NAP

Sitting in your chair at home or at work, close your eyes and allow your body and your energy to flop.

Allow a sinking feeling to move all the way through your body. If it is helpful, imagine yourself going down in an elevator from the tenth floor to the basement. Count yourself down. Ten, nine, eight . . .

Sense and visualize the energies of your brain sinking down, drawn by gravity, into the earth.

Slowly and softly begin to slow down your breathing.

Allow the muscles of your neck, chest and abdomen to sink down.

Take your focus down into your lower stomach.

Now, with no expectations, just wait.

Keep your breathing soft and relaxed.

Sooner or later, you will fall into a state of conscious slumber.

Then, when you feel it is appropriate and without disturbing the sense of slumber, think of your strawberries. Use any of the CEM steps with which you feel comfortable.

Then before you get on with your day, wriggle your toes and send a message of appreciation down into your body.

Stretch and move gracefully into action.

Building Strength

The vital and benevolent energy that comes into you when you rest is stored in the lower abdomen. To people only familiar with Western anatomy this may sound strange but, again, it is common knowledge in Eastern medical anatomy. In many pre-modern medical traditions, the lower stomach was conceived as being like a cauldron or a chalice. Students were taught to imagine that they had a cauldron of warm vitality located in their lower stomach.

This area is the core of the Curled Deer. It is the location of growth in pregnant women – the centre from which the growing foetus emerges.

The foundation of all the exercises in martial arts and chi gung is to become aware of this vital energy in the lower stomach and to feed and amplify it. This part of the lower stomach is called *tan t'ien* in Chinese and *hara* in Japanese. It is the source of strength and vitality for health and fighting. All physical movement in martial arts pivots around the centre of power between the hips. Physically, it is also the strongest part of the body.

Again, it is very important to appreciate that this is not a piece of theoretical knowledge or imagery, but a physical reality and sensation. So alongside the sensation of the Curled Deer there is a second sensation of having a warm and vital storage centre in the body. In a healthy person, this all functions well and does not require special attention. If, however, you need to build up strength or to maintain a steady centre in disturbing circumstances, it is very empowering and supportive to work on your inner cauldron of energy.

BUILDING STRENGTH AND VITALITY

Do this exercise whenever you feel comfortable. (Particularly in relation to this exercise, I recommend that people who are interested read books or attend classes on chi gung.[1])

- **Strawberries – think of some things that you really love.**
- **Inner Smile – switch on your Inner Smile and soft eyes.**
- **Focus down into your body – turn your awareness affectionately down into the great cavern of your stomach and abdomen.**
- **Take a few soft breaths down into your lower stomach.**
- **Go into the feeling of the Curled Deer.**

Become aware that in your lower stomach there is an area of warmth, heat and nurturing fire.

Become aware of the fact that simply because you are in a happy and restful state, benevolent vitality is being absorbed by you. Sense that it is being stored in particular in the region of your lower stomach.

Stay relaxed and allow yourself to receive it all.

Experiment with guiding the energy down into your *tan t'ien* on the flow of your breath. Breathe in and absorb the energy. Breathe out and guide it down into your stomach.

Experiment with visualizing the energy in your abdomen as a ball of golden light or fire.

Do all of this in a soft and comfortable way. If you start to tense

up, release the exercise and return to contemplating your strawberries.

For some people the sensation of all this may be very subtle; for others it may be very obvious.

HARA OR TAN T'IEN

Most Westerners are completely unfamiliar with the importance of the lower stomach and the concept of *hara*. In classical Japanese culture, however, the ability to stay centred within the lower stomach, and to have the vitality and strength that go with it, were considered to be the signs of an aristocratic and spiritually evolved being. To be in one's *hara* was the goal of daily life. Writing at the beginning of the twentieth century, the Japanese teacher Master Okada Torajiro taught:

'*Tan t'ien* is the shrine of the divine. Its stronghold is finely built so that the Divine in us can grow and then a real human being is achieved. If one divides people into ranks, the lowest is he who values his head. Those who endeavour only to amass as much knowledge as possible grow heads that become bigger and so they topple over easily, like a pyramid standing upside down. . . .

Next come those of middle rank. For them the chest is most important . . . . These are the men with outward courage, but without real strength. Many of the so-called great men are in this category. Yet all this is not enough.

But those who regard the belly as the most important part and so have built the stronghold where the Divine can grow – these are the people of the highest rank. Strength flows out from them and produces a spiritual condition of ease and equanimity.'[2]

Be a Parent to Your Body

Accomplished martial artists know how to handle the internal energies and stay in their *hara*. Watch perfectly attuned fighters and you will see great courage, strength and remarkable flexibility. You will also notice calm and fearless observation. The one thing that they are not experiencing is the adrenalin rush of fear. Even if they are in an overwhelming situation, they stay calm and watchful. They flow to dance out of the way of the flying arrows.

But how is this done? How can a fighter be in an overwhelmingly dangerous situation yet experience no tension or anxiety? This is possible because the biological vehicle, the monkey creature, is being carefully looked after by the mind which inhabits it. The mind observes and assesses the situation. At the same time, the mind is humming reassurance down into the body.

- The body stays feeling calm and safe because:
- The *hara* is strong, centred and vital.
- The Curled Deer is in healthy orbit.
- The biological creature of the physical body feels and senses that its master, its mind, is caring for it and aware of it.

This is very similar to an infant being carried by its mother, whether in the womb or in her arms. The external situation may be dire but, providing the mother does not slip into terror or panic, the infant continues to feel safe in the physical warmth and reassurance of the parent. The infant, like the body, is oblivious of the external dangers.

You can see, then, that these exercises create a kinaesthetic sense of safety and strength. This is not a psychological or mental attribute, but a genuine physical feeling. It does not depend on whether you have the stoic personality of a hero or warrior, but on how you manage your internal energy. The best-trained Samurai and infants in their mother's wombs have something very important in common. They know how to curl up their body energy to absorb nurture, vitality and strength.

There is a beautiful teaching from the Taoist tradition that is very relevant here. It says that there is a tiny baby in the lower stomach of all of us. As we build up our inner energy and strengthen our *hara*, this baby begins to feel strong and starts to grow. It continues to grow because it is fed by the benevolent flow of the universe and because it feels completely safe within you. As your practice continues and your calm strength builds, so the baby gets larger and larger. It grows so much, in fact, that it expands beyond your physical body. It grows enormous – strong, safe and innocent – and you are now held *inside* it. The child whom you nurtured in your own womb is now a great being who holds you – but this child is still you.

Maintaining Your Strength and Confidence in the Real World

Of course, it is all very well building and maintaining this stance in the comfort of your armchair or bed, but another thing altogether to maintain and demonstrate it in daily life. For some people the transition from feeling safe in the privacy of their own living room to feeling safe in the public arena of an inner city or busy office is very challenging. Endorphins at home, but tension at work.

There are three key techniques for holding on to your sensation of strength, comfort and safety as you move out into the real world.

- Keep your energy contained and in integrity
- Learn the skill of not reacting
- Assert clear boundaries and be able to push people and energies out of your face

I will go through them one by one.

Keep your energy contained

Whatever happens the most important thing is the ability to stay feeling strong, comfortable and centred in the midst of the pressures of daily life. The key is to keep the primal energy loop contained and functioning within you to maintain endorphin flow. This means that, whatever is going on around you, you must maintain that inner sense of being comfortable. You need to be able to walk around and do the business of your life, whilst continuously maintaining the sensation of the Curled Deer. Even when you are in Blobsville you hold the inner experience of being in Strawberry Land. In more Buddhist language, you are present to the hell state of human suffering, but are centred in the bliss fields of true reality. Or in Christian language, Christ lives in your heart even when purgatory is all around.

This may seem a steep learning curve to many people. It is difficult to imagine being in a threatening situation and having your body feel comfortable at the same time. But if a martial artist can do it in the face of overwhelming odds and imminent death, you can do it on a visit to an overcrowded supermarket, a difficult family, a bank manager or a hectic office. It is partly a matter of dignity, about which the Japanese *hara* Master Okada wrote beautifully:

> 6 When you sit quietly, a good meal and a good bed
> are being prepared. The good cook and the good
> mattress are within yourself. When you sit, a lovely cool
> wind blows in summer, and in winter a cosy fire burns
> on the hearth.
> The cool wind and the warm fire are within yourself. 9

So the purpose of the following exercise is to help you make the transition from feeling safe and comfortable privately to feeling the same way in public situations.

STAYING STRONG AND COMFORTABLE IN THE REAL WORLD

In this exercise, you practise holding your centre as you emerge from a private comforting rest to go back out into public life.

Start by going through the main sequence:
- **Strawberry**
- **Inner Smile**
- **Focus down into body**
- **Curled Deer**
- **Absorb and strengthen *hara***

Keep your attention down in your body and enjoy the relaxation, the comfort and the private space.

Then, staying in that mood, begin to think about the fact that you are about to go out into the public world.

Being realistic, recognize that the stimulation and circumstances of the external world may wobble you out of your centre and your internal sense of comfort. This is the moment in the exercise when you must stay relaxed. Maintain your Inner Smile and have a kind and understanding attitude towards the realities of life and your possible reaction to them.

Some people may tense just at the thought of meeting pressured situations. But you must stay centred and observing the outside world as if it were a movie. Do not let it get through to you. If you cannot handle thinking about it, you will certainly not be able to handle the reality of it. If there is a genuine psychological problem here, the strategies of Chapter 9 will help you.

Then send your body a calm and encouraging message that you will remain aware of it when you are out in the public arena. It is as if you are talking to a young child or a pet animal. You are sending reassuring messages that you will remain with it and look after it.

Amplify your Inner Smile and soft eyes. You may need to think of your best strawberries again. As much as is possible, sink into and enjoy the sensation of the Curled Deer.

Now imagine yourself going out into life, into your home and family relationships, into your work – but always maintaining the internal Curled Deer, always feeling the comfort within you. Visualize and sense yourself in those situations, but remaining calm and comfortable.

Imagine yourself in a situation that might normally disturb you, then imagine yourself behaving with absolute calm and awareness. You do not react to the situation, but immediately turn your attention down into your body and monitor that the inner loop is comfortable. If necessary, you take yourself back through the sequence:

- Strawberry
- Inner Smile
- Focus down into body
- Curled Deer
- Absorb and strengthen *hara*

Again, visualize the situation that may cause you problems and see yourself in it, perfectly holding your centre, perfectly in your Curled Deer.

STRENGTHENING YOUR ENERGY FIELD

Maintaining your sense of inner comfort as you go out into the world can be further helped if you strengthen the integrity of your energy field. Readers wanting further guidance about maintaining their sense of integrity in difficult situations should see my *Psychic Protection*.[3]

Again, this exercise follows on from being in the comfort of the Curled Deer. So, go through the sequence again:

- Strawberry
- Inner Smile
- Focus down into body
- Curled Deer
- Absorb and strengthen *hara*

Feeling comfortable and at ease, imagine and sense your energy field as being like an egg or a bubble around you. It extends several feet, perhaps further, from you.

Sense the energy from your lower stomach, from your *hara*, radiating into and filling this bubble. This bubble is filled only with your energy.

Notice your breathing and how your outbreath is filled with warm and moist air. This warm air is filled with the essence of your own vibration.

On each outbreath, imagine and sense this warm essence moving to surround and cover the whole of your body. Do this for several breaths until you sense that your bubble, your aura, is filled with the essence of your own vibration.

If, later in the day, you sense yourself losing centre and internal comfort, you can then quickly turn your attention down into your body. Notice your breathing and again allow your outbreath to fill your aura with your own vibration.

The sensation of comfort from the Curled Deer inside you must continue no matter what is happening. Your body's sense that you are still aware of it and caring for it must continue no matter what is happening. Your sense of being centred in your lower stomach must continue no matter what is happening.

Learn Not to React

During one of my courses on how to hold a calm centre whatever the circumstances, a woman student came up to me in a break. She complained that she already knew all the techniques that I had taught, but none of them helped her. She had an ongoing situation with three friends. Every time she was with them, she ended up arguing and upset.

I then put to her a very straightforward question: I asked whether she had ever considered simply not reacting to them. She was stunned by the idea. The whole basis of her relationship with them was to be involved in fast, intense and competitive conversations. Her jaw literally dropped as she accepted the absolute relevance of my question. She saw now that she had a choice. She could choose not to react. Her whole problem could be solved simply by staying calm and not being reactive.

I have told this story innumerable times in training sessions and I always see nods of recognition. So many people are caught in the habit, and sometimes the compulsion, to respond and react. This is frequently the case with difficult parents, siblings and children, as well as partners, friends and colleagues. People can be addicted to automatic reaction.

To stop doing so is an easy change for some and a very difficult one for others. It means that, when you do not like something that is happening or being said, you need to be able to stop your normal instinctive defensive, judgemental or aggressive behaviour. You have to understand that, by going automatically into those kinds of reaction, you are depleting and hurting your own energy and integrity. Every time you react or become judgemental, a part of your body freezes and the energy jams up. It feels horrible.

Here is my golden rule: when you feel reactive, don't react. In fact, take it one step further. When you feel reactive, take it as a signal to turn within and look after yourself. When you feel upset, don't go for revenge or into automatic response. Take the sensation as a signal to switch on the Inner Smile and guide your body into the Curled Deer. It is amazingly powerful to recognize that you are reacting negatively to a situation but, instead of flooding with unpleasant emotion, you are immediately comforting your body and maintaining your stability.

I am not telling anyone here to become a passive robot who puts up with anything. I am just stating a clear energetic truth: a habit of reactivity depletes your energy field and creates unpleasant feelings for you. It turns the elixir into acid. What you need here is the self-discipline not to respond. This is not about having a still mind or being passive. It is about keeping your body, your monkey vehicle, happy. Concentrate on keeping your body happy and the endorphins flowing.

> **When you feel reactive, it is a signal to turn your attention inward. Inner Smile. Curled Deer. Look after yourself. Then, from a centre of strength, act.**

DO NOT REACT

When you start to feel triggered by someone, immediately turn your attention down into your own body. Do not react.

Bring your attention down into your body.

Take a couple of soft, quiet breaths deep into you.

Switch on your Inner Smile.

Have a comforting attitude towards yourself.

Go into the safe and nurturing sensation of the internal energy loop.

Be a kind observer to the whole situation.

The result of this new behaviour will usually be very beneficial for other people as well. If you yourself can break the loop of reactivity, it also releases the other participants in the conflict. Like the woman who always argued with her friends, there are many people who have knee-jerk reactions to their parents or colleagues. I have heard innumerable stories from my students of how they just stayed cool, looked after themselves and brought a completely new dynamic into their relationships. As you break the old loops, long-standing triggers will be defused.

Staying cool and centred in this way does not rule out spontaneous behaviour and creativity. Nor does it rule out the possibility that you may need to express anger or become very expressive. It is, however, a basic life skill with which you should be familiar and able to use whenever you want. In my opinion, though, it is not appropriate to withdraw into yourself if you are being abused, which requires more active and assertive behaviour. Therefore, you also need to know how to assert a clear boundary.

Assert Clear Boundaries and Push Away Abuse

It is from a calm and contained body that true strength and power emerge. The men who are considered the greatest martial artists in the world are the famous Shao Lin monks. These are men who practise long periods of meditation and holding their focus calmly down in their abdomen. Some of these monks are so experienced that they can use their *hara* energy to knock people over without physically touching them.

Energetically other people can instinctively sense whether you have a strong centre or not. If your *hara* is not strong, bullies (and your own children) may be inclined to abuse your boundaries just for the hell of it. People who are emotionally involved with you may also intrude upon you if they feel you are weak in your *hara*.

I believe that people have a right to their own unabused space. I also believe that being able to assert this right and effectively tell people to back off when necessary is another basic life skill that everyone should have. It is the other side of the coin from not reacting.

If you have had parents, siblings and/or teachers who have continuously invaded your boundaries since you were a child, you may have developed a habit of letting people in. This is not healthy. You need to be able to communicate clearly with both words and body language that you want a person to back off. But if your boundary is to feel authentic, it must come from a centre deep within your body. The energy of the boundary is then expressed and radiated from your *hara* and your full body. People will sense it and believe it.

I have also watched many parents and teachers telling children not to do something. If the voice is shrill and from the head, the child may be startled but will usually carry on with the undesired behaviour. If, however, the voice comes clearly and assertively from the full body of the parent or teacher, the child energetically feels a very clear and powerful communication. Animals will also register a full body communication but will remain deaf to a shrill squeak that contains protest but no energy. You must be able forcefully to assert your energetic boundary. You must be able to say authentically: 'This is my space! Get out of my field! Give me space!' All this must come from a strong and safe centre.

Some people have trouble imagining that they could ever be so assertive and clear, but you must learn how to do this. Otherwise you are a walkover, not looking after yourself and ignoring one of your most basic needs. Like any creature on this earth, you have the right to the integrity of your own energy field. If that integrity has been damaged, you need to repair it.

In parallel to the exercises in this chapter, I often recommend that people who are not accustomed to asserting their boundaries might do a couple of months training in a hard martial art such as kendo, aikido, kick-boxing or karate. This will quickly give you a clear physical experience of how to work with a strong *hara* and a clear voice.

ASSERT YOUR BOUNDARY!

First rehearse this exercise mentally and kinaesthetically. Then, when you feel confident, experiment with it in real life. You may not be able to pull it off 100 per cent the first time, especially if it is a very difficult situation, but your results will definitely get better with practice.

THE FIRST STEP

Sit or lie comfortably and take yourself through the sequence:
- **Strawberry**
- **Inner Smile**
- **Focus down into body**
- **Curled Deer**
- **Absorb and strengthen** *hara*

Wait patiently until you feel calm and reposed.

Bring into your mind a situation in which you have to assert a clear boundary. Stay calm and relaxed as you contemplate it.

Imagine the person provoking you, but you simply turn your attention down into yourself and do not react. At the same time, your body feels calm and centred. Your stomach is strong and radiant.

From deep within you, a voice begins to roar. It is filled with creative and positive fury.

It asserts with absolute conviction. 'This is my space. It is my birthright to have an integrated energy field. Get out of my field. Stop. Back off. Get out of my space!'

This message must be kinaesthetically experienced as roaring from your *tan t'ien*. Sense and feel it. If you imagine asserting it from your chest or your head, you will experience that it loses its power and effectiveness.

Keep asserting this message for as long as you feel comfortable.

Then relax and bring your focus calmly back into yourself. Make sure your Inner Smile is still humming and turn your attention carefully to any part of your body which may be feeling anxiety or tension. If it feels appropriate, physically touch the tense area.

Softly bring yourself back into the comfortable experience of the Curled Deer.

It is often helpful to practise this exercise with a friend. Ask your friend to feed back to you whether your voice sounds strong and authentic, and whether your body language reflects your clarity.

THE SECOND STEP

Then, when you are feeling confident, begin to experiment communicating with intruders in your new style. Be realistic and patient with yourself. If things do not work out immediately to your benefit, come back to your strawberries and Inner Smile. Then try again. When dealing with difficult and complex situations, it is also very useful to have some training in communications skills and assertiveness.

Stay centred and in your *hara*. From a strong and comfortable body, assert your right to your own space. Let the centred power of your communication push out from you. Assert from your stomach.

LIFE WARRIORS

A Christian knight went to fight in the crusades to keep the routes and holy places safe for pilgrims. He was supremely gifted as a chivalrous warrior, always centred and watchful, always seeking an opportunity to be of service. He was also an extremely effective soldier.

One day on a battlefield where he had been fighting for hours, he was about to plunge his sword into the chest of a Saracen warrior. Suddenly, he held off from striking the fatal blow and stepped back.

'Why do you not kill me?' asked the Saracen.

'Forgive me,' said the Christian knight. 'I was about to strike you in anger.'

'You are forgiven,' replied the Muslim. 'I would anyway not have blinked an eyelid.'

The two warriors looked at each other kindly.

Heaven Is in the Great Cavern of Your Chest and Abdomen

I would like to end this chapter on a more mystical note that will help underline the significance of holding a focus in your body. Many spiritual traditions have denied the body and even propagated the idea that the body is some kind of evil that needs to be transcended. This has led to a terrible fracture between body and soul, body and mind, which runs all the way through Western theological and intellectual thought.

It has also led to an institutionalized abandonment of the body and, therefore, the creation of an ongoing subliminal hum of tension and anxiety. Whatever the sublime teachings of Western religion and philosophy, the culture has been filled with angst. How can the world be lovingly accepted if you do not even accept your own body? This attitude permeates the West and is endemic in commerce, education and almost all organizations.

To include the body, then, is not just a matter of healing an imbalance. Without giving the body some caring and careful attention, your whole foundation for living is flawed. The whole body is a living intelligence that carries your mind, consciousness and spirit. If it experiences alienation and fear, then your whole life too is filled with the acid of those uncomfortable neuropeptides rather than the endorphins of benevolence.

The Taoist tradition understood perfectly how the bliss fields of the cosmos needed to be reflected in the great space of the chest and abdomen. The foetus, curled up in its mother's womb, experiences this ambrosia, soaking in its fleshy warmth and comfort. There is, therefore, this direct connection between the womb and the universe, between the *hara* and the cosmos, which must be carefully cultivated.

Eva Wong's eloquent translation of the classic Taoist text *Hui-Ming Ching* contains a wonderful passage that speaks directly about the wonder of this space that is both in the universe and in the human body.

> ❝ The one cavity is the root of the void. It has neither shape nor form . . . The one cavity is the place where the sacred is hidden. It is the altar of life and it has many names – the Palace of the Dragon at the Bottom of the Sea, the Land of the Snowy Mountain, the Western Realm, the Original Gate, the Land of the Great Happiness, and the Home of the Limitless. If the practitioner of the arts of longevity [long life and health] does not understand this cavity, he or she will wander through thousands of lifetimes not knowing where to look.

> This cavity is great and wonderful. It emerged when
> we were conceived in our mother's womb. In it, original
> nature and life are intertwined like flames in a furnace
> and are united with the Laws of the Celestial Way and
> the Great Harmony . . . .
>
> If you try tens of thousands of methods looking for
> the One cavity outside and do not understand that the
> key to life lies within, you will waste time and effort and
> accomplish nothing. [4]

This text also gives some clear advice:

> If you want to stop the leakage [of energy] and attain
> the indestructible golden body, focus on the radiance
> and do not leave the happy grounds.
>
> Practise diligently to temper the root of life. Always
> keep the true self hidden in its home.

This, in symbolic language, reminds us to stay in a good mood, connected with the benevolent energy fields of the universe, and remain focussed and contained in our bodies.

CHAPTER 9:

The Connection – Breathing the Earth, Nature, Sun and Universe

Let It All In

You can control the production and flow of endorphins in your body. You can harness this to open to the fields of benevolent vitality and absorb them into your body. It is also possible to take this general feeling of pleasure and expand it into something deeper, more expansive and ecstatic. This experience of physical bliss, accompanied by a sense of meaningful connection with nature and the universe, is perhaps the most profound experience that any of us can have. It is the enduring engine of endorphin production. It is both the foundation and the culmination of total health.

Working with endorphins, bioenergetic armour and wavefields, it is possible to manage the whole experience of ecstasy without losing any of its wonder or power. Ultimately, it is always mysterious and awesome.

The connection with the benevolent wave fields of the universe is always there, but most of the time we are either too tense or too busy to notice it. There are times, of course, when we feel the connection and the flow of endorphins without being fully conscious of what is happening. During and after a wonderful experience, we often allow ourselves to soak in the pleasure of the event.

This soaking in pleasure is not limited to sensitive, poetic or receptive types. The toughest and most cynical of men and women can end up soaking in the connection after making love or trekking in the mountains, just as much as the arty types can go into rapture with dance and music. It is a normal human attribute that belongs to all of us. The Endorphin Effect simply harnesses what already happens.

If you already have a religious or spiritual practice, this approach will only enhance, deepen and support your faith and experience. I have also worked with agnostics, humanists and atheists who have a sense of the wonder of life but are uncomfortable with any idea of a supreme individual or being.

Let me just repeat the basic premises:

- Everything in nature and the universe, including the human body, is made of energy
- According to universal experience, the predominant note of this energy is benevolent and creative
- Its natural state is to be in flow
- Normally, you do not feel it because you are too tense
- Any pleasurable event produces endorphins, melts the tension and allows you to experience the benevolent wave fields
- Using your mind, you can guide both the endorphins and the energy

The basic method for deepening and expanding the experience is relatively simple. When you are experiencing a pleasurable moment, you open yourself fully, like a receptive sponge, to the wave fields of earth, nature, sun and universe. The natural state of these wavefields is to flow into and through you. So, you just open a fraction more and allow them to enter you more fully. You then guide them deep into every part of you and allow yourself to 'melt' in the experience, letting the benevolence of the universe permeate you cell by cell.

- Pause in pleasure
- Smile down into your body
- Relax a fraction more
- Allow yourself to let in the benevolent wavefields of earth, nature, sun and universe
- Float in the ocean of cosmic benevolence
- Your whole body is soaked in ambrosia
- Your consciousness feels and knows your connection with all life

Earth, Nature, The Sun and the Universe

After much experience of teaching these strategies, I am certain that the easiest way – once you are in a state of pleasure – of fully letting in the benevolent fields is to focus on a few specific sources: earth, nature, sun and the universe. This also follows the pattern of many energy medicine traditions.

In my experience, the human body and energy field absorb the benevolent vitality most easily in the following ways:

- Earth from below
- Nature from below and around
- Sun from around and above
- The universe from above, below and from all around

It is worth remembering that just as every atom or tree has its own magnetic field and energy, so the sun, universe, earth and nature are also the physical source of huge energy fields, permeated with flowing vitality.

Once again, recognize that it is completely natural to allow these wave fields to come into you and to bathe in them. Two students in one my classes were party animals and had trouble turning up on time. They also had trouble relating fully to everything they were studying with me. But it was the strategies described in this chapter which finally got through to them. They both realized, to their astonishment, that they were fully familiar with the experience. Many times over recent years they had danced through the night at raves in exotic locations around the world, usually close to the ocean.

As the morning sun began to warm the rocks or sand close to the sea, they had finally stopped dancing and lain down on the ground. As the night's rhythm pulsed through them, they tumbled down from an electric ecstasy into a deep collapse on the earth. Lying with their stomachs on the ground, they surrendered every part of themselves and became sponges for the beauty and power of the earth, nature, the solar system and the universe.

The dancing – as tribal and mystic dancers have known for millennia – had shaken them free of their bioenergetic armour and the constraints of Blobsville. Everything about their bodies was now loose, open and fluid. Their busy minds no longer interfered or sabotaged. The two students just let it all in.

> **The earth, nature, the sun and the universe are humming with beautiful, powerful and benevolent wave fields. This is an energetic fact and not a poetic hope. Surrender, relax and open. Allow the wave fields to come fully into you.**

No Effort

Letting in and absorbing the benevolent wave fields happens naturally and with no effort. In fact, it *must* happen without effort because effort creates physical tension and any tension will block the flow of energy.

Allowing the wave fields fully in, therefore, requires your body to relax a little more than usual, so that it gives way, releases, surrenders. There are similar situations with which you may be familiar. When sunbathing, there usually comes a point when, instead of just feeling the sun on your skin, you let the rays come deep into you, warming your core and you feel yourself going into a deeper state of relaxation. In a warm bath, something like this happens when you allow yourself to soak. It also happens during a good massage. A certain level of tension finally gives way and you sink into a more comfortable flow. This is precisely what you have to do when you let in the benevolent vitality.

ABSORBING THE BENEVOLENT FIELDS OF EARTH, NATURE, SUN AND UNIVERSE

What follows looks like a very long exercise, but is in fact very straightforward. Basically, it states:

- **Relax**
- **Enjoy**
- **Absorb**

The connection is natural and automatic.

The initial sequence is the usual one of strawberries and Inner Smile, with special acknowledgement that you are not just a citizen of Blobsville but are also a creature of nature and the universe. After that, you just allow in the benevolent magnetism.

THE FIRST STEP

You have a choice of going into this exercise very consciously and deliberately, or waiting until you just happen to find yourself in a calm and comfortable mood. I will describe the whole sequence as if you are starting from scratch. If you are already feeling good, you can go into the sequence at any point that works for you.

Comfort

First of all, get yourself physically comfortable. Your body posture is not important. Loosen any tight clothing and close your eyes.

Inner Smile

Sit quietly for a minute or two just noticing what is going on in your mind and in your body. Begin to switch on your Inner Smile and have a kind attitude to any part of your body, emotions or mind that are uncomfortable.

Switch on your Inner Smile and soft eyes.

Look kindly down into your body. Be aware of your bone marrow and spinal cord.

Strawberries

Bring into your awareness as many of your favourite strawberries as you want and allow the thought of them just to bob and float around you. Notice the pleasure that comes from thinking of them.

Allow the pleasure to enter you as if you were a sponge.

Breathe the pleasure into you.

Curled Deer

Turn your kind awareness down into your body, into the cavern of your chest and abdomen, and smile kindly down to your lower stomach.

Allow yourself to go into conscious retreat. Your energies collapse and loop into the Curled Deer circuit. Allow yourself to feel that experience of primal foetal safety and comfort.

THE SECOND STEP

When you are feeling relaxed and comfortable, allow your body to sink into a state of deeper relaxation. Imagine yourself as completely permeable. There is nothing to stop the benevolent vitality entering you.

Earth

Allow your heart, mind and body to open and become aware of the earth beneath you.

Allow yourself to become aware of the fire and heat at the earth's core.

Relax the muscles around the base of your spine, your anus, your scrotum or vagina.

Visualize, imagine and sense the nurturing warmth of the earth's vitality.

Allow it to come softly up into you.

Your lower body opens completely to let it in.

It comes up into you and fills your abdomen and lower chest.

Nature and the landscape

Allow your heart, mind and body to move out horizontally across the landscape to the beauty of nature.

If you are in a city, let your heart, mind and body travel far beyond the city.

In all directions, you will find wilderness and pure nature. Animals. Plants. Mountains. Oceans. Forests. Deserts. All of this radiates with the energy of nature.

Allow this energy to come to you and into your body. It comes into you from the side, horizontally, and from all around. In particular it comes into your torso, that whole area from the base of your spine to the top of your chest.

Your torso opens up and allows the energy of nature to flow into you.

Sun

Allow your heart, mind and body to become aware of the sun.

Sense its presence and its power.

Stay very calm and take a couple of soft breaths down into your lower stomach.

The energy of the sun radiates horizontally into you, coming into your abdomen and your chest. It also comes down into you from above.

In particular, your lower stomach and your heart open to the warmth and creative power of the sun.

Allow the sun's wave fields to come into you.

Open yourself fully to allow it in.

Absorb it all gratefully.

Universe

Allow your heart, mind and body to scan upwards and outwards to space and the stars.

Stay calm and grounded.

If you start to feel dizzy, take your focus down into your lower abdomen and take a couple of soft breaths deep into you.

Let your heart, mind and body open to the beauty and mysterious expanse of the universe.

It is filled with creative and benevolent energy. This energy is everywhere, all around.

Allow yourself to feel it all flowing softly into you.

It comes down into your head and your torso.

It can come into you from everywhere.

Surrender. Give way. Open yourself completely. Unzip everything and allow it all into you.

Just relax and stay bobbing patiently in the experience for as long as you like. Allow yourself to feel how pleasant this whole connection is.

There is a wonderful harmonic here. The feelgood of the universe is evoking and creating the feelgood in you. Your endorphins are in full flow. Your bioenergetic armour is melting and you are open to all that is positive and benevolent.

THE THIRD STEP

When you are ready, start to guide the energy. Do not do this too soon. It is important that you allow yourself to soak in the experience.

When it feels appropriate, begin to guide the benevolent vitality carefully around and through you, deep into your bones and bone marrow, spinal cord and brain. Circulate and spiral it. Follow the meridians. Take it out into your energy field and back. Experiment with how fast you move the energy.

Follow your instinct as to where it goes.

Absorb it fully.

Enjoy!

THE FOURTH STEP

Before you come out of the connection and go back into the hustle of daily life, you may need to check that you feel completely secure. Most people will feel fine, but a few may feel too open and vulnerable.

So check whether you do in fact feel energetically open and vulnerable. If you do, take your focus down into your body and spend a while just being aware of the great cavern of your chest and abdomen. Contemplate the warmth of your *hara* in your lower stomach and allow your breath to come softly and deeply into you.

Sense and visualize that you are in a bubble or egg of your own energy, and that it has clear boundaries.

Sense your warm outbreath moving to cover the whole of your body, until you are surrounded and enveloped by the essence of your own vibration.

From your abdomen, allow your energy to radiate powerfully from you filling your field and extending beyond it.

Feel your connection with the earth beneath you.

Sense and visualize your open energy field closing down, like a tulip at night closing down its petals.

Be prepared, if necessary, to assert clear boundaries. (Keep your Inner Smile and sense of humour switched on.)

So the basic points to check as you come out of the exercise are:
- *Hara*
- Integrity of your own field
- Breathe your energy so that it surrounds you
- Close down your field

In case of difficulty

If at any point during the exercise you feel irritable or impatient, remember the two strategies that can help you: strawberries and breath.

As a wilful act of concentration, but without tensing up, hold your awareness on your strawberries. Do not allow your mind to wander away from them.

Turn your attention to how you are breathing. Notice how the air feels as it flows through your nostrils. Just watch your breath. Keep watching it. Be prepared to watch it for twenty minutes. Switch on your Inner Smile and hold on to your sense of humour.

IMPORTANT POINTS ABOUT THE CONNECTION

Always Changing, Subtle and Strong
It is important to be realistic about how your experience of the connection can change
- Sometimes it will be very subtle
- Sometimes it will flood your body with power and beauty
- It depends on your mood and the mood of the moment
- But whether it is small or great, it is still very valuable
- Do not take it for granted

Initial Conditions
Even small experiences of connection and endorphin flow are better than no experience at all, especially during crisis or depression when a tiny light at the end of the tunnel is a thousand times better than no light at all.

Even when the connection is subtle, it can nevertheless be the crucial moment that sets in motion a whole new positive chain of events which will be of huge benefit later. This benefit will be the outcome of what is called in chaos theory 'the result of sensitive dependence on initial conditions'.

Your Motivation and Mood Fluctuate

- Sometimes you will have the time and motivation to sink slowly and deeply into the connection
- Sometimes you will just pause and slip in and out of it
- Be satisfied with however you do it and whatever happens

Use It When Up and When Down

- Remember that you can enter the connection when you are in a great mood and pause
- You can also enter it when you are in a lousy mood and allow yourself to go fully into Curled Deer and conscious retreat

Radiate or Absorb

- When you are strong and healthy, allow the benevolence of the connection to flow through you and radiate generously to others. Strong = Radiate
- When you are tired, absorb the benevolence purely for yourself until you are ready again to give to others. Tired = Absorb

Connecting in the City

Some people have particular difficulty maintaining their connection with nature and the universe when they are in the city. Especially after the peace and calm of the countryside, they get lost in Blobsville. After living for two years high in the mountains of North Africa with no electricity or other modern conveniences, I physically shook for several weeks when I returned to central London. This was not a psychological reaction, but an energetic one.

The 'noise', the vibrations of the city can cause us to tense up with anxiety and block our natural connection. But nature and the universe do not stop existing when you are in the city. Their wave fields do not suddenly stop flowing just because they encounter buildings, cars and concrete. Every atom is filled with life and vitality. Nature and the universe are still there, but it requires a conscious effort to connect with them because the pollution and intensity of the city can be so powerful.

The solution is to remember that there is more to life than Blobsville and deliberately to open to the wider environment. The following short exercise can help. If people who live deep in the countryside, are coming to stay in a busy city for a while, I suggest that they start preparing with this exercise a full month in advance. This firmly anchors the sense of connection.

AWARE IN THE CITY

Sit or lie quietly anywhere that you are comfortable.

Acknowledge that you are disturbed by the intensity of the city vibrations.

Allow your mind to recognize that below the concrete is the deep, rich, fertile body of the earth. Far below you is the core of the earth with its molten rock and great heat. All of this is still there even if you are in the city.

Allow your mind to recognize that the city contains trees and flowers, yards and gardens and parks, ponds and lakes and rivers. Allow your mind to go way out beyond the city to the countryside. Go as far as you like to places in the mountains or by the oceans that you really love. All of this is still there even if you are in the city.

Allow your mind to recognize that the sky above you is precisely the same sky that you would experience if you were lying in an alpine meadow or on some tranquil seashore. The sun above you is the same sun. The moon is the same. The stars are the same. All of this is still there even if you are in the city.

Allow yourself to remember this with your mind and your heart.

Recognize that the vibrations of this greater environment are always there.

Allow yourself to think of them and feel them.

CHAPTER 10:

Managing Distress – First Aid and Long-Term Healing

Noticing the Distress

Working with The Endorphin Effect turns the volume up on a positive experience of life, but it does not miraculously transform all negative psychological and emotional histories. Even those who have had a 'normal' upbringing have been scarred in some way. Parents, siblings and teachers are rarely perfect angels. Life is tough and both children and adults get hurt.

This chapter focusses on how you can manage distress so that it does not sabotage the Endorphin Effect. Sooner or later, old emotional blocks and negative attitudes need to be transformed and integrated. Distress, whether conscious or not, has three negative effects.

- It creates a mood that permeates how you behave. At a psychological level the ancient fears, resentments and anxieties rumble in the background, sabotaging a healthy emotional life.

- It creates anxiety and bioenergetic armour that inhibit and block the endorphin flow. At a physical level, it creates pools of adrenal acid and painful tension.
- It creates an underlying attitude, a magnetic atmosphere, that is unpleasant for other people.

At the risk of being simplistic, I want to categorize distress into two groups: immediate and long-term. Immediate distress is knee-jerk emotional reaction. This happens, for example, when someone provokes you and you become flooded by an emotional reaction. The other kind of distress consists of psychological attitudes that recur all the way through your life, interfering with your ability to experience happiness and fulfilment. These attitudes usually, for example, create repeated anxieties or arguments around particular issues such as money, jealousy or control.

I want to look at strategies that handle short-term reactive distress and then at a method for working with the deeper issues. But first, we need to discuss some general principles.

The Safe Parent Who Cradles

It is difficult for most of us to look honestly at ourselves, at our faults, at our unpleasant attitudes, at how we have been hurt and damaged. Materialistically, this kind of self-honesty delivers few rewards. From inside the competitive world of Blobsville, what advantage is there in being so self-reflective and truthful? It looks like weakness. It does not seem worth the cost.

Most of us were taught to be stoical and get on with life. Now, stoicism is an admirable skill that everybody needs to possess: it is impossible to survive if we break down and blubber at every obstacle. But if it is the only tactic used to manage distress, in the long run it creates further emotional disability.

To be very practical, if you cut yourself you need to look into the wound to see what needs to be done. Not to look is stupidity or cowardice. It is the same with your emotional problems. You need to look at them. And you need to look at them wisely.

Your problems need the kindness of your Inner Smile. I have already described how your mind must have a friendly attitude if your body, your monkey vehicle, is to feel safe. A cold, unfriendly mind sends a frigid vibration through your whole vehicle. Remember that psychological distress causes physical stress which blocks endorphin production.

So, how do you feel about your own emotional problems and negative attitudes? Judgemental, cold, critical and denying? Or friendly, sympathetic, accepting and understanding?

It is clear, surely, that your emotional life needs the same care and friendship as your body. If your mental attitude to your problems is cold, you will experience a double whammy. You will have the scar that resulted from the original injury. And you will have the second scar created by your own unkind attitude – creating, for example, even more frigidity, guilt and all the rubbish that accompanies a cold and judgemental mind.

Your emotional distress needs to be dealt with in exactly the same way that a good parent cares for a hurt child. Slow down and become caring. Pick up the child, hold it and comfort it.

This is the exact opposite of a dysfunctional adult who ignores the problem or hisses, 'You stupid child!' I have seen short-tempered parents hit their children as punishment when they have accidentally fallen over. This is obviously stupid and bullying behaviour. The child is already hurt by the fall. Now he or she has to deal with the aggressive parent. This is exactly what so many people do to themselves when they fall into emotional distress. You feel hurt by someone's aggression and then make it worse by a further internal attack that judges your reaction as pathetic and punishable.

When someone is physically wounded, you have to look to assess the damage and move physically close to comfort. You act in a manner that is both practical and comforting. To be impractical, frigid and abusive is the wrong attitude.

But your mind and attitude need to be more than kind. What is necessary here is a feeling of 'holding' or 'cradling' the injury and distress. This means that your Inner Smile, your warmth and your endorphins actually surround and permeate the distress instead of just looking at it. This maintains flexibility and gives instantaneous healing. Good parents do this automatically with their children, as do good teachers and professional carers. Their attitude *holds* the person needing care. There is a positive embracing of the distress. This is not just a mental concept. It is an actual kinaesthetic sensation, felt in the body.

> **Look at your emotions and negative patterns with a warm and sympathetic attitude.**

Emotional First Aid

Imagine that a situation at home or work has just offended you in some way. You react in a partly emotional, partly physical way. You will certainly feel some distress and tension somewhere in your body. The moment that you notice the unpleasant sensation, turn your attention towards it. Switch on your Inner Smile and have a cradling and comforting attitude towards the distress. Bring yourself into the feeling of the Curled Deer. Biochemically, this strategy counters the tension and toxins created by the negative emotion, and replaces them with feelgood neuropeptides and relaxants. Instead of getting lost in Blobsville and your own negativity, you stay centred and are able to choose how you react – instead of simply reacting.

So, the sequence goes:
- Notice that you have been triggered and are experiencing an uncomfortable emotion.
- Withdraw your attention from the provocation. Do not get lost in any reaction.
- Manage yourself first.
- Turn your attention kindly down to your distress.
- Switch on your Inner Smile.
- Comfort your distress.
- Check your Curled Deer.
- Get on with your life.

To put it at its most simple: Provocation = Inner Smile + Curled Deer. So, whether it's inefficient staff, a pushy boss, intrusive children, a rude partner or dangerous drivers, the moment you feel yourself reacting, notice the reaction, give it kind attention and manage yourself.

> **Whenever you are in distress, turn your attention within. Switch on your Inner Smile. Cradle your distress.**

CRADLING DISTRESS: REHEARSING THE BASIC STRATEGY

Sit comfortably and close your eyes.

Patiently wait until you are feeling comfortable.

Use any or all of the core connection sequence:
- **Recognize your true environment**
- **Contemplate and feel your strawberries.**
- **Inner Smile**
- **Guide the golden flow**
- **Curled Deer**
- **Open to the earth, nature, sun and universe.**

Sitting calmly allow your mind to scan your body and notice how you are feeling. Somewhere there may be tension or distress.

If you notice tension or pain, allow your focus to stay softly on it.

Smile affectionately and kindly at it.

Kinaesthetically experience a warm feeling going towards the tension and sense/imagine that you are cradling this part of you as if it were a child in your arms.

Stay calmly holding it for as long as you like.

Breathing softly into your lower stomach a few times may also help.

REHEARSING FOR REAL LIFE PROVOCATION

Sit or lie comfortably and take yourself through as much of the core connection sequence as you want.

When you are feeling calm and watchful, bring into your mind one of those situations in which you might find yourself emotionally triggered. For instance:
- Provocative friend, partner, child, relative, colleague, stranger, shop assistant.
- Slow post office queue, traffic jam, being jostled in the street.
- Unwelcome invoice, financial error, information overload, deadlines.

Imagine that you are in one of these situations and about to be triggered. Imagine withdrawing your attention from the situation and looking kindly and caringly down into yourself. Feel the Curled Deer. Cradle any reactivity or distress you feel.

In the face of the provocation, you maintain your Inner Smile and the sense of the Curled Deer. You are fully aware that you are in a situation that upsets you, but instead of reacting you are centred and sending endorphins to the stress.

Spend a while contemplating the situation and your new behaviour in it. Do not just visualize it – actually feel it. Go into a kinaesthetic scenario.

Repeat this exercise as many times as you like until you feel comfortable with it.

> **Working with the exercises throughout the book, at times you may experience irritation, disappointment or tension. Cradling your distress is the perfect strategy to use in these situations. Never get cross or criticize yourself because you cannot do the exercises to your satisfaction. Always switch on your Inner Smile, look kindly at the distress and cradle it. Permeate it with endorphins.**

Naming the Armour

To pause and cradle distressed emotional reactions is a temporary but very effective short-term strategy. But there are other wounds, older and deeper, that require more careful attention.

I have seen many friends and colleagues use the Endorphin Effect to bring themselves slowly but surely out of extremely painful psychological histories and behavioural problems. These included being victims of serial abuse as infants, eating disorders, and alcohol and drug dependency, not to mention the more usual patterns of bullying parents and so on. In the long run, the creative power of the universe, anchoring in your body through endorphins, will provide the strength to transform anything.

As a first step towards working with these wounds, it is important to remember that all distress, whatever its particular history, anchors as body tension and blocks the flow of endorphins and connection. If the distress is healed, the result will always be a sense of ease and flow where previously there was emotional and physical congestion. This healing will be psychological, biological and energetic.

It is useful, therefore, in the first place to have a general idea of the bioenergetic armour that you carry. In *Walking the Tiger – Healing Trauma,* the bioenergetic therapist Peter Levine lists the general reasons for traumatized body armour:[1]

- Foetal, intra-uterine trauma
- Birth trauma
- Loss of parent or close family member
- Illness, high fever, accidental poisoning
- Physical injuries, including falls and accidents
- Sexual, physical and emotional abuse, including abandonment and beatings
- Witnessing violence
- Natural disasters such as earthquakes, fires and floods
- Certain medical and dental procedures
- Surgery
- Anaesthesia
- Prolonged immobilization

I would add to his list the more general traumas that come from spending long periods of time in a harsh family, school, work or general social environment.

> **All tragic histories have the same effect. They create tension, block the production of endorphins and sabotage a connection with life's benevolent vitality. All healing restores the flow.**

Cradling All the Wounds

In my courses, I sometimes ask students to name out loud the sources of their bioenergetic armour. I remember, for example:

- 'My mother was on drugs when she was pregnant with me.'
- 'Caesarean section.'
- 'My father hit my mother and me.'
- 'My brother was a jealous bully.'
- 'I was told off for singing.'
- 'I broke my arm.'
- 'School.'
- 'Sexual abuse.'
- 'Endless television.'

- 'My first job.'
- 'My first kiss that was forced on me.'

I then ask students to draw a portrait of their own body and its bioenergetic armour. Often these pictures are of little matchstick men with patches of black and red. They are very dark, dramatic and tragic. Some have small labels pointing to a particular patch of dark armour. Written on the label will be some simple message like those above or: 'Mum died', 'Boarding school', 'Not wanted'.

Then I ask the students to crumple up their drawing slowly and carefully into a little ball. Often they want to do this quickly and throw their drawing into the nearest rubbish bin, but I ask them to slow down. Next I ask them to hold this crumpled ball close to their heart or stomach. I ask them to cradle it as if it were a hurt child in need of care. This is often a poignant and healing moment, as people understand that it is possible to experience their distressed history with understanding and kindness. The background hum of endorphins and the connection with a benevolent universe makes this possible. Their whole emotional history of armouring is symbolically put in perspective and cradled. Again slowly and carefully, their pictures are uncrumpled and straightened out. They look at the images with stronger and more compassionate eyes.

Unlike a psychotherapist or counsellor, when I run these training sessions, I am not interested in these tragic psychological histories for themselves. What concerns me – and what I want my companions to focus on – is that all these histories have the same awful effect. They create tension and armour, and imprison you from experiencing the fluid beauty of life and the universe.

One man was weeping as he looked at the picture of his armour, and I went to comfort him. In his drawing there was a great smudge of grey-red all down his body and I asked what this represented.

'That,' he answered, 'is ten years at a private boarding school. That is my parents who rejected and sent me there. That is the regime of bullying, competition and cold showers.' A few tears were still rolling down his cheeks. 'And,' he said strongly, 'that is not what is making me cry. What is making me weep is this: I have spent years trying to connect with God. But God's energy field has always been there. I just didn't let it in. Sure, I can cry for the little boy who was sent to that school. But my tears are for me, the adult, now – blocking out what I could always let in.'

Giggles in Hell

I want to make the following point very clearly. People's biographical histories are important and need to be understood. But from the perspective of the Endorphin Effect, the most important thing that they sabotage is their natural birthright, which is a flowing endorphin-based connection with the good things and benevolent vitality of life.

In therapy it may take years to unravel and heal the emotional history, but the endorphin flow and connection is something you can nevertheless have now. You can have it – provided that you connect yourself beyond Blobsville and authentically get the whole story in perspective. Yes, people's histories may contain terrible pain and tragedy, but they are not bigger than nature and the universe. So, based in the powerful foundation of flowing endorphins, if you can allow into yourself that connection with a benevolent and creative universe, you have the resources and the 'size' to deal with and accept your history and distress.

The Endorphin Effect is not a strategy for transcending and ignoring emotional pain. It is a way of connecting with resources powerful enough to enable you to create a contented life and to face and heal the distress. People go to therapists and healers precisely because they do not have the resources to deal with their 'stuff' alone. For a while the therapist provides the strength and reassurance, the connection, which supports a positive transformational process.

Although I am deeply sympathetic to people's tragic emotional histories, my major purpose is to get them to see beyond their immediate pain and to experience endorphins and the connection. The strategies of this book can achieve that because experience that they are creatures of a benevolent universe, not prisoners of Blobsville. They can now start to work more consciously and confidently with their negative feelings.

In the longer trainings for my students who also want to coach these strategies themselves, there are sessions when students are asked to be honest about all their own worst attitudes and behaviour. These sessions only take place when every member of the group has worked fully with strawberries, the Inner Smile and the connection over a period of time. In these classes, people end up giggling uproariously as they finally name and announce their own worst 'stuff'. Psychotherapists in these sessions, however, are usually stunned by the self-honesty and humour. 'It can take me months, even years,' therapists say, 'to get my clients to this level of honesty and acceptance.'

I have never led this exercise without people collapsing into wails of giggles as they outdo each other in the awfulness of their patterns. The laughter comes mainly from the relief of finally being honest about this aspect of themselves and letting some light into these dark regions. Years of denial melt away. Endorphins and the connection not only create positive and enjoyable sensations inside your skin, they also create a sense of hope so that you can look clearly at your distress without slipping into further distress or depression.

> **Endorphins and a solid connection with the warm flow of the universe are the greatest resources available for healing and positive change. With these resources, you can accept and cradle any history.**

Holding Others

Being able to cradle your emotional distress is a fundamental skill of emotional intelligence. It allows you to contain your negative emotional behaviour, so that it does not spill over and affect others. Also, it is not at all like repressing anger or impatience, so that the feeling remains seething beneath a calm exterior. Cradling it soothes it. Yes, you may still feel the anger within you, but it begins to calm down because of your internally kind attitude.

This skill is a positive attribute in any social or work situation. To stay centred and cradled in disturbing circumstances demonstrates a mode of behaviour which distinguishes wise leadership. Energetically, it also radiates a pleasant and supportive atmosphere. People who can maintain a positive mood and goodwill put out good vibrations. This should not be underestimated. By its very nature, it is powerful and healing. It encourages people and makes them feel safe enough to take creative risks. (I shall return to this subject in greater detail in Chapter 12.)

Disturbing circumstances, then, are an immediate signal to cradle any distress that you might feel. In crisis, it is important not to have knee-jerk reactions, but to act in an appropriate and strong manner from your *hara*. It is also important to cradle that aspect of yourself which understandably goes into anxiety or impatience.

This sequence, therefore, goes as follows. In crisis or difficult circumstances:

- Turn within
- Strengthen your *hara*
- Cradle your distress

This sequence is equally important when you are with other people who are in distress. As a general rule, I suggest that in such circumstances, your immediate strategy should be first to come back into your own centre, rather than to reach out with your concern. Check first that your own distress or concern is cradled. Then come into relationship with your distressed companion. People who are in trouble need a centred, kind companion, someone who has first managed their own emotions. Then, carefully and with complete openness, you can give proper attention to their problem.

DEALING WITH ABUSE

In cases where you are the subject of abuse, I do not recommend cradling your emotional pain as your first reaction. Your first strategy should be to

---

assert a clear boundary and reject the wounding
intrusion. It requires a strong *hara*, which was
discussed in Chapter 7. It also requires courage. If
necessary, get support from a friend or adviser.
Then, having stopped the abuse, turn your
attention to cradling your distress.

Dealing with Distress

What follows now are the specific exercises for working with old
distress and negative patterns.

MELTING THE ARMOUR

THE FIRST STEP

When you are feeling calm and strong, take yourself into the
connection.

Then take a piece of paper and draw a picture, a simple outline,
of your body. Do not be concerned if your drawing skills are
limited. A few joined up circles or sausages or matchstick men
will be good enough for this exercise.

Select one major trauma from your life and instinctively draw
where you think it may have caused armour in your body.

Write next to it a few words that describe what it represents,
like 'School' or 'Dad hit me.' Keep it simple and short.

Slowly and carefully, crumple up the piece of paper into a ball.

Hold the ball to your heart.

Accept and cradle it for a while.

Carefully unfold the paper and look again at the picture.

Reflect on how this injury has blocked and frozen you.

Recognize that, despite its personal power and effect, it is tiny compared to the grandeur of earth, nature and the sun, that it is minuscule compared to the infinity of space.

Recognize that it has blocked you from feeling the universal flow, but that the flow is nevertheless there.

Recognize that in loving and cradling the distress, you begin to melt and energetically massage it into release.

When you have done this for as long as feels appropriate, end the exercise.

After the exercise, you may want to pin this crumpled drawing on the wall to remind you of the issue that needs cradling. Or you may want to trash or burn it. Follow your instinct.

THE SECOND STEP

If you feel comfortable and confident with the first stage, move on to this second stage at your leisure. It could be in the same session or days later.

Again draw again on a large piece of paper an outline of your body. Then begin to name and place on your body all the major events in your life that would have created your bioenergetic armour – all the historical events logged in your body that block you from feeling the wave fields of benevolent energy. You may need coloured crayons. Do this drawing quite quickly. Do not spend too much time thinking about it all. Just go for it.

Again, if you want, label the wounds.

Be as honest and as open with yourself as you can.

Now pause.

Check that you are in the connection: Inner Smile, strawberries, Curled Deer and so on.

Carefully and slowly take your picture in both hands and look at it for only a few seconds.

Softly and without violence, begin to crumple and squeeze the paper up into a ball that you hold tight in both hands. Do not tear it.

Take the ball of paper and hold it to your heart and to your chest.

Cradle this picture and rock it.

Recognize that the elements in the picture often overwhelm you, but that now you are connected to the greater reality, you can hold and cradle it all.

Do this for as long as feels right.

Slowly and carefully uncrumple your picture. Straighten and flatten it as best you can.

Stay connected. Take a couple of breaths down into your lower stomach. Make sure your kind observer is switched on.

Carefully look at your picture.

Stay connected and look at the armour and the history that you carry.

Have compassion and understanding for yourself.

Notice that you are truly facing your history and your wounding, but that you are far greater than this picture – because you are part of the universe.

Just because you are alive you are part of a
benevolent universe. Your birthright is to feel and
express this connection. You do not need to be a
saint, a therapist, a doctor, enlightened or
anything special to have this connection. It is all
yours – just because you exist. There is nothing in
the universe that is blocking your connection
except your own armour. Any moment, any place,
this armour can melt and you can experience the
flow. The universe is always there, around and in
you. It is all yours. Always remember this.

Specific Traumas

It is also possible to use the Endorphin Effect to focus on particular
traumas and negative emotions. This, of course, can only be done
when you are anchored comfortably in the endorphin ocean. It also
needs to be done very carefully. You may, for example, start working with an issue such as shyness or short temper, only to discover
a whole cauldron of sadness or resentment that requires attention.
This may be temporarily overwhelming.

It is therefore also useful to have a good friend with whom you
can talk, if you find yourself suddenly managing an area of your
own growth that feels too difficult. Talking with a friend or a professional counsellor is always helpful and sometimes essential. So,
move forward carefully with this work and do not try to deal with
too much too fast.

HEALING SPECIFIC WOUNDS

THE FIRST STEP

Take yourself into a calm and relaxed space.

Take yourself through the core connection sequence.

When you are feeling secure and strong, turn your focus towards an emotional issue that causes you distress.

See and sense it as a tiny seed in the distance. This tiny seed is an image or a thought of the distressing pattern.

Hold it at a distance.

Feel compassion and kindness towards it.

Allow it to come a little closer to you and maintain your attitude of kindness.

Recognize that this ability to hold it in your thoughts and to have kind feelings towards it is a powerful step forward in managing and healing it.

Again, allow the thought and feeling of the distress to come closer to you. But the moment you start to feel tense or overwhelmed, push the distress away. Withdraw your attention from it. Focus kindly down into yourself and cradle your distress.

Let your attitude of loving kindness move kinaesthetically down into you.

At any stage that you choose, you can stop the process altogether and come back to it at some other time when you are ready.

THE SECOND STEP

When you feel it is appropriate and you feel strong enough, allow the image and sense of the distress to come fully to you. You will now be experiencing two sensations simultaneously:

- **The pleasure and support of the connection**
- **The distress and pathos of the emotional wound**

At this stage you must remain very calm, kind and observant. You must hold to your Inner Smile and, if you feel agitated, watch and guide your breath so that it remains soft and even.

Recognize that by being fully aware and present to the distress, and at the same time holding the connection, you are bringing great healing into the distress. Stay watchful. Stay patient.

Stay in this space for as long as you feel comfortable. Observe what happens within you.

Do this exercise as often as you need.

When you come out of the exercise, you may find that your body holds some residual tension or you may feel that some emotional baggage is staying with you unnecessarily. You might also feel irritable. I strongly recommend you to give yourself a good stretch and perhaps a shake to release any of this anxiety from your body. Fresh air or a good groan can also help.

After the exercise, you may also feel a powerful release of energy and new vitality. This happens because the distress has been historically clogging up a free flow in your life. As the bioenergetic armour begins to melt, so energy flows into and around you more easily.

Working with your worst wounds and patterns is like a relationship. Your intention is to embrace them completely, but you need to be strategic and patient about how long this might take. Sometimes it will be very fast, and sometimes very slow. The relationship also needs to feel comfortable and never threaten or overwhelm you. So, I shall list the basic principles again to avoid any risk of anyone getting out of their depth:

- Only do this work when you are feeling calm and strong in the Endorphin Effect.
- Carefully monitor how your body feels to maintain your comfort and confidence.
- Bring the emotional issue into your awareness very carefully and keep it at a distance. Observe it with your kind Inner Smile.
- The moment you feel any tension or distress, push the emotional issue far away from you and turn your comforting attention down into yourself. Accept and cradle your reaction.
- Use your strawberries, Inner Smile, Curled Deer and connection to bring you back to comfort.
- Use your breath to stabilize yourself. If you start to wobble, take some soft breaths deep into your lower stomach. If your composure is threatened, spend a while noticing how your breath feels in your nostrils.

Warning

If at any point you feel that these exercises are causing too much emotional and mental excitation, put a brake on them completely. You will know this is happening because you will literally feel too much energy buzzing in your brain and perhaps have some minor feelings of panic. Leave the exercises alone for a while. Make sure that you are eating and sleeping well. Do things that make you feel good in your body. Only come back to the exercises when you are certain that the time is right. If in doubt, do not do these exercises. Talk to a friend. Get support. Or contact us.

Twelve Steps Programmes

There are powerful parallels here with the strategy of the various Twelve Steps Programmes, as used by Alcoholics Anonymous and other groups, which help release people from compulsive and addictive behaviour. This inspired method relies upon a relationship with God, 'as understood by the individual'. An understanding of endorphins and the universal field provides another way of engaging with the Twelve Steps Programme, which may be a useful addition for some people. What is certain is that the Endorphin Effect strategies are absolutely congruent with and supportive of these anti-addiction programmes. Here is the classic text of the Twelve Steps Programme as adapted by Emotions Anonymous. Each passage of their text is then followed by my adaptation in italics.

❧ 1. We admitted we were powerless over our emotions – that our lives had become unmanageable.

2. Came to believe that a Power greater than ourselves could restore us to sanity. *We do not live purely within human society. We live in a benevolent field of universal energy.*

3. Made a decision to turn our will and our lives over to the care of God, as we understood him. *Using all the gateways and strawberries that are available to us, opened and connected with the benevolent fields.*

4. Made a searching and fearless moral inventory of ourselves. *From within the endorphin flow and connection, looked clearly at and cradled our emotional distress and behaviour.*

5. Admitted to God, to ourselves and to another human being the exact nature of our wrongs. *From within the connection, were absolutely honest about our failings and shared all this with another person.*

6. Were entirely ready to have God remove all these defects of character. *Knew that the flow of universal benevolence could heal us completely.*

7. Humbly asked Him to remove our shortcomings. *Retreated into a small ball of nurture and invited in the*

benevolent fields to melt, heal and bring our wounds back into flow.

8. Made a list of all the persons we had harmed and became willing to make amends to them all. *Supported by the infinite connection and flow, we became aware of all the persons we had harmed and became willing to make amends to them all.*

9. Made direct amends to such people wherever possible, except when to do so would injure them or others. *From within the connection, we made direct amends to such people wherever possible, except when to do so would injure them or others.*

10. Continued to take personal inventory and when we were wrong promptly admitted it.

11. Sought through prayer and meditation to improve our conscious contact with God, as we understood him, praying only for knowledge of His will for us and the power to carry it out. *Used all possible gateways and strategies to trigger endorphins, connect with the wonder of life and allow it to manifest through us.*

12. Having had a spiritual awakening as the result of these steps, we tried to carry this message, and to practise these principles in all our affairs. **❥**

Physical Self-Healing

In the same way that the Endorphin Effect strategies can be focussed on particular emotional problems, they can also be focussed on specific physical distress and illness. Essentially, you focus your benevolent mind on the injured area and kinaesthetically guide endorphins and benevolent vitality into the tissue.

Especially with critical illnesses, it is crucial that your positive attitude is filled with warm affection and not coloured by any macho elements. A positive attitude is great, but not if it contains that kind of tension exhibited by a sprinter geared up for the starting pistol or a dog pulling at a leash. The tension will block the flow.

So self-healing requires you to be courageous and relaxed at the same time. This is a different kind of courage from the usual one of fighting on against all odds. It is the courage to surrender – to surrender your tension to the endorphin flow and universal energy fields.

EXERCISE FOR PHYSICAL SELF-HEALING

Take yourself into a quiet mood and go through the sequence for connecting: strawberries, Inner Smile etc.

Staying relaxed and connected take your focus down to that area of your body which is experiencing the physical distress.

It is absolutely crucial that you stay relaxed and retain your kind and compassionate observer.

Cradle the illness and pain. Accept it lovingly.

Allow your awareness to go fully into it, sensing the damaged tissue and cells.

Stay in an attitude of absolute kindness.

Energy follows thought. Recognize that your kind attitude guides both endorphins and the benevolent vitality of the cosmos into your body and the area of illness.

Keep your loving focus on the distressed area. Keep cradling it.

Take your kind Inner Smile fully into the cells and tissue. Sense and visualize your smile warming it all. Sense and imagine all the body's healing agents flowing into the area.

Imagine and sense the area as being perfectly healthy, perfectly manoeuvrable, as good as it possibly could be, in fact better than it ever was.

Keep smiling into the area.

Carefully release the exercise.

**Repeat the exercise as often as you like, particularly before
going to sleep and when waking up.**

Healing Others

The Endorphin Effect also provides a specific healing strategy that
can be used with other people. It is similar to the methods used by
many traditions of spiritual healing, but has a particular focus on
how your own body energy and presence can affect others.

- In general, if you are comfortably in your body, experiencing connection and a healthy endorphin flow, you radiate a
  healing aura. This healing aura is beneficial and supportive
  to all humans, animals and plants around you.
- You can deliberately extend your energy field to hold and
  support a companion. You can then guide their own energy
  field into a connected and integrated flow – leading them
  into a connection with their true environment and the healing magnetism of their own Curled Deer.
- You can also deliberately guide benevolent vitality into the
  distressed areas of your companion's body.

For people who are new to this field, you may need reminding that
everything is energy and that different moods create different
atmospheres.

THE HEALING CONNECTION

**Make sure that both you and your companion are comfortable.
This exercise will take at least twenty minutes. The physical
position is not important – they can lie down whilst you sit
next to them. I particularly like the position used in**

cranio-sacral osteopathy. Your companion lies down on their back and you cradle their head, where the neck joins the skull, in your hands.

The most important thing is for you yourself to go fully into the Endorphin Effect.

Usually, the atmosphere of being in a caring and healing role will take you easily into the connection.

Nevertheless, go through the whole sequence and check that you are as connected as you can be: True Environment, Strawberries, Inner Smile, Guiding the Flow, Curled Deer, Open to the Universe, Cradling any Distress.

When you feel calm and confident, softly extend your awareness to include your companion.

- Allow the strong and warm energy of your *hara* to open and hold your companion.
- Allow the strong and warm energy of your *heart* to open and hold your companion.
- Allow the strong and warm energy of your *mind* to open and hold your companion.

Check that your attitude is absolutely calm, friendly and supportive.

Monitor your Inner Smile to ensure that it remains firmly radiant all through your body.

Kinaesthetically sense and visualize your own benevolent magnetic field permeating your companion's body. Guide this benevolent field into all the energy streams of their body. Take your awareness all through their body: toes and fingers, spine, brain and bone marrow.

Staying calmly and perfectly in tune with your companion, imagine and sense these energies entering them:

- **From the earth coming up.**
- **From nature coming up and in from the side.**
- **From the sun coming in from the side and from above.**
- **From the universe and stars coming down and from all around.**

Very caringly, very parentally, hold your companion in this field. Monitor your breathing. Monitor your Curled Deer.

Sense the golden flows of benevolent vitality building and strengthening your companion's *hara*.

Sense the golden flows of benevolent vitality moving around and settling in every cell and fibre of their body.

Sense and visualize your companion's own Curled Deer.

If there is a particular area of physical distress or illness in your companion, softly guide the warm golden vitality into this area. Sense and visualize all the healing neuropeptides flooding the area. Sense and visualize the body tension and bioenergetic armour melting.

Be intuitive and instinctive, but never lose your connection and never go into a vibration of excitement. Stay quiet and centred.

To complete the session, sense and guide your companion's Curled Deer to be fully looped and very comfortable.

Then imagine and sense that the whole of your companion's energy field is completely contained, has absolute integrity and strong boundaries; that it is safely closed, like the petals of a tulip at night.

Withdraw your own energy and focus completely away from your companion.

Check again that their energy field feels contained and strong. If you work with chakras or any other energy medicine map, use that as a basis for sensing your companion's field to be healthily contained and with strong boundaries.

Let your companion rest for a while on their own.

Being a Healing Presence

If, within yourself, you are centred and connected, you must appreciate your value in any situation. Whether other people recognize it or not, whether you are appreciated for it or not, having a benevolent energy field is profoundly healing for others.

In intensive care hospital units and centres for the dying, patients often seek comfort from hospital cleaners and porters, reaching for their hands, appreciating their smiles. In comparison to many of the stressed doctors and nurses, these auxiliary workers often have calm, benevolent and strong magnetic fields. I remember once being badly injured myself and so grateful for the grounded and caring practicality of the ambulance team. I could feel their genuinely reassuring presence.

Many of my students who find themselves caring for the dying or do this work as a vocation affirm that the most important gift they bring to the situation is an atmosphere which cradles the situation. Words and gestures are superfluous. In fact, some of the most gratifying courses I have run have been on using the Endorphin Effect for facilitating and easing the dying process.

In my own daily life, I do not often work as a hands-on healer, but I do use these strategies with my family and students. I prefer to do it when they do not know it is happening, when we are just relaxing over food or watching a movie. With my close family, I do it while they are sleeping next to me. Essentially, I go deep into the connection and then expand my magnetic field to cradle my companion so that they experience me as a silent and friendly presence. Slowly and carefully, I then kinaesthetically sense and imagine the whole Endorphin Effect sequence happening within their body. This is a very enjoyable gift.

The Man in the Iron Mask

I want to end this chapter with a story about a student who did the exercise of drawing the self-portrait of his armour and emotional wounds. He was in his sixties and his picture was particularly tragic. The entire sheet of paper was filled with an illustration of a head imprisoned behind black bars, but it had no body beneath it.

'This is my head,' he explained. 'I feel nothing in my body. I might be able to feel in my head, but I am caught in this terrible prison. I am like my father and my grandfather. There was so much education, so much intellect, so much criticism. I sabotage everything. I feel nothing.'

He paused.

'Look!' he said dramatically in a voice that was filled with frustration and pain. 'I cannot do it like the rest of you – the connection, the opening. Don't you see how someone like me struggles with it all? I don't feel the same things. I experience frustration. My mind is always working! Sometimes I lie awake at night and my mind goes out into the infinity of space. The infinity of space! Do you understand that? But I cannot understand it. It cannot be understood! It's a complete and absolute mystery. Who knows its end and beginning? Why is it so extraordinary? Why am I so small and insignificant? I understand nothing!'

His head drooped into his hands.

'You sound,' said a woman, 'just like a mystic. Your words are the words of a mystic. Mystics connect with the universe and its mystery and say it is incomprehensible.'

There was another silence.

'You mind is sensing it,' said someone else. 'Your consciousness expands and your mind is an expanding energy field. Even if you are only in your head, your head is getting it! You're doing the connection, but in your own way – like the rest of us.'

'But why do I experience so much tension?' he asked.

'It's just your armour,' a woman responded. 'Others of us have been abused in different ways. I am sorry that it's so painful for you.'

'But you are getting it,' a helpful teenager said. 'You are feeling it – the mystery of the cosmos and all that.'

❝ You do not have to be good
You do not have to walk on your knees
for a hundred miles through the desert, repenting.
You only have to let the soft animal of your body
love what it loves . . .
Whoever you are, no matter how lonely,
the world offers itself to your imagination,
calls to you like the wild geese, harsh and exciting –
Over and over announcing your place
in the family of things. ❞ 2

CHAPTER 11:

Unboundaried Dreaming – Vision, Purpose and Success

Your State of Mind Determines Your Future

When a carpenter builds a chair, he has to start with an *idea* of the chair. Without this mental concept in the first place, there will be no chair. This idea of the chair he will build emerges from all the chairs he has ever seen before, plus his own creative imagination.

You build your own life, you create your future, in precisely the same way. It is based in the ideas of what you think is possible and what you can creatively imagine. Your decisions about what you should do next, how your career should develop, how your relationship should feel, the future of your family – all of these are first envisioned by your mind. To state the obvious, your mind reigns supreme in the creation of what you do next and what will happen next. But what you can envision is limited by the boundaries of your mental and imaginative framework. This is both a conscious and an unconscious process,

The strategy of Unboundaried Dreaming uses the Endorphin Effect to clarify your future and next steps, and harnesses the creative flow of the universe to bring your dream into being. This can be applied to very personal issues, as well as to work and social issues.

> **It is crucial that you assess and understand your mind, its ideas and its boundaries, because it is your mind and nobody else's that imagines and dreams how your life could be. It is your mind that dreams the possible futures, not just for yourself but also for your families, organizations and communities.**

Liberate Yourself From the Two Prisons – the Personal and the Collective

When you ponder your future, when you plan your life, do you do this as a free citizen of earth, nature, the solar system and the universe – or as a limited creature within the confines of Blobsville? Are your thoughts and creative ideas located in the true universal context? Or are they trapped by purely human culture? Are you in the free world or are you imprisoned? Are your ideas locked inside your armour?

It is obvious that, if your mind is trapped inside your armour and inside Blobsville, you can hardly even begin to imagine or plan your future. Look at these two gaols.

The personal gaol

The first gaol is private and very personal. It is the prison of your own bioenergetic and psychological tension, which derives from your emotional history and your distress, both conscious and unconscious. You may seem just fine, but what are you carrying beneath the surface? How can you imagine true success if you are still haunted by the ghosts of bullying and critical parents or teachers? How can you dream of prosperity if you still carry a needy wounded child? How can you become a true leader if you still carry the trauma of abuse? How can you imagine a harmonious and loving relationship if the vulture of fear is sitting on your shoulder?

These wounds, we know, are not just psychological. They sit in the body as pools of subliminal tension, blocking flow, sabotaging imagination and creativity. Energetically, they create a polluting magnetic field within you and around you. This is like a thick and moody fog which both limits and distorts your vision, which permeates how you think and imagine.

This negative field is at its most dense and uncomfortable when you are in crisis or anxiety or depression. In fact, you recognize the presence of severe distress precisely because of how it feels inside you; at its worst, it is an oppressive and overwhelming hell state.

Yet here is one of those terrible human ironies. It is usually in crisis or distress that people want to sort out what should be happening in their lives. You can see the tragic paradox. It is precisely the mood of crisis and distress that locks people more deeply into their limitations and sabotages their ability to imagine freely and creatively what might unfold.

> **Never try to clarify or imagine your future when you are in a mood or in crisis.**

The collective gaol

The second terrible constraint is the collective prison that we have all created – the Blobsville of human culture and civilization. It is the collective energy field and society in which we live and react and plan our lives and it is filled with the actions, effects, vibrations, energies and wave fields of six billion people. It is full of genius and saintliness, but also full of the unpleasant energetic baggage of individual and collective selfishness, greed and nastiness. It is stimulating, complex, brilliant, cruel and often overwhelming, permeated with an increasing urgency and a set of values that rarely reflect the harmonics of nature and the universe.

How can you possibly plan your life in a way that will bring you true satisfaction if your imagining takes place within the confines of Blobsville? You have to liberate yourself from the false consciousness of this purely human reality.

Begin the Dreaming

Time after time, people realize the solutions to their problems when they wake up. Why? Because sleep is a deep state of relaxation in which your consciousness floats in a dimension beyond the two prisons. Liberated from them, you are free to imagine far beyond your normal boundaries. That is why people wake up with solutions and new ideas.

The strategies of the Endorphin Effect take you into that free and comfortable state of consciousness while you are still awake and fully alert. Step by step, they take you easily and simply into the connection. With your body feeling good and your mind observing kindly what you are doing, feeling the connection with the wider context, you can imagine and plan the future with total freedom while still awake. It becomes easy to explore to the full how things might be.

In his book *Everyday Miracles* my favourite holistic teacher, David Spangler, draws a parallel from quantum physics. He points out that we contemplate our various futures in a multidimensional world of infinite *waves*. But, when it comes to grounding these dreams, we have to bring them down and concentrate them into *particles* which must manifest in the three-dimensional solid world. We need to *particularize* the infinite *waves* of our dreaming. To put it concisely:

- Dreams and imagination are infinite quantum waves
- Action is grounded particles

These two worlds – the multidimensional world of waves and the solid world of particles – are substantially different. The solid world is dense and slow, but the inner world is free and fast and full of infinite possibilities. It is absolutely logical, then, that your creative imagining and planning must be as free and as infinite as the quantum waves. But when it comes to grounding and manifesting your plans, this requires the slow careful strategies of the solid world. The waves become particles. The solid world requires real and particular actions. The carpenter may dream his chair in infinite waves, but then must particularize it with careful precision.

> **Creative imagination will not hammer a nail. Particular logic will not dream a future. When you begin the imaginative process of contemplating your future, it must not include any logic or any rules. You do not know what the future holds. Your logical mind cannot grasp it. The dreaming must be free and intuitive – unboundaried.**

In the realm of infinite waves, in the dimension of dreams and intuitions, there are no limits or constraints on how you and the world can be. When dreaming and planning the future, therefore, your mind must have the skill of wild imagination, the ability to dream without boundaries. You must be open to any vision, any dream, any possibility.

You must release your imaginative mind to explore and move into new and unknown territory. It must be free and able to stretch beyond its normal boundaries of what is and is not possible. You must let your imagination expand so that it transcends your usual expectations and is not caught in the personal and collective prisons.

Unboundaried Dreaming allows your imagination to run absolutely free. It is extravagant. It is mythical. It is heroic. It is magnificent. Everything is exaggerated. Everyone wins. The scale is cosmic. It is victorious and overflowing with boundless success. The horn of plenty flows for everyone. Heaven is here on earth.

Examples of Unboundaried Dreaming

Before going into the actual exercise of Unboundaried Dreaming, I want to give some clear examples of what it looks like. From experience, I have learnt that it is helpful to divide Unbounded Dreaming into three types of project:

- Personal – any area of your private life that requires clarifying and developing. It can be to do with physical health, career, relationships, home, hobby, vacation and so on.
- Group – anything to do with your family, leisure or work.
- Global – any social, economic, political or environmental situation.

Each example of Unboundaried Dreaming is followed by some possible practical next steps that will help ground the vision. The format is always the same:

- First, the infinite waves of the Unboundaried Dream.
- Second, the practical and relevant action required to ground and 'particularize' it.

Personal

Financing your business
Your business needs new finance. In your dream, your bank manager actively wants your business. He smiles welcomingly and fights for your custom. You are a very attractive investment. Behind him stands a line of financiers also desperate to invest in you and your project. The *Financial Times* and *Wall Street Journal* carry front page stories of your success. Money is flowing into your business. George Soros, Richard Branson and other financiers all come to you, begging to be let in on your project. They also want you to tutor them in business theory. Bill Gates and Anita Roddick ask if they can come and work for you. Your business is prosperous and good for everyone. You have a foundation that is now funding the United Nations. You are floating in an ocean of warm and creative money. You are a sun god, beaming and glowing prosperity into the world.

Possible practical next steps: Read biography of George Soros. Make new list of possible investors. Get picture of a sun god for display. Have conversation with accountant. Rehearse meeting with investor.

Injured knee

Your knee is strained and painful. You envision the golden oil of healing *prana* and endorphins flowing into and around every cell of it. The swelling is going down and flexibility is returning. The knee is back to its normal health and is beginning to look and feel extraordinarily radiant and flexible. It is now as strong as an oak tree and yet able to spin like a propellor. It is the most wonderful knee in the whole world, flowing with magic vitality. You win several gold medals in the intergalactic Olympics.

Possible practical next steps: You buy and work with an anatomy colouring book. You talk to a friend who does yoga. You watch athletics on TV. You give your knee personal healing for five minutes.

Learning a musical instrument

You want to be better at playing the violin. In your dream, you become good enough to play in the local amateur orchestra. You now move on to play in the ensemble of one the world's greatest orchestras. Then you become its lead violinist. Now you are a soloist of world renown and your playing is phenomenal. In fact, you are the greatest violinist that ever lived. Mozart reincarnates simply to be inspired by you. Yehudi Menuhin pleads to be your student. You feel your music inspiring them and filling them with the healing genius of the cosmic harmonies. The planets dance in new orbits to your playing. You are Orpheus, god of music. You are a god/goddess, playing the harmonies of the universe. You, the violin, the muses and harmonics of the cosmos are one. You create and feel musical bliss in every cell of your body.

Possible practical next steps: Get a bust of Mozart. Buy shower curtains with a musical note motif. Create an altar for the muse of music. Mime to a CD. Join a music club.

Repairing a relationship

You have a relationship problem with your partner, husband or wife, that you want to repair. In your dream, the two of you are having a pleasant meal. You are enjoying each other's company. The sex is great. You make beautiful love. You feel wonderful. The two of you now become the greatest lovers and friends that the world has ever seen. You are teaching relationship skills to Prince Charles and Princess Diana, to Hillary and Bill Clinton. You have your own television show, internationally syndicated in which you share your love and insights. The author of *Men are from Mars, Women are from Venus* is quoting you as his greatest teacher. You feel deeply confident and gratified. You are happy to help others. Your harmony and joint creativity are so great that you can literally fly through the air. Look at them fly! Super-couple! The world gasps as it sees you. The cosmos applauds. The sensation is exquisite. The joy and fun you have together are a blessing to all beings. People are travelling from other planets to learn from you both the secrets of true friendship. You are 1000 per cent satisfied by your partner. You feel fully loved, fully appreciated, connected and satisfied. This relationship is heaven on earth.

Possible practical next steps: Give a present to your partner. Apologise. Appreciate. Take some space. Research the available books on relationships. Talk with a friend.

What shall I wear?

You want to look really good and are going to buy a new piece of clothing, but what should it be? In your dream, you begin to imagine how incredibly attractive this garment makes you look. You are so fabulous in it that *Vogue* wants you on the front cover and *Hello!* wants a series of pictures. You become a fashion icon. You feel charismatic and beautiful. The night skies of the greatest cities are filled with laser-beamed holograms of you, inspiring people with your style and beauty. Vivienne Westwood and Giorgio Armani want to know what you will wear next, so that they can copy you. Hercules and Artemis come to you for new robes, new clothing. Temples are built for you in the heavens. Your glow illuminates the cosmos. Your clothing style is copied by the sun and by the galaxy. The colours and the flows are bliss. You feel extraordinary, confident, radiant, a blessing to all life.

Possible practical next steps: Buy *Vogue, Elle, Harpers* etc. Place a photo of your ideal model on the wall. Look in your diary to see when you can take off time for window-shopping. Ask a friend what he thinks. Draw a picture of how you want to look. Go to a colour stylist.

Group

Teenagers

Your teenage children are giving you harassment and pain. You dream of going on enjoyable holidays and trips and outings together. Your patience is infinite. The teenagers are affectionate, friendly and helpful. Your friends love them and their friends love you. Oedipus comes to you all, begging forgiveness for having misled so many people. You write a book together on inter-generational relationships. You start a family business together. Together you are on the front page of *Time* magazine, *Newsweek* and *Hello!*. The sun and the galaxies are singing praises for the harmony and blessing that you are giving the world. You feel fantastic and satisfied. You have done a great job of parenting. Everyone is celebrating and grateful.

Possible practical next steps: Watch MTV. Give unexpected money. Buy something youthful to wear. Celebrate an untidy room. Give them a day off school. Read a book on parenting teenagers. Have a moan with another parent. Take them to McDonald's.

Business meeting

At a forthcoming business meeting to discuss a new product line organizational politics and conflicts are going to surface. Envisage the meeting ending in productive harmony. All the members are pleased to be with each other. You are centred and strong in your *hara*. Your Inner Smile is on full beam. Your energy is affectionately extended to hold the whole group. Throughout the meeting, you remain centred and alert. Everyone is interested in everyone else's ideas. There is useful and creative discussion. People are listening with great care and communicating with great clarity. There is a real sense of a coherent group purpose. There is a relaxed but efficient and creative flow. Everyone is in their *hara*, supportive and confident. Participants are going home and telling their partners what a great day they had. This group can now benefit the whole world. It is a model for organizational cooperation and synergy. All stakeholders in the universe are satisfied. There is great added value from the meeting that benefits everyone.

Possible Practical Next Steps: Identify possible trouble makers and greet them positively in advance. Make sure the meeting room is cleaned and aired. Read again the mission statement of the organization. Check the Agenda carefully. Say a prayer to Mercury, god of communications and healthy business. Read a book on group dynamics.

Christmas with the whole family

Spending Christmas with the whole family is often a distressing and boring experience as family feuds and prejudices surface. You sit quietly and envisage the family coming together. They are smiling and greeting each other. You are centred and strong in your *hara*. Your Inner Smile is on full beam. Your energy is affectionately extended to hold the family. Throughout the whole day, you remain centred and blissfully holding the situation. The spirit of Christmas is flowing into you and spilling over to touch the hearts of everyone there. Old enemies are embracing and joking together, holding hands while watching television. The radiance of the family is benefiting all the neighbours. In fact, it is radiating to the universe.

Possible Practical Next Steps: Phone each member of the family in advance. Give care to special diets. Make a list of your family's foibles and buy goodies to keep them quiet. Get extra boxes of crackers. Make sure there are plenty of flowers. Create a flop-out space for watching television.

Global/Social

War, Famine and Destitution

In this Unboundaried Dream, you focus on a region undergoing a terrible crisis. Gradually, you envision weapons being put down, soldiers shaking hands, children being fed, families being reunited, communications functioning, food being distributed, corruption ending, schools working, hospitals up and running. Slowly you build a picture of a decent society in which everyone is cared for, supported and respected. Then you begin to quantum leap the dream. The previously warring factions have devised methods of conflict resolutions that attract students from all over the globe. The previously ravaged land is now a model of environmental harmony and abundant organic farming. The schools are cosmic models of loving education. People come from many countries to be nurtured and inspired by the brilliance of their culture.

Possible practical next steps: Get information on charities working in this field. Read a book on global history. Donate money to a relevant organization. Make friends with a neighbour. Choose to be friendly and smile.

Destruction of the rain forests

In your dream, the destructive developers appreciate that their previous policies have been misguided. They understand the wisdom of the environmentalists, the non-profit activists and the tribal peoples. A clear and expanding boundary is created that protects the forest and a programme of reforestation is initiated. All across the globe, the great expanse of ancient forests begins to breathe freely again. Laboratories are set up in which researchers study the great medical and ecological lessons inherent in Gaia's natural universities. A great forest movement begins to ensure that in and around every city there are pockets of woodland for animals, plants and people to enjoy. Throughout the cosmos, earth becomes known as the Forest Planet.

Possible Practical Next Steps: Audit how green your home is. Buy some recycled loo paper. Get organic food. Boycott McDonald's. Donate to a relevant charity. Plant your own garden or window box. Get involved in a neighbourhood planting scheme.

Children at risk

This dream is about creating a safe world for our children. Healing and therapeutic programmes are set up which fully understand the deep historical, family and social sources of child abuse. Any person who carries the slightest vibration of bullying eagerly enters into transformational therapy. Society as a whole begins to recognize that the most important thing in life is to welcome and celebrate children, to make them feel safe and encouraged. The pavements become safe and everywhere you go there are children playing happily. The roads become safe and pollution-free. Every child is welcomed into a multi-cultured family and network of carers and friends. Every two hundred yards in every city there is a community area of grass, trees and plants where families and children congregate to play and picnic. Throughout the world there is a general sense of calm and enjoyable comfort between adults and children. The general love for children is so great that people cannot even consider beginning ventures that might prove hazardous or polluting for children. The earth becomes a paradise for children which adults are proud and satisfied to have created.

Possible practical next steps: Read a book on child development. Reach out to a child you know. Check that your own psychological issues around children are managed and talk to a friend or counsellor. Support a children's charity. Help out in a local school.

Kinaesthetically Feel the Future

It is crucial, when you are enjoying the Unboundaried Dream, to feel it in your body. You are having not just a mental fantasy but a full-body experience of what it would feel like when the dream is fulfilled – before it is fulfilled in three-dimensional reality. Your body and psyche do not care whether the fulfilled dream is imagined or real – they cannot tell the difference. From their perspective, the imagined fulfilment *is* the real one! This is obviously very strengthening and encouraging.

In a famous prosperity exercise for people who want more money, the client is led through a long and careful visualization sequence in which he imagines how much money he really wants in order to live the life he really wants. Enough for a few houses, a lifetime income, creative business and philanthropy, travel and so on. The client is carefully led into visualizing and experiencing what it is like to have all that money and freedom.

At the end of the visualization, the client writes down all the details of the exercise, including the feelings that were experienced when the client had everything he wanted. The coach then presents him with another reality. 'Suppose,' he says, 'that life will not deal you that twenty million pounds – do you still want the feelings that went with it? In fact, supposing God came down out of the sky and said, "You have a choice. Do you want the money or the feeling?", what would you say?'

Without exception, in answer to this question, people say that they want the feeling. (A few, of course, say they want both.) The coach then says, 'Well, you already had the feeling – just now and *without* the money!'

You may not be able to change the physical realities around you, or you may have to wait a long time, but you do not have to wait for the sensation and the experience of the fulfilment. Moreover, from a strategic point of view, if you are carrying the attitude and the atmosphere of someone who has already achieved their goals, it is much easier to fulfil them. If you feel prosperous, it is a thousand times more likely that someone will finance you than if you feel poor.

Leadership too is about holding the sensation of a fulfilled dream whilst the work is still being done. 'I have a dream . . . .' These words echo with charismatic power from someone who has faith in the dream, an inner certainty in its fulfilment precisely because that person is already experiencing the dream as fulfilled. It is a joy to be inspired by and follow such a person. And those of us who are not public leaders must still lead ourselves forward into our dreams.

> **In Unboundaried Dreaming the unconscious mind does not know that the fantasy is just a fantasy. All the neural pathways and neuropeptides are popping away as if it were all here-and-now reality. The inner experience is as authentic as a physical event.**

If, for example, you want to create a better relationship, within the Unboundaried Dreaming there is a physical experience of how the good relationship would feel. A bad or good relationship, by its very nature, is defined by its unpleasant or pleasant feelings. If you can fully imagine and sense how the perfect relationship would feel, then two very important things are happening.

First, regardless of how the relationship is in reality, the exercise privately allows you a 100 per cent positive experience of it. In the privacy of your own dreaming, you completely transform your experience of it. This is a full endorphin-based kinaesthetic experience anchoring down into your body. Obviously, this shifts things. If you felt oppressed, you will feel liberated; if you felt unappreciated, you will feel appreciated. Your dreaming cuts through emotional injury and replaces it with a more positive experience.

Second, there is also a purely energetic change. In the exercise, you transformed the mood, atmosphere and vibrations of your attitude to the situation. You therefore carry a much more positive energy towards the situation. In fact, you carry around with you the energy field of fulfilment. This renders you much more attractive, congruent and magnetic, and this makes it easier for you to create in real life what you want.

Experience the Support

It is also crucial to allow yourself to *feel* the support of the universe. There is more momentum to fulfilment than your own private desire.

Sometimes, people are so lost in their psychological history that they are embarrassed or unable to admit that they are an intimate part of this brilliant unfolding cosmos. You have to push past that and just accept it as reality. By definition, nothing is separate from the cosmos. Just as the tiniest flower or amoeba is part of it, so are you.

Like a tree or a galaxy, people are drawn through time and space towards fulfilling themselves. There is, in fact, no other direction. You need to let this feeling into your dreaming and into your general experience of life. It is part of choosing to live in the universe and not in Blobsville. It is part of choosing to feel the real dynamics of an endlessly changing but benevolent cosmos.

> **The power of endless change permeates the universe. It permeates you. Whether you like it or not, you are inevitably changing and transforming. Do nothing and you will still transform. You cannot exclude yourself from the cosmic process.**

Monitor Its Benevolence

It is important to monitor that your dream is harmless. There are two reasons for this.

The first is a simple matter of morality and congruence. The whole flow of the universe supports the growth and fulfilment of all life forms. If you do anything that obstructs or weakens that growth, you are doing harm. Indirectly, you are also doing yourself harm because you are part of this system and the extra tension you create in its fabric will, sooner or later, come back to you.

The second reason is energetic and practical. In order for the core connection to flow fully through you, you yourself need to be in harmony with its essential dynamic. That dynamic is benevolent. If your dream and your intention are not benevolent, the universal benevolence will not flow through you and your dreams and goals will remain unfulfilled.

You need, therefore, to monitor your dream and assess that it hurts no one and nothing. If it does, you need to adjust it and experiment with new scenarios. You must carefully assess the ecological, emotional and social costs of your fantasy. Sorry to be a spoilsport, but there's no point in dreaming about how you can become a billionaire if your core idea is dehumanizing or ecologically abusive. Equally, a perfect romantic relationship is meaningless if children are abandoned or friends betrayed.

Shout Your Desire

You may not be accustomed to getting what you want. You may think you do not deserve it. You may have several inner critics and saboteurs in your conscious and unconscious mind who would all be deeply upset and embarrassed if you achieved your goals, received what you wanted and created a happy life for yourself.

There is one sure way of making certain that the background drone of these inner saboteurs does not suck the vitality out of your goals and dreams. This is to assert clearly and loudly that you really and truly desire your dream.

There are many different dreams and possible futures. You will create yours only if you really want it. If you do not really want it, no energy will flow into its manifestation – and someone else's dream will come true.

Look at the earlier examples again: good relationship, finance, musicianship, attractive appearance, parenting teenagers, health. In Unboundaried Dreaming, you can take yourself into a clear vision and experience of how you can fulfil each of those perfectly. But you now need to check that you have a genuine passion actually to fulfil them.

The natural flow of the cosmos may support your dream, but do you support it yourself? If not, your apathy alone may sabotage its actualization. You want a good relationship or environmental harmony? Then put some energy of desire into the dream. Magnetize it with your emotional commitment.

> **Do you have the inner ability to state with absolute clarity, with power and with passion, that you really want the fulfilled outcome? Do you have the motivation to commit yourself?**

But many people were not brought up or educated to feel free to express their passionate desires, even in private. To do so was too often labelled as selfish, self-centred or theatrical. It is, however, 100 per cent appropriate, and has absolute integrity, to desire with passion that which is good for you and for other people. This is righteous passion. It is the force behind great visions and liberation movements. It is the force of creative achievement. Some will demonstrate this passion quietly and with great endurance. Others will shout and be public. But whether you are a noisy or quiet person, your dreams must be supported by your clear desire to achieve them.

Poignantly, there are other people with whom I have worked who are frightened to assert their desire because they do not want to be disappointed. They have wanted things in the past, only to be disappointed and hurt when they did not come. I encourage these people simply to cut through memories of disappointment and go for it.

In the actual exercise, however, the desire is not held on to. It is released to the cosmos and allowed to happen in its own good time. You have to shout the clear desire and, having asserted it, let it go and return to being a compassionate, philosophical, kind observer. It may happen. It may not happen. Whatever the circumstances or outcome, you remain connected and centred. You stay with the good feeling of the fulfilled dream.

> **Your dream is meaningless if it is not fuelled by your passion.**

Particularize the Dream Waves

As you experience the full-body enjoyable sensation of fulfilling your dream, it is very easy to scan for a congruent and useful next step for actually manifesting your goal in real life. 'What small and easy thing can I do immediately that is congruent with my dream?' You do not need a full strategy, but you must be able to come up with at least one simple action, one easy first step – a step so easy that you will have no excuse to ignore it. That first simple action begins the physical process of bringing the dream into reality. If you do not start to act, nothing will happen.

This simple first act is the exact point at which the infinite dreams enter into manifestation in the solid world. Sometimes you may already be doing the congruent actions. I have worked with many people who were trying to build a career or an organization and were already doing everything they needed to do. But they were not dreaming or experiencing the fulfilment of their project – they were lost in short-term goals and realities. I have also worked with many idealists and environmental activists who had almost the same problem. They were all doing the right things, but with the wrong attitude. They were always worrying about their projects rather than envisioning their fulfilment and being inspired by their dream. These people had no inspiration and felt they were getting nowhere.

Unboundaried Dreaming:
The Full Sequence of Exercises

Let's look now at the actual exercises of Unboundaried Dreaming, after which I shall clarify some of the points. We shall start with casual daydreaming and then go into a description of the more detailed work. One of the most important points to remember is that this work can also be done when you are tired or in crisis, if you allow yourself to go into conscious retreat.

CONSCIOUS DAYDREAMING

The next time that you are relaxed and in a mood to daydream, check that you are in an endorphin flow. Then slowly turn your attention to an issue that requires clarity and solutions.

Keep this issue at a comfortable mental distance.

It is a small seed, which you are contemplating in a relaxed and completely patient way. You have no expectations. You are just looking at it. Do not allow the mental image or thought to be big or overwhelming. Maintain space between you and it.

Have a warm and kind attitude towards the issue.

Staying calm and confident, begin to imagine what that issue would look and feel like if it were perfectly transformed.

Stay relaxed and allow your mind to play around with possible outcomes and different courses of action. Allow any fantastic ideas to surface into your awareness. Be open to anything that might come.

Do not be impatient for clarity. Do not frown or get earnest. Keep the whole process playful.

If at any time you feel any tension or disquiet, cradle your distress and maintain your Inner Smile.

Notice and remember any interesting impressions or ideas that come to you.

UNBOUNDARIED DREAMING

This is the full sequence of the exercise when you want to give deliberate attention to an issue.

CONNECT

For this exercise it is essential that you are in the endorphin flow and connected. So go through the sequence carefully and relax into it. If you are impatient, you are just going to have to wait until the tension subsides.

FOCUS

Pause and bring into your mind that aspect of life which you want to change and about which you want clarity. Hold it as a distant thought, like a seed or picture in the distance.

DREAM

Carefully allow yourself to contemplate how you would like it to unfold. Allow the daydream to become an extravagant fantasy. Remove all boundaries from your dreaming. Enjoy the dreaming and imagining. Let it go anywhere, into absolute fulfilment.

MONITOR ITS BENEVOLENCE

Staying completely relaxed and open, check that your vision cannot harm any living being, including yourself. Nature and the universe are intricately intermeshed. Make sure that your dream supports the growth and fulfilment of any other life that it touches.

EXPERIENCE THE SUPPORT

As you enjoy contemplating the brilliantly fullfilled dream, turn your attention again to the benevolent and supportive energies of earth-nature-sun-universe. Gently allow your body kinaesthetically to sense their support.

Allow yourself to recognize that earth-nature-sun-universe are all positively, actively and enthusiastically supporting you and all life in change and fulfilment.

Turn your attention to all the strawberries in your life. Sense them floating around you. All your strawberries are also positively, actively and enthusiastically supporting change and fulfilment.

There are also many people and communities who will be served by the successful transformation. Notice and be aware that they support the change.

Recognize that the whole universe is perpetually changing and fulfilling itself – and that, just because you exist, you are part of that.

The power of change and fulfilment is emerging through every cell and fibre in your body – and through everyone else.

The whole thrust of the universe carries change forward and supports vision and transformation.

Allow yourself to bathe in the comfort of that support.

CRADLE ALL DIFFICULTIES

If you feel any tension or resistance to the exercise, smile towards it. Cradle it. If your mind starts to sabotage your flow, smile at your chattering mind and its judgements. Cradle all difficulties.

ANCHOR IT DOWN INTO YOUR CELLS

When you are fully enjoying the experience of the Unboundaried Dream, notice how good you feel.

Notice also whether there are any smells, scents, colours or sounds that are accompanying the experience.

Relax a fraction more and allow the whole experience and sensation to land down into every cell and fibre of your body. Allow the whole dream softly to anchor and dock into you.

You are having a complete kinaesthetic experience of the fulfilled dream. You are not just dreaming but actually feeling the complete transformation.

SHOUT YOUR DESIRE

Staying within the great feeling, allow a voice to emerge from deep within your chest and abdomen. It emerges clearly and powerfully. This is your core voice and, in relation to the dream and the feeling, it roars telepathically out to the universe: 'I want this. I want this. I want this. The universe supports me and this fulfilment and I want this!'

Do this for as long as feels comfortable.

After having shouted your desire, bring your attention back down into yourself. Notice any tension or reaction within yourself and cradle it.

RELEASE

Now make absolutely certain that your Inner Smile is switched on and that you are watching the world and yourself with warm and affectionate compassion.

Release your sense of passionate desire completely. Give it up. Allow it to flow outwards. Trust the universe to support you.

NEXT STEP

Allow yourself to contemplate possible next steps. It can be anything, no matter how small, which is congruent with the dream and will help to anchor it down into real life. The infinite waves of the dream must particularize into some specific action. Make sure it is something that you can do easily and immediately.

SUMMARY OF UNBOUNDARIED DREAMING

Core Connection: True environment, strawberries, Inner Smile, guiding the energy, Curled Deer, breathing the earth-nature-sun-universe, cradle the distress.

Conscious Daydreaming: Allow your mind to watch that part of your life that needs to change and patiently observe and play with possible ways forward.

Unboundaried Dreaming: Have absolutely no limits on your dreaming. Let them be as fantastic and extravagant as possible. Stretch your boundaries.

Experience the Support: Feel the whole dynamic of the universe supporting you in your changes and your fulfilment.

Kinaesthetically Feel the Future: Allow yourself fully to imagine your most wonderful possible future. Experience it in your body here and now.

Monitor its Benevolence: Check that the dream and the plan do no harm to you or any other living being

Shout Your Desire: Do you really want this future? If so, clearly express your desire.

Particularize the Dream Wave: Think of one small action you can do immediately which is congruent with the dream and begins to anchor it into real life.

Choosing Your Future

One of the facets of Unboundaried Dreaming is that it allows you to experiment with different possibilities. You can fully examine a possible course of action without actually doing it in real life. This provides you with a way of checking out whether or not you really want to do it.

If, for example, you are thinking of a career in education, you can use Unboundaried Dreaming to take you into a total experience of being the absolutely fulfilled teacher. Having experienced this dream, wait to see whether you have the instinct or motivation to repeat an Unboundaried Dreaming session focussed on education. If you do not want to repeat it, you can be fairly clear that you do not really have an inner passion or calling for it. If, on the other hand, you find yourself being called back to the dream, it is obvious that there is a strong attraction towards that future.

This approach can be applied to all areas of your life, including changes in your job, relationship, where you live and where you go on holiday. It can be used for something as mundane as selecting your next car or something as meaningful as choosing which social issues you want to support. There are only so many projects in which you can be involved, and they ought to be the ones that are continually attracting your attention.

The body and unconscious psyche cannot distinguish between physical and imagined reality. Fully imagining and feeling possible courses of action, therefore, provides you with a short cut to enriching your life with experience and clarifying what you really want. Having the Unboundaried Dreaming sensation can defuse your urge or neurotic desire for a particular outcome. You might, for example, be exploring making money. In the Unboundaried Dreaming you can have the full experience of absolute prosperity, but afterwards you might assess that it is not worth all the work and dedication. You have other things you want to do with your life rather than chase financial status. The sensation of the successful imagining is enough to bring you to a point of intelligent stabilty and realism.

I have seen several people do Unboundaried Dreaming around their marriages and, having had the inner experience of how they wanted it, decide not to continue in their marriage. They go fully into the experience of a completely fulfilled relationship and then look realistically at what they have to do in order to achieve it. After the process, they assessed that it would be impossible to achieve in real life and it was not worth compromising. Others, however, chose to stay with their partners and to be led by their dream.

Robert Holden, who founded the first National Health 'Laughter Clinic', once told me about one of his challenges: he often had too many book projects in his mind. He said,

> ❝ To ease the self-imposed burden of thinking I "must" publish every idea I get, I bought a beautiful piece of computer software, and simply created jackets, covers and sleeves for all the ideas I *imagined* I had written. I was therefore looking at the finished product. Doing this seemed to enhance my creative flow even further. But, also, it left me free to focus on the creative projects I am most passionate about. ❞

So, if something is genuinely part of your life's purpose, you will find yourself continually wanting to dream about it. If you want that wonderful career or marriage or vacation, you will keep coming back to it. You will find pleasure in taking it often into the space of Unboundaried Dreaming. Your passion for it will remain. You will still be able to roar, 'I want this! The universe supports me in wanting this!' And if it is not something you really want to do, it will fall away. You will have fulfilled your curiosity by allowing yourself a full experiential fantasy and be free now to move on.

The Metaphysics of the Dream

I want to end this chapter with some thoughts on the metaphysics of this strategy. The importance of this aspect was brought home to me by an environmental activist on one of my courses. He had mixed feelings about doing the training in the first place. He felt that he should be doing something more practical for his cause and that the whole day was possibly just a time-wasting indulgence. He was openly cynical about doing Unboundaried Dreaming for his particular environmental concern.

'Positive thinking or flaky visualization won't achieve anything,' he protested. 'The disaster is already happening. It needs practical action.'

But he stayed with the training and did his dreaming around the

destruction of the rain forests. By the end of the day, his whole attitude had turned round. There was one point when he was almost in
tears.

'I felt useless,' he explained, 'but I can feel some power now. I
always believed in the power of every individual's actions, no matter how small. But now it has a whole new dimension.'

The new dimension was the energy that is created by consciously
dreaming a positive and fulfilled future. When the mind thinks
something, energy is being generated and used. Following the
normal laws of physics, this energy does not just disappear but
continues to exist in its own right. So, when you put mental energy
into thinking, this energy continues to live – like a cloud of mental
vibrations. Ideas, therefore, float around in the psychic atmosphere
– a core concept in most energy medicine.

These 'thoughtforms' obviously have different vibrations and can
affect people – for instance, depressing or inspiring them. It is
important, therefore, to create ideas that are filled with a positive
and not a depressive vibration. If you energetically moan about the
destruction of the rainforest, it only adds moaning vibrations to the
already unpleasant scene. You do not want to walk around accompanied by the atmosphere of a depressed and distressed idea. This
does not serve anyone or anything. It has been suggested, in fact,
that worrying is a way of praying for what you do not want. It feeds
energy into a scenario that you do not want to create.

A depressed vision leads people nowhere. It actually makes
things worse. If you were in trouble, would you want people sending you worried energy with visions of further doom and disaster?
Or would you want a positive vibration with visions of hope? A positive thoughtform, a vision of a fulfilled solution, inspires people.

'Just by staying true to my dream of humanity caring for its rain
forests,' the environmentalist said at the end of the day, 'I am doing
good. In my own small way, I am doing something to change the
whole energy of the situation. Of course, I will carry on being an
activist. But this gives me so much hope.'

SUMMARY OF PART 2

Throw Away the Rules –
Do What You Want with the Exercises

You have now been taken through all the exercises of the Endorphin Effect. I encourage you to be flexible in the way you use them. Follow your instincts and intuition. Do them in the way that suits you.

- You can do them in any order you like
- You can just do one or a mixture of them
- You can focus on them for long periods of time
- You can give them just a second's attention
- A tiny taste of one can shift everything – if not immediately, then later

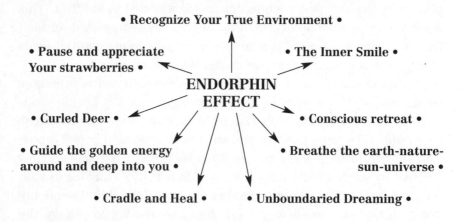

• Recognize Your True Environment •

• Pause and appreciate
Your strawberries •

• The Inner Smile •

**ENDORPHIN
EFFECT**

• Curled Deer •

• Conscious retreat •

• Guide the golden energy
around and deep into you •

• Breathe the earth-nature-
sun-universe •

• Cradle and Heal •

• Unboundaried Dreaming •

Let your underlying attitude be full of goodwill and generosity. It is only with this goodwill that the Universal flow will pass fully into and through you. In this way, there is true health.

PART 3:

Integration

CHAPTER 12:

Waves on the Ocean – Managing the Highs and Lows

A Stitch in Time

Earlier I told the story of the yogi who emerged from his twelve-year retreat only to be overwhelmed by irritation when some young boys crashed into him. I have never met anyone who has not experienced this seesaw duality. We have all been like this yogi: one moment feeling calm and positive, the next flooded with negative agitation. This polarity is part of the human condition. We are an amazing species, strung out on a spectrum of experience. At one end we have the glands and nervous system of a highly sensitive ape; at the other end, a consciousness that can expand and dream the greatest glories of the universe. We are simultaneously frail and magnificent, neurotic and brilliant.

Integrating this duality is the fundamental struggle of self-development. The struggle does not disappear when we practise the exercises in this book. In fact, the duality may intensify as we expand our experience of feeling good and notice even more clearly when we feel bad.

In this chapter, therefore, I want to devote some attention to the challenges that you may face with this work. My purpose is not to dampen enthusiasm, but to be realistic about the challenges that some people may encounter. Because I discuss what may go wrong, some personal development trainers have accused me of being pessimistic – but what happens if people find the work difficult or hit a trough or a depression with no warning? I would rather they were forewarned and prepared.

There are four particular challenges that may arise:

- *Moods:* Everyone has moods, so your experience of the connection will not be consistently wonderful. There will be ups and downs.
- *Deeper problems surface:* As you increase your flow of endorphins and deepen your connection, it will make you feel safer and stronger – and this may allow deeper and older psychological problems to surface.
- *Some problems endure:* Whilst some problems may dissolve easily as they meet the Endorphin Effect strategies, other problems are more deep-seated and will require much longer to transform and integrate.
- *The inner critic:* Faced with these moods and more difficult problems, an inner critic may appear. This critic may produce a self-sabotaging sense of failure when things do not go as well as you want and you may stop doing the exercises all together.

The Mystic Marriage

When people first work with their strawberries and the Inner Smile, they begin to have some very deep, pleasant and useful experiences. Not surprisingly, but naively, many of them then want or expect every negative memory and aspect of their psychology to be swiftly transformed.

And sometimes for some people, everything does change for ever. They manage to unload one level of tension, and beneath it they find a calm, happy creature ready to take over the whole of their life. I remember a senior civil servant who took the CEM training. His whole life had been disciplined and dedicated to service. He expected and was at ease with self-sacrifice and stoic devotion. He was also frozen and unhappy. Within months of doing the basic Endorphin Effect exercises, the whole veneer of an almost military personality had melted away. Beneath was a calm and creative man carrying very little psychological baggage. Fellow students looked at him and said, 'Good karma. This man has good fortune.'

In general, though, this kind of easy and immediate life transformation is not realistic. Bad moods and negative feelings that have a history.

There are the original traumas that created them and then there are the grooves of attitude that you have furrowed, sometimes for decades. It is therefore obvious – and it is wise to acknowledge this – that you will continue to experience some inner negativity whilst at the same time you enjoy the experience and benefits of the Endorphin Effect.

You need these two aspects of yourself – the negative history and the endorphins – to integrate and work together in some form of cooperative co-existence. To bring the extremes of our psyche and our behaviour into harmony was known in Western mystical traditions, such as alchemy and Rosicrucianism, as the Mystic Marriage. We might call the two partners who are being brought closer together here the Armoured Personality and the Inner Smile. A fabulous couple!

- *The Groom:* the Armoured Personality, stuck in its patterns of survival and self-gratification and living in Blobsville.
- *The Bride:* The Inner Smile, endorphin based and connected to the benevolent wavefields of Nature and the Universe.

This relationship is the source of numerous myths – Beauty and the Beast, the Frog and the Princess, the Dragon and the Maiden, the various heroes of many cultures and the terrible monsters they must vanquish, Dr Jekyll and Mr Hyde. They are all an archetypal description of the inner duality that exists in all of us.

Keeping them separate is easy. It can be tough work and uncomfortable as you bring the two partners closer and they get to know each other.

Heaven and Hell Simultaneously

So be realistic. You will experience the endorphin flow and the connection. You will enjoy the fabulous sensations of Unboundaried Dreaming. But you will still have to meet and experience the wounds that you already carry. They will not just disappear, but will continue to pop up until they receive the compassionate attention and integration that they need.

Sometimes, like everyone, you will oscillate between feeling good, feeling neutral and feeling bad. But, increasingly, there may now be periods when you experience both the good and the bad at the same time. Recognize that it is completely normal and good to have both experiences at the same time.

You may find yourself sitting quietly, working with your strawberries, feeling the connection and the endorphin flow, whilst elsewhere in your body or mind, there is still murderous tension or endless compulsive babble. These moments of simultaneous heaven and hell may feel deeply uncomfortable, but they are also times of great growth. It is in these moments that Dr Jekyll and Mr Hyde are truly meeting, that the princess is kissing the frog, that the truly transformational inner marriage is happening. Supported by the whole endorphin dynamic, the Inner Smile expands to accept, cradle and integrate the inner monsters. All aspects of yourself are being accepted and given space.

It is when the two aspects meet that real growth is happening. The energy of loving consciousness is coming into the wounded patterns. When your inner kindness meets your inner negativity, that is when creative transformation is taking place. Yes, it feels uncomfortable, but that is the friction of the two fields meeting. At the point of contact, there is uncomfortable physical and psychic chemistry. Endorphins are permeating frozen tension.

The only comfortable way of dealing with this friction is to go as best you can into the Inner Smile. Accept and watch compassionately. Have a kind attitude towards your discomfort and psychological process.

The old patterns are lodged deep into the body and psyche. To experience them again in order to release them is not comfortable; sometimes it is hellish. Someone who carries the scars of continuous childhood abuse cannot avoid, at the appropriate moment of healing, re-experiencing the events precisely so that they may be integrated and released.

This marriage, this simultaneous heaven and hell, is recognized by many mystical traditions and is illustrated in their art. From all around the world you will find images of a holy person looking absolutely beatific but surrounded and tormented by demons and monsters. These demons are not external: they describe what the saint is feeling. Yes, there is bliss and connection. But there are also the monsters of bad moods and feelings, snapping and flaming around and within you.

This is what the Inner Smile and cradling teach you to do gracefully – to be both in the bliss state and in the hell state. When you are having both experiences simultaneously, you are doing the practice perfectly.

The important thing is to maintain your Inner Smile. *Just because you do not feel 100 per cent good when you are doing the endorphin exercises, do not judge that you are getting anything wrong.* Be pleased with yourself that you are maintaining your composure whilst still wading in the mud of your particular difficulty.

Again, be realistic. Some of your bad moods have a momentum that is too powerful to be seduced easily by the Endorphin Effect. It is like trying to stop a stampeding elephant. You need patience and endurance.

> **The real art of personal transformation is to experience, as a kind witness, both your bad mood and your good mood at the same time. This may be uncomfortable, but it represents the true inner marriage and a time of great development.**

This, I believe, is the quintessential art or power skill of the core energy work – the ability to stay centred and kindly observant whilst feeling bad. The power skill is to feel terrible and yet at the same time also be totally in the Inner Smile and connected.

If you do not develop this skill, you may judge that you are doing the exercises ineffectually simply because you do not feel great every time you do them. Expect the exercises to take you easily into a good feeling when you are already feeling great. But if you are feeling lousy or in the groove of a negative mood, expect the exercises to work more gradually.

The Peaks and the Troughs

Using the Endorphin Effect exercises to achieve a full flow and connection is not always easy; sometimes it is extremely difficult. There will be periods when your experience of the endorphins is brilliant and totally fulfilling. At other times you will barely catch a taste of them and you may lose the connection completely for a while.

These fluctuations are not due to some inherent ineptness or unworthiness in you. They happen in the same way that they happen to everyone else. We all have moods and highs and lows. This is completely normal.

Our moodiness is partly psychological but also partly reflects the fluid nature of all life. There are many moods and rhythms: biorhythms, monthly periods, lust, astrology, weather, seasons, sun spots, cosmic rays, weekends, sleepiness, hunger and so on. These moods and rhythms permeate nature and the universe. Space is filled with emerging waves of energy, black holes collapsing, universes expanding. Nothing in the universe is at rest. The metaphor of the ocean is useful. Oceans do not stay calm, nor do they remain stormy. There are crests and troughs, tidal waves and calms, different temperatures, currents. One wave will throw you on to the beach and another will pick you up.

Do not judge emotional moods as being bad and unnecessary. They are a totally normal and acceptable part of life. They do, however, affect how easy it is to trigger endorphins.

It is obvious that if you are in a good mood it is going to be easy to trigger endorphins. Equally, when you are in a trough it may be more difficult to find your strawberries meaningful and to make the connection. But that is what it is like to be in a trough. It does not mean you are doing anything wrong or failing. You are just being human. Have kind thoughts and stay with the Inner Smile.

The most experienced energy workers recognize only too well how subject they are to the rise and fall of their moods. They know that there will be difficult times, but from a psychological perspective this is bound to happen as people encounter their wounds and their negative patterns.

The greatest mystics in the world – those who have committed their lives to achieving and living permanently in the connection – have never claimed that the journey of integration is easy. In the Christian tradition, for instance, there is the famous Dark Night of the Soul when the most devoted saints descend into a lengthy mood of despair and depression. In fact, educated 'saints' know that at some point they must meet the darkness of the human character.

> **Everyone has moods and cycles. That is just the way it is to be human and part of this universe.**

Rumi, considered by many to be the greatest of all Islamic and Sufi mystic poets, wrote comfortingly of all this.

> ❝ *This being human is a guest house*
> *Every morning a new arrival*
> *A joy*
> *A depression*
> *A meanness*
> *Some momentary awareness comes as an unexpected visitor*
> *Welcome and entertain them all*
> *Even if they are a crowd of sorrows who violently sweep your house empty of all its furniture*
> *Still treat each guest honourably*
> *They may be clearing you out for some new delight*
> *The dark thought*

The shame
The malice
Meet them at the door laughing and invite them in
Be grateful for whoever comes
Because each has been sent as a guide from beyond **9** [1]

Real Life

We are also, of course, directly affected by what life throws at us. Two months after her CEM coaches training, Kate MacDuff, an Australian herbalist, wrote to me. I reproduce a substantial part of her letter here because it illustrates so well the ups and downs of integrating this work.

> **6** I enjoyed 10 days at Findhorn [in Scotland] following the workshop and each day used the connection to nature, the strawberries (although I didn't need them much being there!), being in my body, pausing, guiding the flow, Curled Deer, inner loop, cradling the hurt and some Unboundaried Dreaming. This was all TOO EASY because I had unlimited time, I was alone, had no commitments and I could focus completely on integrating all that we had done.
>
> I returned home totally revitalized and within a short time have been faced with two major episodes in my life - one personal/family and the other work related. In the first instance, during the actual crisis time, I tried to connect, use the strawberries, be in my body, Curled Deer etc. It felt as if nothing worked - I couldn't feel the endorphin flow. The first time my body went into adrenalin/acid rush for several days and I resorted to a session of acupuncture to restore my energy balance and this helped (as it usually does). This was all from a major hurt that had been stirred up by a decision my daughter was considering . . . .
>
> Following this challenge, I smiled (Inner Smile) instead of berating myself for not being able to make

your tools work on my own, when they were really being tested. Two weeks later the second major challenge came (around my work) and I took your advice – relaxed and drank a glass of red wine first! Then, I connected and throughout the whole episode, which is still continuing 10 days later, I am feeling connected to the benevolence of the bliss fields. I do not always feel the endorphin flow in my body, but there is a distinct awareness that I am not handling this crisis in the usual way. Somehow, although I can't consciously feel it all the time, the connection is there helping me to rise out of Blobsville. I observe that although I did "react", the reaction lasted a very short time and I have recovered so much more quickly than I normally would.

I am also using the connection of the inner loop, then looping my energy out into the universe, inviting strawberries and feeling their presence when working with clients and the atmosphere is electrified.

So, I think I'm "doing the practice"! What do you think? 〞

I replied that I thought she was doing brilliantly.

The Chief Saboteur – The Inner Critic

In my experience, the biggest reason why people stop working with their strawberries and making their connection, is that they expect it to work perfectly all the time. This is understandable. You have a high experience that feels great. You are pleased with yourself for getting it right and the reward was the feelgood. You judge yourself a success. Then, when it does not work perfectly, you do not get your reward and you judge yourself a failure.

You forget that there are natural ups and downs in life. You feel that the exercises do not work properly for you or that you are no good at them. You start with enthusiasm and then slip into lethargy. A major part of this light depression, which saps people of motivation, is caused by an inner critic condemning you as inadequate and failing.

This inner critic belongs to a competitive culture filled with the notion that if something is not perfect, it is not good enough. You get it right or you get it wrong. You do well or you are mediocre. Our culture, our education and our working lives are typically filled with tests, failures and successes. It is easy to see this macho approach, this lack of emotional and spiritual intelligence, running all through our society, including many religious approaches. You are either a saint or a sinner, enlightened or ignorant, graced or damned.

This sense of failure, created by the inner critic, is rationalized into many different reasons. During training sessions, I have asked students to name the possible reasons why they might not continue with strategies that are so obviously beneficial for them. In sharing this list with you, I want you to be amused and reassured as you recognize the common difficulties that people share and the innumerable reasons for them.

The inner critic's reasons for not continuing

- Resentment (that I have to do anything at all)
- Too busy
- It's too soft. I'm a toughie.
- More tasks
- No time
- I like tension
- Need support
- Exclusion/ alienation
- Elitist
- Escapism /addictive behaviour
- Mean with time (I've spent enough time on this)
- Too nebulous
- Avoidance / denial
- of feelings
- Nausea/fear/ tension
- Fluffy head
- Exhaustion/ tiredness/ overwhelm
- Laziness/ inertia
- Depression
- Self-judgement
- I always fail
- No confidence / disempowerment
- Lack of skills
- Ignorance
- Weakness
- Insecurity
- Pomposity
- Undisciplined/no rhythm/no routine
- Too much hard work for too little reward
- No short-term rewards
- Not valuable/not important/ intangible
- No material rewards
- No status
- Lack of love
- Guilt
- Self-indulgence
- Projection / misperception
- Humourless
- Too earnest
- Stuck
- Hostile
- Angry

- Closed to the idea that life can be better
- Arrogance
- Bolshy/rebellious
- Forgetful
- Other people
- No self-love
- Impatience
- Universe is horrible
- Delusion
- Unworthy
- Disbelief
- Duty to others
- Cynicism
- Internal mockery
- Lost the plot
- I need a facilitator
- I need a supportive environment

- Sick
- Don't believe it
- Other people don't believe it
- People will think I'm flaky
- Neurotic
- Spaced out
- Pollution
- Talk, talk, talk
- Too high expectations
- Displacement
- Leave it till tomorrow
- Moody
- Astrology
- Biorhythms
- Weather
- Apathetic
- Prefer my addictions

- God is angry
- Eaten too much
- New Age bullshit
- Too poignant
- Needy partner
- Too orgasmic
- Too wired
- Theology
- TV
- Distractions
- Lust
- Workaholic
- Amnesia
- Worry
- Embarrassment
- Physical pain
- Wrong time
- Untidy environment
- Devoted to more formal tradition

You must learn how to observe these critical thoughts with some shrewdness and wisdom. It is very easy to buy into the criticism and feel that it is completely real, when the truth is that you have gone unconscious and the inner critic has just taken over.

When your mind tells you that you are wasting your time, you have to learn the art of detaching from that inner voice and observing it with kindness. Regard it as an evasive child who requires your affection. You must not let it overwhelm you. This wise detachment is made much easier if you remember, when doing the exercises, to guide the endorphin flow deep into your brain. It can be entertaining to imagine that you know exactly which brain cells are producing the excuses, and then to flood that area of the brain with endorphin feelgood.

Whatever excuse the inner critic produces, the trick is to maintain a sense of humour and detachment. Keep coming back to the

Inner Smile and the kind witnessing. Don't take the excuse seriously. Observe it. Cradle it. Do not buy into it.

Tough Love, Kind Attitude

Of course, life and transformation are difficult. That is just the way that it is. And sometimes pain and frustration are experienced, but the point here is not the pain itself. The significant point can be highlighted by asking this question: what is your attitude towards your difficulties? Your difficulties are one thing, but far more important is your attitude towards them. The content smile on the face of a Tibetan Buddhist is derived not from the fact that he has no problems but from his basic attitude towards these problems. He recognizes the true reality and has them in perspective.

I was coaching a good-looking man who suffered physical disability following a brain tumour in his twenties. Having done a weekend's training with me, he was still pissed off about his disability and wanted counselling. I agreed that fate had dealt him a terrible hand and that his situation was indeed tragic. I was very sympathetic, but he kept going on and on and on, feeling victimized and sorry for himself. Finally I asked what was more tragic, the disability or his attitude towards it – the fact that he kept on complaining? On top of the genuine tragedy, he was heaping the bitter feelings of compulsive resentment and self-pity.

It was awkward as he realized that I was really challenging him. After a while, he appreciated the insight. This was appropriate tough love on my part. It is precisely the kind of tough love that you sometimes need to apply to yourself. You cannot hold off doing what is right for you because you are waiting for the right circumstances.

Your fulfilment, success and happiness are not dependent upon your circumstances. They are dependent upon you, the person in the driving seat. Do not be fooled by the usual excuses: I would feel better if I had the right relationship . . . more money . . . a better body . . . the right job and so on.

You will only feel better when your attitude to yourself and to the world has changed. This is not a change that will happen once and for all – it requires consistent and gradual effort. The effort involved may seem great to you, but there is no greater reward in the universe.

> Get on with the exercises and be kind and generous to the part of you which is sad and resistant.

The Need for Courage

Working with the Endorphin Effect is also bound to pose some challenges, because it will raise your awareness of physical and emotional tensions that you previously ignored or tolerated. I do not want the reader to underestimate how uncomfortable it is to become aware of issues that are frozen within you – in my own growth, I know about it only too well. The background hum of adrenal anxiety, which you thought was normal, now becomes intolerable compared to the freedom of the endorphin flow.

For many people, to look honestly at themselves is an act of courage. It is also an act of courage to be kind and caring towards oneself. Self-honesty and self-care are profound emotional skills, which are usually only developed over time. We are rarely taught them as children and as adults only grasp them with difficulty – often after some crisis.

I have watched many students and clients become slowly aware of the anxiety that they are carrying in their bodies, and whose emotional significance they want to avoid. Over and over I have seen them understand that their childhood histories cannot be ignored or transcended or denied. Such histories fester, intrude, sabotage and constrain people's freedom and energetic flexibility. It can feel daunting as they appreciate that their histories have to be fully acknowledged and worked with, for it is only by working with them that the full endorphin experience can flow.

In fact, a colleague once said that the core energy work needs to be given out with a health warning. This is because the power of the connection, the new safety and strength, allows ancient emotions long buried to surface for healing.

People may be tempted at that stage to stop working with their strawberries and their connection. They do not feel ready to face and accept their own troubles. This is understandable and sometimes caution is indeed appropriate, but the courage to face your emotional reality is a life skill that people must be able to use when needed.

It is, however, a wise courage, for it is balanced and supported by the Inner Smile and the skills of holding and healing distress. The toughest and most poignant case I have observed is that of a woman who as a child endured consistent sexual abuse from her parents. When I first met her, she just wanted to feel good. As she went into the endorphin flow and connection, she increasingly realized how deep her wounds were. She then used the strategies in this book as a foundation and went into various forms of therapy to meet and clear her terrible history.

Several years later, I was stunned when she told me that she had spent an enjoyable Christmas with her parents. A part of me could hardly believe her.

'You sat on the same sofa watching television?' I asked.

'Yes – and it was completely fine,' she reassured me.

Some inner wounds and patterns can be transformed in a twinkle of an eye, but others take so much longer. To bring a full cellular experience of endorphins into the traumatized area may take years. It is important to be realistic about the timing, to safeguard yourself against possible disappointment and to prepare yourself for the sustained work that is needed.

In my own life, I once became aware of some emotional grief stuck like a ball of concrete in my solar plexus. Despite years of talk therapy and self-reflective meditation I had no idea what it was about. All I could do was keep on loving it, cradling it and moving energy through it. Over the years, it finally warmed and began to dissolve. I am still not clear about its source.

Given how deep and difficult some of your wounds may be, it is a sensible strategy to be aware of when you might need support from a friend, colleague or therapist. There are times when wise, friendly companionship can be invaluable. Do not be proud about getting support when it is needed. (A friend of mine, a psychotherapist, once lived in an area of the United States where, he said, people would rather go to prison than see a therapist.) It is better to use the tools that are available than to stagnate as an emotional dinosaur. (You can always contact us for further support or advice. See Appendix.)

The Butterfly Effect

Please, never get so overwhelmed or despondent that you think it is not worthwhile pursuing the exercises. You may feel that you lack the motivation or stamina to do them properly and that it is therefore not worth doing them at all. Don't feel like this. It is when you are in crisis or in trouble that you really need to keep up your practice.

Remember the Butterfly Effect of chaos science. One flap of the wing can create a typhoon on the other side of the globe. A small initial event can have a tremendous long-term effect, even if the short-term gains seem minimal. The slightest use of these strategies is better than none. The slightest attempt to trigger endorphins, to remember your location in a universe beyond Blobsville, to smile internally, can create the minuscule leverage that ultimately sets change rolling.

Even in your worst mood, on a day when you are cursing all creation, you need to remember the power of a small gesture in the right direction. Remember the power in the tiniest act of connection. The slightest glimmer of a good vibration may unfold to redeem the whole situation. What a terrible mood needs is a glimpse of light at the end of the tunnel. What a person in depression or crisis needs is a ray of hope.

The Two Styles

You also need to remember that there are two styles for doing this work, and to know which style is right on which occasion. Like a good martial artist you need to know when to push forward and when to give way. These two styles can be compared like this:

• Ying	• Yang
• Passive	• Expressive
• Retreat	• Advance
• Soft	• Hard
• Yield	• Push

The soft style

This style is that of the conscious retreat, which was described fully in Chapter 7. In this mode, you consciously allow yourself to withdraw from the world of activity and relationships. You choose to 'fall' down into yourself and retreat fully from a world that gives you no pleasure. Contained in your own space and energy field, you then begin to play with your strawberries, Inner Smile and Curled Deer, and allow the endorphins to flow and the good vibrations to come into you.

The hard style

The other style is expressive and upbeat. You simply cut through any inert energy or attitude and connect actively, expansively and positively with the strawberries and the beauty of life. It is obviously the style that is easiest when you are feeling healthy, strong and positive. It was epitomized for me by Sir George Trevelyan, a handsome man with a large white handlebar moustache and one of the fathers of the holistic movement in Britain. He used to describe how he woke up in the morning. He said that he sprang out of bed, threw the windows wide open whatever the weather, spread his arms wide, took in a huge breath and then exclaimed in a round, loud and echoing voice, 'Welcome! Welcome! Oh, wonderful day!'

The expressive style does not need to be followed in quite so extrovert a fashion. Some people can only greet the day with enthusiasm two hours and a cappuccino later. But it is the style that accompanies a strong, centred and positive attitude.

Choosing the right style: basic guidelines

In general I would suggest using:

- The extrovert expressive style when feeling up and positive
- The introvert, contained style when feeling down and negative.

When you are feeling down, I do not want you thinking that you should be singing arias on mountain tops. When you are up, I do not want you feeling that you have to retreat boringly down into yourself. Do what is right for your mood.

Working with Your Mood

But you do need to notice that you have changing moods. Observe your personal rhythm – when are you in an expressive positive mood and when are you more inclined to retreat?

If you can identify the pulse and inclination of your own personality, it can really help you choose your style. For example, when travelling to work, is it best for you to be in retreat or advance – staying quiet within yourself or aware of the things of beauty around you?

Here are a few questions that will help you recognize your own rhythm and decide when best to use the yin or yang approach.

- In what mood do you wake up?
- When do you begin to get tired at night?
- When do you like to wake up?
- When do you like to start work?
- How often do you like to take a break?
- When do you like eating?
- Do you like to rest after eating?
- How long a working day suits you?
- How long does it take you to relax at the end of the day?
- On what days of the week do you work best?
- When do you get fed up with work?
- When do you relax at weekends?
- How often do you need exercise?
- How often do you need an outing?
- Do you have a monthly rhythm of moods?
- Does the lunar cycle affect you?
- Are you affected by the weather?

- Do astrological influences affect you?
- Are you affected by your biorhythms?
- Do the seasons affect you?
- Do religious festivals and public holidays, such as Easter, Ramadan or Jewish New Year affect you?
- How often do you need a holiday or long rest?
- Are there points in the year or month when you regularly get ill?

In general, I have suggested that when you are tired or in crisis, you should curl up and use the technique of conscious retreat. And when feeling good, you should expand positively to widen the connection.

> **Tired, withdrawn, overwhelmed –> Turn inwards, retreat into yourself and the Curled Deer. Then softly use strawberries and the connection.**
>
> **Energized, extrovert, flowing –> Pause and embrace everything fully and enthusiastically.**
>
> **Balanced and centred –> Use both approaches together as best suits you.**

But it may often be useful to go against these guidelines. For example, if you tend to wake in a bad mood, perhaps you need to try cutting dramatically through it by jumping out of bed, greeting the day and noticing the things you love. Equally, if you are always bubbling and extrovert, perhaps it is time to start experimenting with a more contained style. There will be times, for example, when you are tired and feeling sorry for yourself and what you really need is to dance or walk or go to see a friend or a movie. Move your energy. There will also be times when you are feeling energized and active, and what you really need is to slow and centre in your Curled Deer. Centre and nurture yourself.

I cannot know what is best for you as an individual, but I do know that it is healthy to be able to use both styles and to experiment with them to discover when each is most useful for you. They are both basic life skills and to be able to do only one of them, and not the other, is not balanced.

CHAPTER 13:

The Hero at Work and at Home

Emotional and Energetic Intelligence

In this chapter I shall outline how the Endorphin Effect strategies can be used in all aspects of your daily life, to benefit yourself and those around you. In particular, they create the foundation for a high level of emotional intelligence and provide effective new life skills for self-management and working with others.

The crucial importance of emotional intelligence is well recognized. Daniel Goleman's research, for example, has demonstrated that the leading performers in all working situations are those whose emotional intelligence quotient is high even if their intellectual intelligence is not. In his book *Emotional Intelligence*, he writes:

> ❝ For star performance in all jobs, in every field, emotional competence is twice as important as purely cognitive abilities. For success at the highest levels, in leadership positions, emotional competence accounts for virtually the entire advantage . . . . Given that emotional competencies make up two thirds or more of

the ingredients of star performers, the data suggests that finding people who have these abilities, or nurturing them in existing employees, adds tremendous value to an organization's bottom line. But how much? In simple jobs like machine operators or clerks, those in the top 1% with emotional competency were 3 times more productive (by value). For jobs of medium complexity, like sales clerks, or mechanics, a single top emotional competent person was 12 times more productive (by value). **❞** [1]

Emotional intelligence, which provides such startling improvements, contains certain core skills – listening, adaptability, self-honesty, cooperation, empathy and so on. They can be learnt theoretically, but to practise them effectively requires them to be authentic. You simply cannot be adaptable or open to criticism, for example, if you feel bad or anxious.

To demonstrate emotional intelligence requires a basic confidence and personal feelgood. An ongoing healthy endorphin flow and sense of connection provides the most powerful foundation available. In fact, if I list the Endorphin Effect strategies, you can see how they directly transfer into the life skills that are the essence of emotional intelligence.

- With endorphins flowing and the benevolent vitality of the universe anchored down into your cells, it is easy to feel confident and strong.
- With the Curled Deer and Inner Smile, you can stay centred and flexible during crisis, change and urgency.
- Cradling distress, you can positively manage the most extreme disturbance.
- With Unboundaried Dreaming, you give vision, hope and leadership.
- As a centred and connected creature, you are a safe and encouraging presence for all those around you.

These skills make it possible to manage the worst challenges of modern life, such as pressure, changing circumstances, too much new information, fatigue, frustration, uncertainty about the future, a sense of entrapment and conflict. They are replaced with endorphins, connection, vitality and all the positive attributes of this work.

Strong and Flexible

ENDORPHIN
EFFECT

Visionary and Purposeful   **Supportive and Inspiring**

The centre of inner strength from which these attitudes arise produces a very different result from a thoughtless compulsion to achieve. Please note:

- Strong and Flexible is not the same as Pushy and Cunning
- Visionary and Purposeful is not the same as Ambitious and Driven
- Supportive and Inspiring is not the same as Manipulative and Controlling

> **Emotional intelligence requires an authentic foundation of goodwill, which endorphins and the connection provide.**

Genuine Warm Support

If you have a good endorphin base and connection, your body and attitude radiate warm, encouraging support. This warmth is not just attitudinal, conveyed by words and body language, but is also energetic too. People can genuinely sense if someone has friendly, supportive vibrations.

I have never met anyone who cannot occasionally 'sense' the mood of other people. Even before the front door opens, they can feel the mood of their partner or family. The boss's mood can dominate an organization. A cold person can ruin a party.

There is a clear logic here. The physical body is both solid and electromagnetic. The tone of its energy field, like brainwaves, changes according to its emotional mood. Adrenalin or cortesol generate one kind of feeling and resonance. Endorphins generate another. This magnetic tone is then 'felt' by other people.

Looking back at your life, which teachers, colleagues, bosses, friends and relatives do you remember with gratitude? It is almost certain that those who come to mind had a warm attitude towards you. Whether they were pushy or passive, they genuinely sought the best for you – and you could *feel* it.

These people, in my opinion, are life's true heroes. They carry a supportive and positive attitude that endures, especially in times of crisis. They do not drop away when the going gets tough or when there is a period of failure and struggle. They remain constant, seeing the best, supporting and accepting even when things are at their worst. They are good leaders, companions and friends.

This business of warmth is crucial when it comes to teaching, coaching, leading and supporting. If you have ever been coached or given personal tuition, you will know the significant difference between a coach who is genuinely supportive and one who is efficient, but just wants you to acquire the skills as quickly as possible. The warm coach creates a psychological ambience which makes learning easy and humane. The efficient coach can stimulate embarrassment and anxiety in which the learning is tough and unpleasant. I wonder how many people have dropped out of courses or learnt nothing because of their teachers' cold personality.

In ten years of tutoring adults and teenagers with physical and psychological disabilities, I watched at first hand the effect of the other counsellors and teachers. Without exception, the students responded positively to humane warmth and not cleverness. Indeed, some research done in the United States in the 1980s showed that students in adult literacy classes learnt faster with tutors who had relaxed brainwaves than with tutors who were skilful but had more agitated brainwaves.

Benevolent, positive figures are crucial for people's healthy growth and performance. Warm, supportive companions are like sunshine to a plant. Cold companions are like frost – people wither in their presence. We need trainers who boost our self-esteem and make us feel good whilst at the same time cajoling, pushing and inspiring us. We need precisely the same from our bosses, teachers, colleagues and parents.

Carl Rogers, one of the fathers of humanistic psychology and the counselling movement, understood this well and stated that the fundamental key to being a good therapist and counsellor is attitude or quality of presence. Technique and experience were secondary. He identified three key factors that made up this attitude:

- *Positive regard:* Unconditional positive regard and goodwill for the client.
- *Genuine:* Being absolutely genuine and who you really are with the client.
- *Empathic:* Understanding, feeling and being truly sympathetic and present to the client's problems.

Positive regard and empathy are not communicated simply by body language and the spoken word, they are also communicated energetically. People sense their presence.[2]

> If you are in a situation of leading, teaching, caring or supporting, first check your own state and attitude. Monitor how you feel. How you feel spills over. Ensure that you feel good within yourself. This will create a positive, encouraging and productive environment.

Warmth in Organizations

A positive radiation is crucial when it comes to creating a productive and enjoyable team. People can sense if you are genuinely on their side or whether you want better performance or different behaviour just because it serves you and the organization. A genuine positive regard for your companions will create an organizational culture in which people feel valued. This will make it safe for them to accept change, take risks, be creative and generally fulfil their potential while also benefiting the whole situation.

Organizations and communities function well when people communicate clearly and listen carefully. This cannot happen if the atmosphere is filled with hostility, competition and resentment. Most of us are only too familiar with what a dysfunctional home or workplace feels like. The moment you go into that environment, stress hormones begin to run, your body starts to tense and there is an expectation of conflict. This interferes with clear thought and can create a spiralling situation of resentment. Creating a safe and encouraging atmosphere is the fundamental solution.

> **A modern organization is dealing with an ever-changing environment.**
> **Modern leaders must therefore create a warm, flowing environment.**
> **This does not mean that you drop goals or the pursuit of excellence.**
> **It means that you understand that safe, happy colleagues will deliver what is needed most effectively, creatively and productively.**

Strawberries at Work

People who support others, but who do not receive support themselves, often burn out. If you are going to radiate warmth to others, you need a solid endorphin flow and connection that does not stop when you are at work. So bring your strawberries into work. Make sure that you have ways of making the connection inside your work environment and that you do not forget to use them. You need images and reminders of strawberries, just the thought of which is enough to give you pleasure and make you smile. You also need the self-discipline to pause and use them.

A therapist came to me one day to discuss a patient whose presence overwhelmed him. He did not know why, but there was something about this person that made him anxious and agitated, even frightened. In such conditions he obviously could not create a therapeutic ambience.

We decided to experiment with a very simple strategy. He would move his chair so that he could see out of the window when working. The sky and clouds were strawberries for him. When he started to feel overwhelmed, he would withdraw his attention from the patient, calm his breath and look out of the window. He would pause and allow the sky and clouds to trigger his endorphins and connection. He would breathe in their comfort, use his Inner Smile and affirm his Curled Deer.

It worked. When he used this simple method to stabilize himself he became able to care for his patient.

Desk tops, walls and screen-savers can all be used to carry images of the places, people and activities which, if you pause with them, will take you into the flow. Wealthy and powerful people instinctively use these strategies. Their offices are usually comfortable cocoons that support them. They have the largest rooms and the best views – and because they control their own time, they can enjoy them.

> **Be practical about bringing strawberries into your workplace. Pause and use them for your benefit. Replenish your energy and give to others.**

The Skill of 'Holding' a Situation

The amount of safety and encouragement you radiate can be pumped up by consciously deploying the strategy of 'holding' the situation. This is very similar to the technique of accepting and cradling your own distress. In this case, however, from a strong and connected centre you switch on your Inner Smile and then expand your kind and compassionate attitude so that it encircles and cradles the situation and people around you. We are talking here about a definite energetic effect. Your positive energy field expands to surround the people you are with, and it helps to make them feel safe and welcomed.

EXERCISE IN HOLDING A SITUATION

The basic strategy is very simple. It comes from a strong personal centre where your Inner Smile and Curled Deer feel comfortable.

You need also to be aware of your true environment – earth, nature, sun, universe – and allow yourself to be connected and supported.

With kind eyes and a compassionate heart, imagine, sense and feel that from your torso – from your hips, abdomen and chest – you are softly radiating a warm and safe energy. It extends like wings from either side of you. It must feel completely relaxed.

This warm and loving energy radiates and encircles the situation.

You do absolutely nothing except hold the situation in your warm and supportive energy field.

Some people instinctively and unconsciously hold situations. They are solid and have a basic attitude of goodwill. They are patient. They have a sympathetic awareness of what is happening. They are tolerant of human weakness. They encourage the quiet ones to speak, and mellow out the noisy ones. In many tribal situations this is the role of the elders, who often remain silent through important meetings but in fact are actively holding the tribe and creating a safe and encouraging atmosphere.

If a difficult situation is not held, speedy people can precipitate stupid and thoughtless events. In political psychology it is well

known that groups of people, especially in crisis, can slip very easily into a state called 'groupthink'. In the urgent atmosphere, they
stop thinking clearly and put their excited energy behind any course
of action with which they all agree. This leads to blinkered and stupid decisions. Groups need people who can keep them centred and
calm. This is invisible but highly effective work.

I learnt the skill of holding through a dream. I was about to host
a week-long gathering of one hundred strong individuals, each with
their own agenda and nearly all of them group leaders in their own
right. I wanted to create a very open and flexible event, but this
would be difficult to achieve if the participants wanted more structure or were impatient. I was nervous.

Then, a few weeks before the event, I had a dream in which I
found myself in a very pleasant jungle, having fun with a family of
gorillas. Suddenly, the mother of all gorillas appeared and sat
directly opposite me. She looked into my eyes with incredible kindness and telepathically communicated, 'Do it like this.'

She held her arms out wide as if cradling some huge object. But
in her heart and mind she was cradling me and my energy field. I
could sense a wave of love and warmth radiating from her stomach
and torso, moving all around me and cradling me. Her *hara* was
strong, warm and loving. Her aura penetrated into the cells of my
body. She could hold and cradle any trouble or crisis. All the time,
her eyes remained smiling and compassionate. 'Do the same with
the group,' she told me.

I put the practice into effect and the conference was successful.

You can practise the art of holding in many situations, especially
those that might otherwise irritate you, and experiment with how it
changes both your mood and the atmosphere around you.
Supermarkets, post offices, traffic and bank queues are great places
to practise. (A post office counter clerk once said to me, 'When it
feels bad on your side of the counter, it's worse on our side. So
please extend the holding warmth to include us as well.')

Several people I know who run businesses spend time every day
strolling around their workplaces. Their sole purpose is to generate
an attentive warmth. In their offices, they also sit quietly and energetically holding their situations. Employees do not feel intruded
upon, but cared for. Holding a situation is the very opposite of

controlling. Its essence is to create a safe atmosphere which actively *allows* creativity and innovation.

> **If you have responsibility for a situation, then extend the warmth of your energy field to hold and cradle it. This mature activity will actively support everyone involved, encouraging creativity and emotional intelligence.**

In Healthcare

I would like to quote from two letters that illustrate the practical relevance of this work in healthcare. They are both from coaches who have trained with me in core energy management. The first is from Hilary Thomas, a nurse working in a geriatric ward:

> ❛ At work, I've been using the strategies with the patients and it does help them to relax in stressful situations. For example, on Monday I was with a gentleman with cancer of the larynx who needed a nasogastric tube passed because he is unable to swallow even liquids. This is normally done in an operating theatre but as it was an oncology emergency it was done on the unit. As you can imagine, the patient was very agitated and frightened (having already experienced the ordeal a few days previously).
>
> I was able to get him to trust me enough to follow my instructions and got him to breathe into his lower abdomen while the registrar was passing the tube. At the same time I connected with my strawberries and a sense of it happening perfectly, and I could feel the presence of peace and calm. The patient could feel it as well – I am sure of that – and he managed to swallow the tube without too much distress. Even the doctor

complimented me afterwards on how easily I calmed him down. **,**

The second is from Michael Epple, a medical doctor practising as a psychotherapist.

' My personal experience is that in general it helps me from getting lost in "Blobsville" in my everyday life and being more consciously aware of the cosmos, of nature, of my strawberries. There are times when the exercises don't work immediately, but if I go on practising, at least after a few days the flow, the bliss, the golden honey … are with me again. And sometimes it's just a thought, a little pause, a breath – and immediately it shifts. I more and more find that the kind of thoughts my brain is producing just depend on what is going on in that body of mine down there. If the body is bathed in adrenalin, there are fearful thoughts, sorrow, anger and so on. If the body is bathing in endorphins, there is less thinking and the thoughts are peaceful, calm and dealing with nice and pleasant things.

In my work, I have been using a lot of different elements of core energy management with different patients. Every time that I have used one or more techniques, it has been helpful, especially with "difficult" clients for whom other approaches had not been helpful. It is amazing. They often react to the exercises and my explanations about them in a way that shows me that they spontaneously feel understood and accepted, and that I understand their problem and am offering them the appropriate tool/answer that helps them deal with it. **,**

Flexible

Family and work life can be really challenging with their constant stimulation, demands and pressure. Bringing the core energy and endorphin flow deep into your bones and nervous system produces an underlying strength and vitality to carry you through difficult times. It will help you feel good regardless of pressured circumstances and this will create a general hum of flexibility. One thing is certain: it is always easier to be flexible when you feel well and strong.

Nevertheless, there will probably still be occasions that irritate and upset you and make it especially difficult to remain open and flexible: someone is rude; you are misunderstood; there are too many urgent demands. In these situations, you feel your body tensing with irritability and an unpleasant reaction. You either release it into the situation, attacking other people and spreading the negativity, or you sit on it and it rumbles along inside you, pickling you in frozen adrenalin and cortesol – which is also horrible for you and those around you. Sitting in these frozen hormones is not a good place from which to radiate humane warmth or to hold a situation.

It is in times of particular stress that you can use the strategies of the Inner Smile, Curled Deer and conscious retreat. Do not react to provocation. Turn within. Look after yourself. This sequence needs to be put into action as soon as you notice the provocation. Comfort your body. Keep it feeling calm and protected. You can then look at the situation and choose an appropriate strategy rather than being controlled by your emotional reactivity.

Do not waste energy responding and fighting.

> **You cannot hold a situation if you yourself are wobbling. Connect. Hold yourself. Then hold others.**

Imagine a stressed parent preparing the evening meal. One of the children suddenly behaves atrociously. The parent feels stung and angry, and there is an immediate choice. Blow your top and set in motion a whole train of hysterical events that will consume more time and energy – you will have made the situation worse by becoming a victim of your own reaction. Or pause, breathe into your lower stomach, think of a strawberry, come into your Curled Deer and comfort your own distress. The core energy strategy places the real power and authority back with you.

Again, imagine a stressed office where everyone is working to tight deadlines and dealing with too many people and too much information. Someone comes to you – it does not matter whether it is a messenger or the boss – and dumps some extra task on you in a manner that is both thoughtless and rude. Within a split second, you are flooded with a defensive/aggressive feeling. If it was the boss who brought you the message, you probably keep quiet, stomach your feelings and stew; perhaps you pass them on to your partner or family when you get home. If it was a lowly messenger, you might bawl him out immediately and perpetuate the bad energy.

And there is the third strategy. The moment that you notice your negative reaction, turn within and comfort yourself. Send endorphins to the reaction. Acknowledge your distress and cradle the reaction. Then respond from a place of choice. Exercise your spiritual muscles and be emotionally literate. For general strength and flexibility, keep on working with your strawberries and connection. In provocative situations, immediately notice how your body is feeling. Pause. Turn your attention within. Breathe. Switch on your Inner Smile. Cradle yourself and your distress. Strengthen your Curled Deer.

PREPARING FOR PROVOCATIVE SITUATIONS

If you find yourself having to handle many provocative situations, it can be worthwhile rehearsing how you want to manage them.

Sit quietly and let your mind travel forward and begin to contemplate what the situation will be like. Allow yourself to imagine the worst case scenario in which someone or something might cause you real distress.

Imagine and *feel* yourself remaining centred, absolutely not reacting. All that you do is turn your attention inwards.

Switch on your Inner Smile.

Check your Curled Deer.

Make sure that you are cradling any distress.

Allow your awareness to go beyond Blobsville and give yourself permission to let in the benevolence of the earth, nature, the sun and the universe.

Keep your *hara* strong and stay centred.

Clearly imagine and kinaesthetically sense yourself staying in that mood in the provocative situation. The unpleasant stuff is happening around you, but you are behaving and communicating in the way that you want to.

You are fully centred and in control of your own feelings, attitude and behaviour.

Rehearse this as many times as you want, until you feel confident.

Holding the Vision

The strategy of Unboundaried Dreaming can also be used practically and effectively in all aspects of your life. This technique works so well because the dreaming is supported and dynamized by your endorphins and your sense of the universe's benevolent and creative flow. There is no greater support.

The dream anchors in a real here-and-now experience of the fulfilled future. Your mind and imagination need to *know* the dream, but every cell in your body needs to *feel* it. It is easier, for example, to make money if you already feel wealthy. It is easier to win a race if you already feel like a winner. You need therefore to maintain both the vision and the sensation of its fulfilment. In this way, you create and sustain an earthed energy field of the dream. It is not just an idea in your brain cells, but is fuelled by universal energy and exists as an aura that you carry with you.

Great leaders, friends and colleagues always have an Unboundaried Dream. They maintain a clear vision and sense of how things will turn out for the best. Friends and good parents also always see the best in you. Gardeners, even while planting seeds or dealing with crises of bad weather or infestation, always have an inner picture of the perfectly grown plant. This is what Carl Rogers meant by the unconditional positive regard that therapists should have for their clients: whilst working with their difficulties, they still see the very best in them.

Effective leaders continuously put forward a purposeful vision and their charisma comes from the fact that they really *experience* that it is possible. Somewhere in their psyche the project is already complete, successful and fulfilled. Their communications are filled with a power and authenticity that is more than just a mental idea. It radiates from every cell of their being.

And they hold the energy of the fulfilled project whatever the circumstances. When times are tough, good leaders and companions do not get lost in pessimism or in short-sighted reactions to immediate stimuli. They do not get lost in the imprisoning dynamics of Blobsville. They know the troubles will pass. All organizations, families and projects need people who maintain and hold the vision. The beauty of this approach is that, even when your family, friends or colleagues are in a negative mood or depressive crisis, you hold and feel the vision of their fulfilment. You hold it psychologically and energetically even if they themselves have temporarily lost it.

Be clear about this. If in a crisis your emotional, mental and energetic attitude is moody and negative, you yourself are feeding bad energy into the situation. A group in crisis needs people who maintain the vision.

Nelson Mandela and Winston Churchill, for example, were great leaders precisely because in the darkest hours they did not lose their hope and vision. Their Unboundaried Dreams of a positive future were fully anchored in every aspect and cell of their being. It could be no other way for them. I dare to suggest that they also felt that the flow of the cosmos was on their side in their struggles with oppressive forces. The benevolent, liberating creativity of the universe could not tolerate the constraints of racism and fascism.

> **For any project with family, friends or work, make certain that you have a clear vision of how perfectly fulfilled it can be. Make sure that you have a body-based kinaesthetic sense of its fulfilment. Whatever the circumstances, hold this vision for the project.**

HOLDING THE VISION

THE FIRST STEP

Go into your connection.

When you are feeling comfortable, allow your mind to be aware of the greater environment.

Remember that everything is always changing and emerging anew. Everything is in flow and everything is in the process of unfolding to its full potential.

THE SECOND STEP

Allow your colleagues, family and friends to come into your mind.

Stay very calm and holding the Inner Smile.

Allow yourself to imagine all of them growing and unfolding perfectly.

This is Unboundaried Dreaming. Think the best of them. Imagine them all as being totally perfect and wonderful.

Stay for a while with this vision and experience of them.

Allow this experience to land in your body.

Tell yourself that you will not forget this experience of them and that you will hold this vision.

THE THIRD STEP

Staying in the connection and the mood of Unboundaried Dreaming, allow yourself to imagine just how extraordinarily wonderful your business or family or organization could be.

Allow yourself to imagine this team humming perfectly.

Allow yourself a complete Unboundaried Dream and experience of the group's potential.

Stay deeply relaxed as you observe this wonderful dream.

Allow the experience to fall into your body.

Tell yourself that you will not forget this and that you will hold the vision.

THE FOURTH STEP

Staying in the connection, be compassionate and understanding about the challenges of human reality.

Recognize that achieving this dream in real life may take effort.

It will certainly require your support, your goodwill and your holding.

See what immediate and congruent next steps you could take to ground the vision.

Holding Both the Situation and the Vision

We have described two kinds of holding.

- *Holding people:* From your torso, you radiate a warmth that energetically cradles and holds the individual or group, making people feel safe and encouraged.
- *Holding the vision:* In your mind and in your whole cellular being, you hold the vision and the sensation of the project's perfect fulfilment.

To be really effective, they need to be practised together. If you want people to cooperate with a vision, you need also to hold them as human beings. This means that you are a good visionary and a good people person.

This combination can be practised both for one-off events and for long-term projects. Let me give a very practical example of a single event – a family moving home. This is a time of high tension. After the fear of death and public speaking, moving home is said to be the most stressful experience in people's lives. (The fourth most stressful was preparing for a vacation.)

The move can be prepared for well in advance. Sitting calmly in an endorphin flow, you envision and physically experience everyone behaving perfectly; the whole procedure of packing and closing down your old home happens harmoniously, happily and efficiently. The transportation is smooth. The arrival in your new home is easy, efficient and comfortable. The new home is heaven. Everything is unpacked and arranged. All is wonderful. You hardly notice the bother of it at all.

This whole scenario needs to be carefully rehearsed and run through your imagination and body many times, until you feel that you clearly and confidently have the full vision and experience. At the same time, you begin to extend your energy field so that it warmly holds your family and the removal men; you envision yourself continuing to hold the family during the actual move.

When the actual move comes, you are absolutely ready – holding the family, holding the removal men, radiating from every cell of your body that the move has been successful and easy. Even if a crisis does happens and you feel distressed, your first reaction is to cradle your distress rather than blast off or stew in acid. Having managed yourself, you continue to steer the situation.

The preparation means that you carry the vision on a great tidal wave of intention and energy that you have built up over time. When there are difficulties, the wave itself carries you. Whether you take an explicit leadership role or not, your whole demeanour is dynamized and oriented towards that fulfilment.

Let's look at an example. A friend and CEM coach runs a property development company in London. With his partner, he owns several buildings that provide rented accommodation. His intention is to be the best landlord in the world, providing great apartments to satisfied tenants. This vision is anchored fully in his psyche and body. Nothing will alter it.

One day a phone call comes through to his office from one of his apartments that is shared by a group of postgraduate researchers from abroad. They need a larger refrigerator and are calling to ask for advice on where best to buy one. Without hesitation he buys them a large new fridge and installs it for nothing. Before working with the Endorphin Effect and Unboundaried Dreaming, he was a mean, profit driven businessman. But now, he asks, how can he be the best landlord in the world if he does not provide suitably sized fridges?

Of course, he is never short of people wanting to rent from him or do business with him. He is prosperous and other people are benefiting – he is both making money and doing good. But his work ethos and generosity derive from an inner attitude that is endorphin-based and connected to the wider flow of life. His happiness would continue even if his business did not.

Another friend works in the non-profit sector, building community projects. Sometimes these take a very long time to form, but he determinedly holds the vision and the group for years until the projects are realized. His wife says that he is like a medieval cathedral builder – patient and understanding that the fruits of his labour may not be complete until after his death.

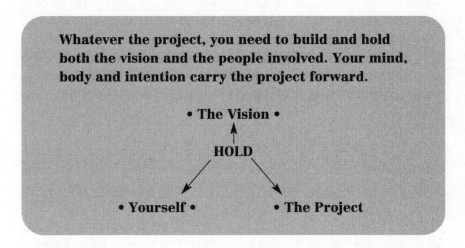

Whatever the project, you need to build and hold both the vision and the people involved. Your mind, body and intention carry the project forward.

Clarifying an Organization's Vision

Unboundaried Dreaming can also be used in corporate and organizational situations for developing a common vision, team-building and problem solving.

My colleague Ashley Akin-Smith uses this procedure in the most commercial and demanding of situations – when large organizations are purchasing new information technology systems. There is always a struggle here as the visionaries compete with the realists and everyone battles to protect their turf and future jobs – and they are all, of course, battling with the finance director.

To clarify the vision and next steps Ashley calls into the meeting all the key players, usually a group of between twelve and sixteen people. Without any unnecessary preamble, she takes them all through a quick relaxation procedure and facilitates them using their strawberries to make the connection. One of the features of working with a group is that the core energy field builds up very quickly and groups usually slip easily into a connected and very supportive atmosphere. This can be done with or without explaining the whole package of how the endorphins are triggered or the connection made.

The group is then led into dreaming and envisioning for their organization the most wonderful and perfect IT system in the cosmos, a system which suits and serves everyone, adding value to all facets of the organization and maximizing everyone's productive and creative potential. To loosen up the group's creative power and to go into an unboundaried space beyond Blobsville, Ashley encourages the team to imagine what this IT system would look like if it were a fantastic animal or a cartoon space vehicle, or a dragon with many brains and wings, or a luxury liner that can both fly and fit in your pocket.

In silence, everyone does their envisioning.

This is followed by an open brainstorming session as people share their magnificent visions, sometimes creating a huge diagram of their amazing machine or beast. Three-dimensional reality, the laws of physics and budgets are not part of the discussion. This process is creative, liberating and very effective at communicating absolutely relevant needs and potentials. The players get to express clearly but mythically what they want, and everyone is allowed to co-create the product. This is a win-win team-building process. Because the mind is in a free and multi-dimensional space, it is not limited by the usual psychological and organizational constraints. Many more options and opportunities can now be seen.

Although it is an imaginary beast, all present understand that every aspect is symbolic of an actual need or real life idea. But in this imaginary world in which everyone is enjoying themselves – like children building a sandcastle or playing with Lego – they can all *cooperatively* hear and play with each other's ideas. In this world of endorphin-supported Unboundaried Dreaming there are no limited resources for which they have to compete and there is no organizational culture to which they must conform.

> **Resources – the resources of the imagination and of the connection – are infinite.**

When the fantastic envisioning is complete, only then, do they get on with the actual work of interpreting and grounding the vision in a workable model and seeing how to turn it into reality. But again this is not done via the usual tense, competitive negotiations of office politics. The group is taken back through their strawberries – very often football victories – into a relaxed and connected state. They are allowed to contemplate and feel into their creature, their plan. Staying in the calm atmosphere, each member of the group is invited to look at what she or he can do immediately to bring that vision into actuality.

They then come out of the relaxed state and all listen carefully and patiently to each other, as each person talks about what she or he could do next to implement the strategy. This is not a brainstorm but careful listening. Within an ambience of cooperation, the group hears every member. Some very realistic assessment and negotiation follow.

The major part of this process, however, can be done in less than a day and save an organization months of internal consulting and confusion. Moreover, all interested parties feel as though they have fairly and fully engaged in a major decision. Having created the vision together, they also hold the vision together as they go into the future.

If the team is also holding the group and cradling the members' own problems, it becomes a very emotionally intelligent team capable of truly excellent work. Sometimes, of course, this happens naturally in groups. There is a shared vision, a loyal and caring team, and it is heaven to work with them.

A Friendly Warning

This process of leading a team in Unboundaried Dreaming sounds straightforward, so you might want to try leading one yourself in an organization. Be cautious.

Group dynamics can be very tempestuous. If you have no experience of leading groups that contain conflicting ideas and personalities, you may be overwhelmed by the fall-out. You must be fully able to hold both yourself and the group, and the vision of the group's success.

Sex For Pleasure and For Healing

And now, from the office to the boudoir. Why not? Let us focus briefly on lovemaking, an amazing source of endorphins and pleasure. The Endorphin Effect strategies can be used to deepen that pleasure.

The trick here, as with all endorphin work, is to pause, notice the pleasure and allow it in more deeply. Imagine first of all that, that before you go into the bedroom, you have spent some calm time working with your strawberries, centring in your Inner Smile and Curled Deer. You have also opened your imagination to an Unboundaried Dream of how beautiful, exciting and satisfying the lovemaking will be. You then go into the bedroom with your energy affectionately and warmly holding the space and your partner. At the same time, you hold a kinaesthetic sense of how perfect it will be.

With care and affection, you then begin to connect with your partner. The love, the energy, the erotic sensation and the pleasure begin to flow. Then, when the pleasure begins to become exquisite, you stop moving and pause. You and your partner are in the middle of a great strawberry experience – erotic endorphins. Pause, relax a fraction more and allow the pleasurable flow to enter you more deeply. Circulate and guide the golden energy. Guide it through your body and energy field into and out of your partner's.

Then allow yourself to open even more and let the benevolent wave fields of earth, nature, the sun and universe come into the two of you. After a while you will feel the need to move again, so allow yourself to go back into physical rhythm. Pause again as often as you like.

Then at the moment of orgasm, pause again, surrender yourselves completely to the flood of endorphins and open yourselves to the beauty, power and benevolence of all life. If you do this together you will have a profound, erotic, ecstatic and healing experience.

In Practice

From a senior executive in a media group.

❝ Having been promoted to lead a larger team I have to use my core energy skills daily in this speedy and high-powered media environment. Whether it is team-building or managing a busy enquiry desk, the strategies help me to stay centred and focussed. In a quiet, discreet way they have helped me to "walk my talk" by empowering me to challenge the status quo – to envision and bring into being a workplace where creativity, connectedness, compassion and clarity sit at the core. I would be a nervous wreck without it. ❞

From a senior manager in a national museum

❝ My job is to care for a national art collection and I manage a department of sixty-five people. I use the Endorphin Effect and am constantly aware of being grounded, breathing and in my body, especially when under pressure. I often manage to get problems into perspective by holding onto the larger picture and being connected despite the immediate crisis. Before I enter any potentially difficult situation, I set it up energetically, assure myself of a positive outcome and try to work subtly with the dynamic of the group. I try to support my staff by actively listening and encouraging them to envision ways in which they could be happy and fulfilled in their work. ❞

From a senior civil servant

❝ In my corporate work in government and in the media, core energy management enables me to 'control the temperature' in energetic terms of what is going on around me and to adjust my own behaviour accordingly. It has given me a new pair of eyes with which to see my colleagues. My heightened awareness of their needs and wants allows me to work with them more effectively, with greater sensitivity and less selfishness. The net result is that people are seeking me out more and more for advice, ideas and vision. **9**

> **The greatest gift that you bring into any situation is your own supportive and encouraging energy and vision.**

You Are the Strawberry

If you give yourself permission to experience the flow of endorphins and absorb the core connection, you inevitably become a magnificent person. The logic is infallible. The power and benevolence of nature and the universe are flowing into and through you. Centred and content, connected and with an attitude of goodwill, you quietly radiate a strong and benevolent atmosphere into your environment. You bring creative flow into any situation. You may not be the extrovert life and soul of a party, but energetically your presence is a profound blessing in any situation. Your colleagues and friends may never speak of it or actively thank you, but your presence always supports and encourages them. This attitude also expresses itself in your relationship with nature and the environment.

CHAPTER 14:

A New Life, a New World

The Primordial Soup

Sometimes I look at a person and I see a mammal made up of millions of cells. I then remember that the most basic single-celled organism is capable of producing endorphins. I find myself smiling at the idea of a happy single-celled organism, wallowing in neuropeptides of feelgood. It cannot add two and two or distinguish between the *Mona Lisa* and a Spice Girl, but it feels good.

Many millions of years ago there was a primordial soup out of which the biological life of our planet evolved. Who knows what it was really like and what actually happened? But it would seem clear that those single-celled organisms, which can manufacture endorphins, were amongst the first to emerge. In fact, we could safely hazard that endorphins were ingredients in that primordial soup. Built into the origins of biological life on earth is the experience of pleasure.

So, here we are – modern humanity. Very sophisticated, very civilized, very high tech. But our biological ancestry reaches far back into the ocean of that thick, steaming, potent liquid and we still carry its initial imprint. The evidence beneath the skin is overwhelming – from the red blood and gastric juices to the oozing marrow, the great soup continues within us.

We have here a great paradox. Human beings are simultaneously extravagant cultural beings and primitive life forms. At one extreme we might put Louis XIV with his Versailles Palace, poodles and wigs, at the other extreme, we can perceive people as blobs of organic juice oscillating from mood to mood.

Many people find it difficult to appreciate the beauty of their biology. There is even a Buddhist mantra, which is supposed to help people grasp the nature of reality, which runs: I am a sack of skin filled with unpleasant things. I used it myself for a while. Many other religious sects also dislike the physical organism, the body.

In its own way, modern culture teaches us the same thing. We give attention to our creations beyond the skin: cars, clothes, homes, televisions; movies, music, fashion, lifestyle and celebrities; careers, mortgages, relationships, families, projects and organizations; sport, music, art, science, dance. And we ignore the juices.

But it is in the juices that we feel our moods and recognize how we respond, for example, to beauty. The mood in this case is a form of consciousness, perhaps even a foundation, of consciousness – for it allows us to feel our response to beauty. The thinking mind that observes the feeling is perhaps just an over-rated commentator.

To all of this, a neuroscientist would nod, 'Of course!' because in the worldview of biology we are indeed *only* biological creatures.

Weird But Beautiful

Normally, because I am so engaged in psychological and spiritual development, I dislike the academic schools of sociobiology, behaviourism and evolutionary psychology. They assert that we can understand human behaviour, development and motivation if we focus on human biology and evolution. This, of course, is true from some perspectives. But it can also be a crude analysis if it is applied to the deep suffering or ecstatic genius that people experience. This biological approach also can have little sympathy or support for the abused and disenfranchised. What else, it might say, would you expect in a society of apes?

The biological approach also suggests that human beings learn how to behave through responding to punishment and reward. Suck on the breast in a certain way and you are rewarded. Defecate in the wrong place and you are punished. And so on. Again, that explanation may be part of why people behave the way they do, but it is so restricted, mechanical and unappreciative of how eccentric, different and weird human beings really are.

It is, I hope, obvious from *The Endorphin Effect* that I deeply appreciate the wonder and complexity of people and the universe. Yet the propositions and strategies of this book are predicated upon the simplest of biological mechanisms. This mechanism is that certain activities and thoughts will reward you with pleasure, through the production of endorphins. Other thoughts and activities will have you linger in tension, pain and apathy. Now, there's a basic behavioural and biological mechanism if ever there was one! Pain/No Endorphins. Pleasure/Endorphins.

Of course, the triggers that stimulate the production of endorphin are incredibly variable, discriminating and filled with psychological and cultural influences. But beneath the differences there is always the same mechanism, the delivery or non-delivery of endorphins.

Star Dust

Not just in beautiful mountains or when looking at the stars or making love, but in any place at any time endorphins can flood you into the soup of primordial pleasure. Within that pleasure, by virtue of that ancient and shared biological mechanism, you are in a state of solidarity with nature.

But there is more than that. All things on earth and in our solar system are coagulated stardust, which came from the mysterious explosion or breath that brought this universe into existence. This is not romance, but solid fact. Where else did all matter – the atoms and molecules, particles and waves, including those in our bodies – come from? Once there was nothing and then there was creation. The unassailable logic is that every cell, particle and atom derives from this same cosmic source. We are stardust.

How perfect and logical, then, that when people flood with endorphins they not only experience a harmonic and pleasurable connection with nature, but feel the same way about the universe. Everything is included in the package of ecstatic pleasure.

I cannot prove that the endorphin flood is an energetic vibration that descants through every energy field of the cosmos, though I am sure that Pythagoras could have proved it with his theories of harmony. But you simply cannot ignore the fact that pleasure spills over into a profound sense of beautiful connection with every aspect of earth and the heavens. This is partly a mental recognition, but it is mainly based in a flood of total knowing that permeates every cell of the body and satisfies your deepest intuitions.

Celebrate the Research

Look, then, at the circle of theory that is now created. We can start with a purely biological approach. But, through observing what actually happens to people when they flood with endorphins, the biological approach to understanding human nature ends up transcending its own biological boundaries. The human creature, in the biochemical state triggered by endorphins, changes consciousness, mood and sensation – and connects beyond itself with all life.

Thus, there is no division between the most basic biology and the metaphysics of a cosmic bliss and consciousness. Biological science has no choice, then, but to expand its focus into the more refined realms of emotional intelligence, psychoanalysis and energy medicine. Indeed, this is happening. I celebrate the fact that we have reached a stage in our evolution when we can be reflective, investigative and conscious of these profoundly important dynamics.

Paradise and Revolution

It is not an original idea, but perhaps the primordial soup is the origin of the myths concerning heaven or paradise. Perhaps that original soup, experienced also in the womb, is the source of a poetic nostalgia for a lost golden age and experience. To satisfy this yearning, people have dreamt of and planned social and cultural utopias, heaven on earth.

But regardless of the possibility of some past paradise, huge crises today are forcing our attention towards building a better world. Thirty thousand children die every day because of an unjust distribution of resources. We face ecological disaster. Warfare. The mad tension of contemporary working life. Both parents forced to work. In our frenzy of population growth and technological innovation, we have managed to create the dysfunctional global society of Blobsville.

Personally, I prefer to take a positive view and even be excited about what we have created. I prefer to believe that it is meaningful. As a species, we have been through an adolescent growth surge and have produced fantastic social, cultural and technological structures. We did not know the problems we would create. We have built great tension into our lives, but this has been a springboard for fantastic human effort.

So, how do we fix all this? To begin with, there must be a recognition that there is a problem. That recognition is growing which is a start at least.

Political and social actions that work to humanize and create a benevolent system should, of course, be initiated and supported. But if we look at history, economics and politics, we have to be realistic. A revolution that ushers in everlasting human paradise would be great, but there have been no revolutions like that. Humanity is always pushing its boulder up the mountain. The juggernauts of global commerce, technology and population growth carry a forceful momentum. There is still greed and bigotry. Humanity still has to work through its mass karma.

So there is another kind of change that is possible, and this is one that lasts. It is the revolutionary change that happens in people's hearts and minds. It then spills over to touch other people, and history can be made.

The Serendipity of Our Age

What incredible timing, then, what serendipity, that just as we face these gargantuan global crises a revolution in information is also happening. Through books, libraries, computers, travel and telecommunications we now live in a global village of free-flowing information. Combinations of knowledge never previously possible are now taking place and giving us new insights into how we are constructed and function. We are now provided with concepts and strategies for managing contemporary reality. Our understanding of human nature and the human condition is quantum leaping. The biological, psychological and energetic/spiritual streams of knowledge that create the holistic understanding of human nature are here. So we have the tools and concepts for creating a revolution in our hearts and minds.

Creating Heaven

Biologically, we never left paradise. The creation of heaven on earth is of course to be found in new social and ecological circumstances, but we will know that it has arrived when everybody feels okay. As a social activist I will work as best I can, along with millions of others, to create those circumstances – but in myself I want to feel okay *now*. Within myself, within the private realm of my own biology and consciousness, I want to reclaim my paradise. This is possible. Change your inner experience and then express yourself as an agent of transformation into the world. This is powerful medicine, for yourself and for everyone else.

Be clear that all this is not a form of evasion, denial or opting out. Finding that personal bliss is accompanied by a deepening compassion and sense of solidarity with all life. Finding that bliss provides the fuel, the flow and the strength to address, understand and be more effective with the realities and suffering around you.

Finding that sense of connection and contentment, once considered mysterious and exclusive, is now a practical project. We understand its structure – endorphins, bioenergetic armour and benevolent vitality. The work is to find pleasure, surrender and allow yourself to feel the kind of cosmos in which you truly live. This is a welcoming project. Become free of the tension and limitations of the purely human environment to sense that you are truly in a benevolent universe. Ultimately, your flow will be continuous and never-ending, but in the first place it will be through ever-deepening gateways.

Whatever kind of life you lead, you have to learn to pause and monitor how you feel. The organ of perception for this job is the whole human body and so you must come into the driver's seat of your own body. Steer the experience. Take responsibility for your own sensations.

A Personal and Social Revolution

This form of self-management is a personal and social revolution. Let me spell out exactly how it works. Our problems, surely, are due to people chasing short-term gratification with no eye on the wider implications. With six billion people on our planet, jostling each other for resources – food, fame or fortune – that are either scarce or unfairly apportioned, it is obvious that not everyone can get what they want. Even as the global economy grows and general wealth expands, the curse of relative deprivation and the need for identity-affirming status symbols remain. As long, therefore, as people depend upon external circumstances to assess whether they are 'happy' and 'successful', we are in danger. Money and status are great, but not if competing for them leads to selfish and destructive behaviour; or if failing to achieve them leads to a sense of failure, anxiety and depression.

The political and social effects of *The Endorphin Effect* strategies are, therefore, obvious. People find a genuine sense of feelgood, security and satisfaction inside themselves. This is not to call for the end of creative competition or of striving for success and achievement. It calls for balance, for a win-win situation: happy, creative and productive people giving value at work, at home and in society generally.

Sustainable Healthcare

Holistic healthcare is both personal and social. It provides a solution to the growing financial nightmare of public healthcare. In the West there are currently ever increasing demands for medical services, deriving from a rising proportion of old people in the population, higher expectations and stress-related illnesses. The growth in demand leads to rationing and cruel choices about which patients should receive which resources.

All of these problems are predicated on a system that delivers back-end care. Most medicine kicks in only when the person is at the stage of collapse. All the money goes into identifying and dealing with problems and illnesses after they have occurred, which is incredibly expensive. This problem cannot be solved through more high-tech hospitals and more money, as that policy deals only with the symptoms and not the causes.

The problem can, however, be mainly solved by 'front-end' holistic healthcare, which teaches people the basics of a holistic approach – physical, psychological, spiritual – to self-care. A body that experiences flow at all levels will be healthy. This is not an abstract philosophical or spiritual issue. It is to do with the flesh and blood reality of your physical and mental health.

One of the greatest beauties of this hollistic approach for modern people is that it does not force you to sign up to a particular belief system or set of strategies. It proposes general principles about the interdependence of your body, psyche and environment – and then suggests ways in which you can work with that package.

Your body, for example, needs to experience movement, but you are free to choose how you do that movement. Your emotions and mind need to open to the pleasure and flow of natural life – but again you are free to choose how you do this. Another general principle is that you are part of your local and global ecology and you affect it; but how you behave in relation to this information is a personal choice.

- Millions of people are turning to a holistic healthcare approach because it works.
- It encourages and empowers individuals to participate in their own healthcare and cures.
- It understands the relationship between body and mind.
- It understands the relationship between the individual and the wider energetic environment.

This is effective preventative medicine. It is bound, in one form or another, to become the foundation of healthcare in the twenty-first century – not just because it works, but because it will also cure the economic nightmare of rising national healthcare costs.

Lest You Become as Little Children Again

When Jesus counselled that we will only enter heaven if we become again like little children, he was a stating a core truth. He surely did not mean us to return to a naive and primitive infantile state, but was recognizing the qualities that children possess. Without armour, infants and children bubble with a creative life force. It emerges through their bodies and their imaginations.

Without losing any maturity, experience or wisdom you may have gained, you will enter heaven by allowing your body and mind to flow back into that childish state. In a world of perfect families, teachers and social conditions, you would anyway never have lost that state.

What, then, can we do to retain it for our children? If we know how to do this, we can create generations of healthy people. The answer is simple: provide an environment that causes no tension. Have parents and teachers who are warm, welcoming and encouraging; otherwise children freeze and disconnect.

The social ramifications are huge, but we have to create a world where mothers, parents and families can give babies the lengthy, totally loving, welcoming and affectionate reception into life that they need and deserve. Babies crave touch and warmth. Without it they begin, from birth, to tense and lose their flow. Babies need to be loved in the womb. As they emerge at birth, they need a calm, warm, mellow and sensitive reception. And they need constant physical holding.

What is normal amongst apes is for the young to be held all the time in the physical contact and warmth of their family. Babies and children need almost continuous physical warmth and presence. This is the preventative medicine that provides a foundation of psychological security and avoids later neurosis. It is this medicine that forms the core of holistic health. It does not spoil children; it keeps them sane and cooperative. When I hear people say that they do not like babies or children, or that they need controlling, my heart melts as I imagine the frigidity of their own childhood.

It is not normal to place a baby in a cot and distance it from touch. Historically, it was only royalty and aristocracy who tried to avoid the intimacy of child-rearing by using wet nurses and nannies. They were not concerned with supporting their children to maintain a connection with the wonder of the universe. They wanted rulers, leaders and effective warriors. Frozen and alienated human beings make perfect soldiers.

Babies and infants need to sleep in the physical warmth of their family. It is tough on nuclear families, let alone single parents, to give this time and physical energy. It requires sacrifices. The saying 'It takes a village to raise a child' is totally right. It is mainly right, not just because the baby demands such resources, but because the immediate parents need them if they are to care for the child properly.

One of my colleagues, Chris Storm, was a nurse for many years in an intensive care unit specializing in premature and damaged babies. These vulnerable little creatures were placed in heat regulated incubators, but Chris and the other nurses knew that they needed lifting and holding close. Distressed babies would die if they were not given this physical touch. So, in the middle of the night when the doctors and administrators were not there, the nurses would take the babies from their warm but sterile cocoons to hold and hum them into healing and survival. Physical warmth, the beat of a heart, is the foundation of health.

Once, a set of twins was born prematurely. Each was placed in its own little incubator. One was weak and not expected to live. A nurse ignored hospital rules and placed the babies together in one incubator. When they were laid alongside each other, the healthier of the two threw an arm over her sister in an endearing embrace. The smaller baby's heart rate stabilized and her temperature rose to normal. Both babies survived.

Jean Liedloff's book *The Continuum Concept* describes how tribal peoples care for their children and stay in continuous physical contact with them through their early years.[1] There are tribes where every single member enjoys that comfort and naturally passes it on to the new members. In Papua New Guinea, for instance, there is a tribe that has a special ceremony when an infant is first allowed to touch the earth and loses physical contact with its family. The child is placed gently on the ground, surrounded by a circle of caring and singing relatives.

Society has come to a point of terrible confusion when, as in the UK, we applaud policies that 'support' parents by providing more nursery places, thereby freeing the potential wage-earner from parenting. This is not family-oriented policy. It is do with the work ethic and has no real regard for the children. With such policies, countries are creating swathes of confused and anxious two-year-olds – brave little warriors who will operate well in the cogs of social technology, but are frozen and emotionally illiterate.

If I have a rant within me, it is about the need for our society to awake from the frigid spell that has been cast upon it. I am dumb-founded by the ignorance around children's needs for ongoing and consistent warmth. If I could wave a magic wand and change just one thing in life, it would be the modern idea of a family bed. I have saved many relationships, including my own, by the simple expedient of creating a large bed. Families need beds that are at least nine feet wide, so that everyone can be in them and sleeping comfortably. (Two double beds, or a king size plus a single. If you have a small room, run them wall to wall. If you are worried about children falling out, use mattresses on the floor until the children are older.) End of rant!

Dostoyevsky once wrote that if a child is within your sight, then your primary responsibility is for that child regardless of what other 'important' things you are doing. People do not develop civic good-will because they have heard a good idea. It needs to emerge authentically from within them. In the long term, this change will come from the generations who have been brought up with this warmth and encouragement. There is no other source for the kind of changes that most of us truly want.

Holistic Studies

Imagine, then, a new subject area in education, one that merges religion, health, emotional intelligence, social skills and citizenship

– holistic studies. It could begin, perhaps, in the slot reserved for religious education or liberal studies.

Of all the school staff, it is the teachers of this subject who know how to radiate supportive warmth and how to hold their classes with unconditional positive regard. They teach and are role models. They are connected to the flow and benevolence of the universe. They teach the basics of holistic health and self-management, the connection between the mind and the body, between attitude and health. They support and encourage children in discovering the activities and thoughts that give them pleasure and trigger endorphins and connection. They teach the significance and practical usefulness of all this. They also model and teach the Inner Smile and Curled Deer, which are not complex subjects.

These teachers acknowledge and understand children's crucial relationship with nature and all the things within it that they find beautiful and inspiring. They support and encourage a child's flow and sense of connection.

They show the pleasurable spiritual activities of other cultures and other personality types. They encourage children to taste different ways so as to broaden their experience and tolerance. There are songs, dances, nature experiences, arts – the whole range of strawberries that open people to the beauty of life.

Children learn to appreciate that, beneath the different forms and ceremonies, something universally human is happening. They learn that all the different religions are expressions of the same basic truths and instincts, clothed in different cultures. They learn that any person who helps you to come into connection and flow is a spiritual teacher – and is also simultaneously a teacher of holistic health and an effective life coach.

They become realistic about the essential goodwill of religious organizations, even when that goodwill appears to be offset by the politics of insecure and often aggressive men. There is no exclusive truth, no exclusive revelation – but each form is to be respected as unique in its own right. These teachers honour different world religions as cultural expressions of the same reality. Individual men and women have plugged into the overwhelming beauty and communicated it to their own societies in the language and culture of their situation. This relativism may be shocking to people who are deeply identified with only one religious approach, but there is a need today to expand and embrace the whole human family. This is the way of the future.

From this basis it is possible to explain the intimate interconnection and dependence of all living things. Within the web of life, it is possible to show children the harmful activities that damage other creatures seeking to reach their own fulfilment. A sense of morality and ethics can be developed from this way of understanding life.

When parents ask me how best they can teach these things to their own children, I respond that if they are practising these skills and attitudes themselves, their children will naturally adopt them. The smallest of examples will demonstrate this. If a child accidentally drops a glass that shatters on the floor, the parent can respond in two ways. He can be scolding and irritated; or he can stay calm and affectionate whilst philosophically clearing up the dangerous mess. The child will absorb whichever attitude is displayed.

If a parent's behaviour and attitude are calm and holding from the earliest months, this is what the child will absorb – and later, as an adult, give to others.

Senior Citizens

And what about the other end of our life, our later years?

There is a wry television commercial that shows a group of retired people giggling at their freedom from the pressures of having to work. The commercial is for an investment company promising a secure and prosperous pension. I certainly wish all of us a comfortable retirement, but this can also be a period of great personal growth and meaningful fulfilment. In many Eastern cultures, it is only in one's senior years that true spiritual growth and wisdom are thought possible. In Hinduism, many men who have retired from work give up all their belongings, renounce materialism and turn to the divine search.

In the West retirement also brings a complete change in lifestyle, but one that is not always comfortable. There is often confusion about a suitable role and many retirements are followed too swiftly by death. But the senior years can be seen as an opportunity fully to explore the meaning and wonder of life, to investigate strawberries and the connection.

What could be more normal, having experienced a pressured life, than to relax into the endorphin connection and then pass the goodwill on to family and friends? There is the possibility here of decades of a new and meaningful kind of life.

The Endorphin Effect also provides a comforting way of approaching death. The endorphins, the Inner Smile and the Curled Deer all bring complete comfort to the biological creature that is about to enter the surrender and release of death. At the same time, the connection with earth, nature, the sun and the universe – everything beyond Blobsville – will facilitate the transfer of consciousness easily and gracefully across into a new dimension. It is absolutely certain that, from an endorphin-based connection, death can be happily received and passed through. [2]

The Sufi poet Rumi once likened dying to sugar dissolving in warm water. 'Dissolve me,' the mystic happily requests at the right moment. This, in a way, is the quintessence of the endorphin experience. It feels good regardless of the circumstances. People who understand death in this way live a much easier life, with no anxiety about what seems to be the greatest of challenges. In fact, the right approach is almost casual. But the whole approach of the Endorphin Effect is indeed casual and relaxed. It has to be, or else there is no flow.

This reminds me of an elegant student who had difficulty at the start seeing how relaxed an approach this is and claimed that he just could not do the endorphin work. 'It's all too spiritual and pure,' he protested. 'The best I can do is sit in the garden with a glass of wine.'

He was, in fact, doing the practice perfectly. Garden and wine – two sources of immense pleasure. In many mystic poems, the state of being in paradise is described as being in a flower garden drinking heavenly wine. This way of connecting with beauty is very appropriate for older people who are more easily prepared to relax and enjoy their surroundings. Done with goodwill to all life, it is a skill that should also be adopted by middle-aged and younger people. And, of course, if you prefer to rave and connect through rock and roll, this is – as a musician friend says – a freewill universe.

Is It All True?

Some people find it hard to believe that the holistic perspective and the Endorphin Effect are true. This is understandable. We are living through that precise historical period when this new understanding is emerging. It is not yet embedded in our culture in the same way that brushing our teeth twice a day or washing our hands before meals have been absorbed from childhood. We have not yet had a whole generation of parents and educators who accept and pass on these kinds of ideas.

Halfway through one of my coaches' training sessions, a brilliant and successful woman who had thoughtfully committed her time and resources to the course suddenly exclaimed, 'I don't really know if all this is true!'

Several members of the class nodded in agreement, grateful that she had openly named the problem.

'I want more proof!' she exclaimed. 'I'm working with thousands of men and women in a competitive commercial environment. I want proof that I can show them!'

'But you know it's real,' I replied. 'You've seen the effects over and over again. And you even have the theories and concepts to back it up.'

'Yes, I have,' she agreed. 'But I still doubt. My brain and mind are still filled with the maps I learnt at school and university. I was taught them as if they were absolute reality. The people I work with still take them for granted. When these maps are challenged, they feel attacked. When I push the new perspective, I meet resistance. I don't like it. They feel threatened. I feel threatened. No wonder I feel pissed off.' She paused. 'I don't want proof. I just want to feel more comfortable about living in the two worlds at the same time! And even though I know it's all absolutely true and effective, a part of me is still hanging on to the old way of looking at things.'

Her feelings are understandable. The unconscious mind hangs on to old ways even when the conscious mind has understood a new truth. The unconscious mind likes to hang on to the stuff it learnt in infancy, at school and over many years. But the most fundamental principles of knowledge and belief change with the passage of time. Flexibility is a sign of life. Rigidity is a symptom of death.

But, along with all the other reasons listed in Chapter 12, do not let that stop you changing. That is the crux of the matter. For the sake of your own health and the wellbeing of everyone else, please change. The longer you hold off from accepting and acting upon the holistic perspective, the longer current problems will last. You do not need to transform everything in one great gesture, though that may be your style. Nor do you have to stop being yourself. Just begin to introduce a new dimension.

Expand your horizons beyond your immediate pressures and concerns, and notice where you really live. Celebrate and go deeper into everything that makes you feel good. Allow the strong and creative vitality of the universe deep into you. Inner Smile. Curled Deer. Dream and hold the vision.

A Conclusion to the Strawberry Story

The use of the word 'strawberry' comes from that story of the terrified man, about to die, who suddenly saw a wild strawberry and reached out to pick it. This was a metaphor for how turning your attention to something pleasurable can turn moments of hell into experiences of heaven.

But there are always people who are not satisfied with the symbolic explanation of the story. They cannot rest easy until they hear what actually happened.

'Whatever happened to that terrified man hanging from the bush above the abyss with the mouse nibbling at the bush's roots?' I have been asked. 'Did he fall? Did he die? What did the wild strawberry really do for him?'

Well, once I did hear the end of that story.

Without falling, he managed to pick the strawberry and place it in his mouth. The taste of that fruit was so delicious that he immediately dissolved into a delirium of pleasure. His whole body flooded with ecstasy and he lost consciousness.

He awoke a little while later to discover, of course, that the whole terrible chase through the jungle and his possible fall had all been an awful nightmare – a nightmare with a strange ending. He had been dreaming.

Lying there, he pondered the experience. He remembered learning once in a psychology class that dreams, especially nightmares, reflect the events of the previous twenty-four hours. So he turned his mind back over the previous twenty-four hours.

Yes, it had been a tough day. His work had been pressured. His relationship was challenging. The stock market had fallen fractionally and there had been more news about climate change and war.

But it was also the day on which he had started experimenting with his endorphins. The previous night, before he went to sleep, he had listed everything that gave him pleasure – people, places, activities, memories – and had been astounded at the length of the list. With a certain healthy scepticism, he had then closed his eyes and allowed his consciousness to play with all his strawberries. To his satisfaction, he noticed a distinct and pleasurable change within him. Endorphins were beginning to flow. Tension was melting. Connection was happening.

He switched on his Inner Smile to comfort any part of him that had been disturbed by the nightmare. The whole dream was now understandable. It did reflect the previous day. First there was pressure, and then there was pleasure. There was constraint and then freedom. The wild strawberry now made perfect sense.

APPENDIX A

Twelve-week Programme

What follows is a possible twelve-week programme for learning and putting the Endorphin Effect strategies into practice. It is in no way a definitive programme, but puts forward some basic guidelines which you may find useful.

Weeks 1 and 2
Every morning as you wake up and every evening before you go to sleep, pause and look kindly down into your body. Touch your body to reassure and comfort it.

Week 3
List your strawberries. Begin the practice of pausing and absorbing the pleasure every time that you experience a strawberry.

Week 4
Place next to your bathroom mirror an image of some person, place or activity that you love. Place similar images in your workplace. Pause regularly with them and absorb the pleasurable experience.

Week 5
Plan an activity that will take you to one of your very best strawberries.

Week 6
As you wake up and before you go to sleep, recognize the beauty of the earth, nature, the sun and the universe. Relax and let their benevolent energies come deep into your body.

Week 7
Whenever you feel like it begin to experiment with the Inner Smile, especially when you are experiencing either a strawberry or stress.

Week 8
Whenever you like, switch on your Inner Smile and begin to focus on your Curled Deer. Sense the strength at your core. When you feel exhausted, turn within and connect with earth, nature, the sun and the universe.

Week 9
With greater consciousness, begin to circulate the endorphins and benevolent vitality through your body and energy field.

Week 10
Switch on the discipline of not reacting and begin to cradle your feelings when you are irritated or upset.

Week 11
Begin to experiment with Unboundaried Dreaming about your future and about anything that worries you. Allow your mind to enjoy totally positive and perfectly fulfilled scenarios for yourself and all life.

Week 12
Strongly centred and connected, begin to experience how your energy field can hold people and situations.

APPENDIX B

Daily checklist

Day	Wake up/go to sleep with awareness	Aware of nature and universe – not in Blobsville	Using Strawberries	Inner Smile
1				
2				
3				
4				
5				
6				
7				
8				
9				
10				
11				
12				
13				
14				

∪ = Remembered very well
∪ = Remembered well
— = Neutral
∩ = Forgetful
∩ = Lost it completely

Curled Deer	Moving and absorbing vitality deep into the body	Holding yourself, holding others	Unboundaried Dreaming, holding the vision

APPENDIX C

Exercise and Diet

Exercise

I go the gym twice a week and do some stretching exercises, yoga and chi gung nearly every day. But I have also worked for many years with people who have physical disabilities, and some of my best friends and teachers are wonderful couch potatoes. I am, therefore, very reluctant to tell anyone what to do with their bodies or how to exercise.

The most important thing is to keep your energy warm and moving. That said, I do believe that it is very helpful for most people to get regular physical exercise. In my opinion, it should consist of these three major components:

- Stretching
- Aerobic
- Weights

They will all, after a few minutes, begin to stimulate endorphins and move your *prana*. It is also very effective to do exercise and at the same time work with strawberries, Inner Smile, Curled Deer and guiding the golden streams. This adds a completely new and holistic dimension to exercise.

Diet

I am also reluctant to tell people what they should or should not eat. People have widely varying temperaments and different kinds of bodies. My own body likes to be vegan, but I cook fish and meat for my young daughter when her body needs it.

I do believe, though, that there are certain ground rules:

- Eat what gives you pleasure
- Eat what makes you feel physically good
- Eat what gives you energy and flow

Some people, of course, are not very good at assessing what is good for them. Let me suggest a couple of methods.

- Whatever you are eating, pause while it is in your mouth and notice how much pleasure the texture and taste are giving you. What do your instincts tell you about this food?
- Twenty minutes after you have eaten, notice how you feel. Do you feel good? Do you have more energy than before you ate? Ask yourself the same questions two hours later.

APPENDIX D

Meditation

The Endorphin Effect strategies are an easy way to start meditating or, if you are already meditating, to deepen your practice. In fact, if you pause long enough in any of the strategies it will become a form of meditation.

In classical meditation you have to be calm, compassionately observing everything you feel and everything that passes through your mind. Through any disturbance, distraction or turmoil, you remain observing the process and maintaining your relaxed breath. This feels good and its biological foundation is high endorphin production.

All meditation traditions teach that its purpose is to experience reality – your true nature and that of the universe. This is done by sitting calmly and observantly for long periods of time. In this state you begin to understand and experience that you are more than just your everyday personality. There is a different you at your core.

Meditation, then, is about spending enjoyable and lengthy time allowing yourself to open more fully and to sink more deeply into the experience.

Different schools of meditation have different opinions about the nature and meaning of your core self, but without exception they assert that this core is a wise and loving consciousness that merges with the bliss fields of universal consciousness. The Inner Smile, the

Curled Deer, contemplating strawberries, breathing earth-nature-sun-universe – these are all gateways to meditation. It is simply a matter of stretching how long you stay in the exercise and attitude. The pause can expand from seconds to minutes to hours.

It is my belief that the classical systems of energy medicine – such as Kabbalah, chi gung and kahuna – were actually discovered by meditators who were particularly sensitive to energy flows. Sitting quietly day by day, they could not help but notice the subtle feelings and changes. Instinctively and intuitively, they must have experimented with what felt best, what expanded their consciousness and what released pain and blockages.

Sadly, this ultimately led to a division amongst meditators. On the one side were the purists, such as practitioners of vipassana and zazen, who maintained that meditation should always be passive and observant. On the other side were those who were sensitive to the flows and wanted to cooperate with and guide the feelings and energies. Both styles, however, always require a deep calm and compassionate awareness.

APPENDIX E

Notes and Further Reading

Chapter 1: The Elixir of Life

1. This poll was conducted by the Opinion Research Business (ORB) for the BBC Television programme *Soul of Britain* 25 April – 7 May 2000.

For a general overview of the holistic field see my reader *The Penguin Book of New Age and Holistic Writing,* Penguin, 2001.
For an introduction to holistic medicine I suggest Richard Gerber, *Vibrational Medicine,* Bear & Co, 1988; and Deepak Chopra, *Quantum Healing – Exploring the Frontiers of Mind /Body Spirit,* Bantam, 1989.
For a rigorous introduction to the field of energies and consciousness see William A. Tiller, *Science and Human Transformation: Subtle Energies, Intentionality and Consciousness*, Pavior Books, 1997.

Chapter 2: The Feelings Factory – Understanding Endorphins

1. Candace Pert, *Molecules of Emotion*, Simon and Schuster, 1999.
2. Antonio Damasio, *The Feeling of What Happens*, Random House, 1999.

3. Norman Cousins, *Anatomy of an Illness,* W.W. Norton, 1996.
For more information on laughter, see Robert Holden, *Laughter – The Best Medicine,* Thorsons, 1993.

Chapter 3: The Metaphysics of Feelgood

1. David Bohm, *Wholeness and the Implicate Order,* Routledge, 1980.
2. 'The Missing Energy of the Universe,' *Scientific American,* January, 1999.
3. Fritjof Capra, *The Tao of Physics*, Wildwood House, 1975.
4. Gary Zukov, *The Dancing Wu Li Masters,* Rider, 1991.
5. *Nature,* vol. 405, p. 707.
6. Jerry I. Jacobson, William S. Yamanashi et al, 'Effect of Magnetic Fields on Damaged Mice Sciatic Nerves', *Frontier Perspectives*,Vol. 9. 1, pp.6-11.
7. Richard Gerber, *Vibrational Medicine,* Bear & Co, 1988.
8. Wilhelm Reich, *Function of the Orgasm,* Souvenir Press, 1983; Alexander Lowen, *Bioenergetics*, Penguin/Arkana, 1994.

Chapter 4: Your True Environment – Your Body and the Universe

1. Alan Watts, *The Book: On the Taboo Against Knowing Who You Are,* Vintage, 1989.
2. Andrew Harvey (trans), *The Essential Mystics*, Harper San Francisco, 1996.

Chapter 5: Your Strawberries, Your Gateways

To help focus on how you feel in your body and begin the process of absorbing the feeling, I recommend two classics: Eugene T. Gendlin, *Focussing*, Bantam, 1982; and
Herbert Benson, *The Relaxation Response,* Avon Books, 1976.

Chapter 6: The Inner Smile

For a classic modern approach to the Inner Smile, see the writings of the Buddhist teacher Thich Nhat Hahn, especially his *Being Peace*, Parallax Press, 1995.

Chapter 7: Absorbing and Guiding the Golden Streams

1. Guy Brown, *The Energy of Life,* HarperCollins, 1999.

Chapter 8: Curled Deer, Strong Centre – Conscious Retreat, Clear Boundaries

1. It is worth looking at almost any book on chi gung. In particular you might try the following titles: Mantak Chia, *Awaken Healing Light of the Tao*, Tuttle Publishing, 1993; Mantak Chia, *Bone Marrow Nei Kung*, Tuttle Publishing, 1991; and Bruce Kamar Frantzis, *Opening the Energy Gates of Your Body*, North Atlantic Books, 1993.
2. Karlfried Graf Von Durkheim, trans. Sylvia-Monica von Kospoth, *Hara - The Vital Centre of Man*, Mandala/Allen & Unwin, 1977.
3. William Bloom, *Psychic Protection*, Piatkus Books, 1997.
4. Liu Hua-yang, *Cultivating the Energy of Life*, trans Eva Wong, Shambala, 1998.

To communicate clearly in a way that makes people take notice of you, are the skills taught in assertiveness training. There are many books in this field, but you might start with Gael Lindfield, *Assert Yourself*, Thorsons, 1992; and Gael Lindfield & Malcolm Vandenburg, *Positive Under Pressure*, Thorsons, 2000.

Chapter 10: Managing Distress – First Aid and Long-Term Healing

1. Peter Levine, *Walking the Tiger–Healing Trauma*, North Atlantic Books, 1997.
2. From 'Wild Geese' by Mary Oliver, *American Primitive*, Back Bay Books, 1983.

In the field of spiritual healing, I recommend Barbara Brennan, *Hands of Light*, Bantam Books, 1988; and Alice Bailey, *Esoteric Healing*, Lucis Press, 1953.

Chapter 11: Unboundaried Dreaming – Vision, Purpose and Success

Two books that I warmly recommend in this field are David Spangler, *Everyday Miracles – The Inner Art of Manifestation*, Bantam, 1995; and Jane Roberts, *The Nature of Personal Reality*, Bantam Books, 1978.

Chapter 12: Waves on the Ocean – Managing the Highs and Lows

1. I cannot source the translator of this Rumi poem and would welcome the information so as to credit it properly.

Chapter 13: The Hero at Work and at Home

1. Daniel Goleman, *Emotional Intelligence,* Bloomsbury, 1996.
2. For research and further strategies, see Doc Childre and Howard Martin, *The Heartmath Solution*, Piatkus, 1999.

Chapter 14: A New Life, A New World

1. Jean Liedloff, *The Continuum Concept,* Penguin, 1986.
2. On the subject of death and dying, I have produced a supplementary pamphlet for people who have read *The Endorphin Effect* or are familiar with the CEM strategies. This is available free from Holistic Partnerships or can be read and downloaded from my website (see p.297).

I also recommend Richard Boestler and Hulen Kornfeld, *Life to Death – Harmonizing the Transition,* Healing Arts, 1995; Sogyal Rinpoche, *The Tibetan Book of Living and Dying,* Rider, 1992.

Resources

Holistic Partnerships

This is the training organization for all the work in this book and core energy management. It provides individual, group and corporate coaching/trainings/courses. It also manages William Bloom's educational programme and has details of his other books, materials and cassettes. For further information or to be on the mailing list, please contact:

Holistic Partnerships
10 The Murreys
Ashtead
Surrey
KT21 2LU
Tel/fax 01372 272400
Welcome@holisticpartnerships.com
www.holisticpartnerships.com

**For more information about William Bloom, visit
www.williambloom.com**

Index